ON THE INCLUSION

Changing labour markets and social exclusion in London

David M. Smith

First published in Great Britain in September 2005 by

The Policy Press
University of Bristol
Fourth Floor
Beacon House
Queen's Road
Bristol BS8 1QU
UK

Tel +44 (0)117 331 4054
Fax +44 (0)117 331 4093
e-mail tpp-info@bristol.ac.uk
www.policypress.org.uk

British Library Cataloguing in Publication Data
A catalogue record for this book is available from the British Library.

Library of Congress Cataloging-in-Publication Data
A catalog record for this book has been requested.

ISBN 1 86134 600 X paperback

A hardcover version of this book is also available.

Cover design by Qube Design Associates, Bristol.
Front cover: photograph supplied by kind permission of www.third-
avenue.co.uk
Printed and bound in Great Britain by MPG Books, Bodmin

Contents

Acknowledgements

First, thanks are due to the Economic and Social Research Council for funding the research on which this book is based (award no: R00429734632). Many people have helped in making this book a possibility. I would like to thank Professor John Macnicol for his invaluable support from the completion of the research proposal, until the writing of the final draft. Similarly I would like to thank Richard Smith and Bernice Martin at Royal Holloway College, both of whose advice and encouragement to undertake the research I am extremely grateful for. I would also like to thank my family for their encouragement and Saniye Dedeoglu at Southampton University whose practical support proved vital. I am indebted to my friends who still live on the estate, and who have maintained the contacts that made my research methodology feasible. Finally, my greatest thanks go to the research respondents without whom the book would have been impossible.

Foreword

Social exclusion and poverty

In the past 10 to 15 years, the term 'social exclusion' has supplanted 'poverty' in British social policy discourses. Its recent origins are probably to be found in the European poverty programme of the 1990s and, before that, in French social debates (where the term was used to denote those on the margins of society, who had slipped through the social insurance safety net). Soon after taking office in May 1997, Britain's New Labour government established the Cabinet Office Social Exclusion Unit and shifted governmental and academic analyses of poverty in a new direction. Labour's ostensible rationale was that whole sections of the British population – in particular, the long-term sick and disabled people, single mothers and the economically inactive – had been 'written off' in the massive economic restructuring that had taken place since 1979. Income inequality and social polarisation had widened. What was needed was workfarist policies to re-socialise these marginalised groups back into economic independence, raise their self-esteem and lift them out of poverty and social exclusion.

The idea of poverty having a cultural and lifestyle element has, of course, a very long history. Arguably, it has been regularly reconstructed over at least the last 100 years. But the modern usage of 'social exclusion' can be traced to several influences. First, theorists of relative deprivation (notably Peter Townsend) have long maintained that poverty must be viewed as 'exclusion from common social activities', objectively measurable by a 'deprivation index' (Townsend, 1979). In this sense, social exclusion means 'inability to participate', perhaps even involving a denial of full citizenship (Dean, with Melrose, 1999). It can be argued, therefore, that the concept takes relative deprivation one stage further. It examines poverty as multidimensional clusters of disadvantage (for example, the combined effects of poor health, low skills, family breakdown, substandard housing, economic inactivity, and so on). The spatial distribution of such disadvantage is mapped, as are poverty dynamics and lifecourse effects. Social exclusion also explores relational issues, placing poverty in the context of wider social relationships and cultural expectations. Social exclusion is said to open up questions of agency, although the causal factors – often termed 'drivers' in government publications – tend to be located within broadly 'supply-side' analyses: for example, the emphasis tends to be on the personal factors that constitute an individual's 'employability', rather than on sectoral labour market demand.

A second, and contrasting, tributary of influence is the 1980s and 1990s 'underclass' concept. New Labour undoubtedly tried to shift the focus from the broadly conservative 'underclass' idea, with its coded eugenic assumptions, towards a more acceptable terrain. Some of the deterministic elements of the 'underclass' idea live on – for example, the emphasis on early childhood experiences profoundly affecting underachievement in adulthood (Hobcraft, 2002) – but, in contrast to the pessimistic, do-nothing conclusions reached by conservative commentators such as Charles Murray (Murray, 1990, 1994), New Labour maintain that one *can* legislate to reduce social exclusion. The key question that remains is how far many of the 'underclass' assumptions still linger, but in a more subtle form.

A third, and relatively minor, influence has been the concepts of 'social isolation' (most notably posited by William Julius Wilson to describe the 'concentration effect' of extreme poverty when a collapse of the economic base in a locality leads to a disruption of social networks, support systems, personal and collective resilience, and so on [Wilson, 1987]), and 'social capital' (Putnam, 2000). Fourth, there is much thematic continuity with the 'cycle of deprivation' research of the 1970s. This also examined the intergenerational dynamics of multiple deprivation (including early childhood effects), and attempted to explain the behaviour of the poor in terms of the limited opportunities available to them (Coffield et al, 1980).

Finally, it must be remembered that New Labour ultimately tends to see social exclusion in terms of 'worklessness'. There is a veneer of social justice arguments: citizens, it is said, should all have "the opportunity to achieve their potential.... Our aim is to end the injustice which holds people back and prevents them from making the most of themselves" (SEU, 1999, p 1). But 'participation' usually means participation in waged labour, and definitions of poverty and social exclusion tend to carry this secondary agenda. For example, "the most significant factor" in the increase in child poverty in Britain over the past 20 years is said to be "the growth in the number of households with children in which no adult works" (DSS, 1999), and "worklessness and low income" are "two of the most important causes of social exclusion" (ODPM, 2004, p 9). In fact, the number of 'working poor' has grown in all Western economies over the last 30 years, with the expansion of low-paid and part-time jobs. Hence in Britain, 52% of children in poverty now live in households where at least one adult is in paid employment ('Key Facts', 2004).

It is important to remember that this redefinition of poverty has taken place against the background of a broader macro-economic strategy of achieving economic growth by expanding labour supply (in both a quantitative and qualitative sense) via 'active labour market' policies. The aim is to achieve non-inflationary economic growth and a 'flexible', skilled and motivated workforce, which can respond to the challenges of globalisation and rapid changes in demand. Re-branding poverty as 'social exclusion' mainly caused by worklessness legitimises the workfarist remedies of the New Deal. This strategy is not confined to Britain: it is now a European Union aim (enshrined in the 2000 Lisbon Agreement) that member states should achieve target employment rates of 70%.

Indicators of social exclusion

There is now a long list – indeed, a bewildering list – of social exclusion indicators. The main areas identified by the Social Exclusion Unit are: children and young people; crime; employment and opportunity; health and care; homes and neighbourhoods; and transport. But these encompass many social problems, such as: teenage pregnancy; lone parenthood; inadequate parenting; children in care; mental health; benefit dependency; low birth weight; children in workless households; educational underachievement; rough sleeping; school exclusions and truancy; neighbourhood renewal; and antisocial behaviour. The Social Exclusion Unit's overall strategy has several elements: prevention (in which early childhood intervention is seen as vital); human capital (equipping individuals with the personal 'resilience' with which to cope with economic changes and 'shocks'); examination of poverty dynamics, measuring outcomes by longitudinal studies; and a focus on multidimensional disadvantage (factoring in all its interlocking components).

An even more detailed list of no less than 50 indicators has been constructed by the Joseph Rowntree Foundation. Many of these – such as low income, low birth weight babies, or overcrowding – are relatively uncontentious, and have long been key elements in objective indicators of social deprivation. But others seem to cast the definitional net extraordinarily widely: anxiety among older people, burglaries in communities, or obesity among adults (JRF, 2003). There must now be a danger that the concept of social exclusion has become a vessel into which almost any social problem can be poured. Even more disturbingly, it may be in danger of becoming an ever-more elaborate concealment of the basic problem of widening income inequality and social polarisation (Hills, 2004). A final criticism is that the concept of social exclusion focuses on the symptoms of poverty, rather than its real causes.

Not surprisingly, there have been many critical analyses of the concept of social exclusion. The early classification – highly detailed and nuanced – by Hilary Silver (Silver, 1994) of the overlapping yet contrasting 'social exclusion' discourses was followed by Ruth Levitas's celebrated threefold typology of a 'redistributionist discourse' (which, like the 'economic' model of the underclass, argues that the problem is located in changes in labour market demand), a 'moral underclass discourse' (which analyses the problem in behavioural terms), and a 'social integrationist discourse' (which focuses on unemployment and economic inactivity, viewing the solution as moving more people back into work). Levitas criticises the third of these – the Blair government's version – for fetishising paid work, neglecting the importance of unpaid work (including childcare), and ignoring wider structural inequalities of gender, class, race and age by implying that the 'included' are a homogenous group. By this definitional process, she argues, "attention is drawn away from the inequalities and differences among the included"; social exclusion "appears as an essentially peripheral problem, existing at the boundary of society, rather than a feature of a society which characteristically delivers massive inequalities across the board and chronic deprivation for a large minority" (Levitas, 1998, p 7).

Other critics have offered a modern version of the classic Marxist 'reserve army of labour' critique that those labelled 'socially excluded' are actually *functional* to post-industrial, globalised capitalism, which will increasingly require docile, low-skilled, flexible workers. Hence David Byrne argues that "advanced industrial societies are converging on a norm of social politics organised around a flexible labour market and structural social exclusion" (Byrne, 1999, p 70). Further studies have examined the empirical underpinnings of the concept, attempting to tease apart its many meanings (Hills et al, 2002).

The perspectives of ordinary people

Much of the discussion of social exclusion has therefore been 'top-down' in nature, with the poor and the excluded remaining relatively voiceless. There is, accordingly, a need for studies that present the views of ordinary people, articulated in their own words. How has the massive economic restructuring of recent decades impacted upon ordinary people's lives, and how do they rationalise the resultant changes at the level of their local economies? How far do ordinary people accept and internalise, or reject, prevailing 'expert' poverty discourses and concepts like social exclusion? What 'survival strategies' do those living on the margins employ in dealing with the impact of economic restructuring and the growth of low-paid jobs? And how have these economic changes affected family formation behaviour?

This book explores these key issues. It is written by a young academic of great promise who has extensive personal knowledge of a South London housing estate, and who has interviewed local residents there with skill and sensitivity. The perspectives of these residents are presented and analysed in a sympathetic, non-judgemental way, taking account of the restricted choices open to them and the difficult ethical dilemmas they face. These personal narratives are set in the context of the interaction between the local economy (with its increasingly complex, overlapping and segmented labour markets) and global economic changes. This book therefore stands in the great tradition of ethnographic studies of poverty, continuing the approaches developed in works such as Elliot Liebow's *Tally's corner* (1967), Douglas Glasgow's *The black underclass* (1980) and Nicholas Lemann's *The promised land* (1992). At a time when the concept of social exclusion has become central to governmental anti-poverty policy, this book reminds us that we need to take account of the perspectives of ordinary citizens. They are the ones who experience social exclusion at first hand, even if they do not always write about it.

John Macnicol
Visiting Professor in Social Policy
London School of Economics and Political Science

ONE

Introduction

This book examines the impact of changing labour markets and social policies on the life chances and working lives of a group of economically marginal individuals, on the locality that they inhabit and on their social relations. Anthony Giddens (1990) has argued that central to an individual's sense of 'ontological security' is the confidence that people have in the continuity of their self-identity and in the constancy of their social and economic environments. The "intensification of worldwide social relations which link distant localities in such a way that local happenings are shaped by events occurring many miles away and vice versa" have removed citizens from the familiar and traditional cultural patterns that are the basis of this security (Giddens, 1990, p 64). The material presented explores the 'adaptive reactions' of residents of one largely white, working-class housing estate in outer south London to wider societal changes, and how they attempt to maintain a positive sense of self and material stability in the context of local labour market conditions, low wages and the workings of social policy. Community studies have the potential to act as testing grounds for abstract theories of social change through illuminating the local expression of large-scale social processes, and revealing the active involvement of individuals in the shaping of their social worlds (Crow, 2002). The emergence of new social formations in response to socioeconomic changes and the ways that they are transforming the nature of social relations in low-income areas is a closely related and central concern of this book, given the role attributed to 'social capital' by policy makers in rejuvenating local communities. In attempting to avoid a reductionism that views these phenomena as a mere response to global processes, I adopt O'Byrne's perspective that:

> Stress(es) the relative autonomy of both globalization and class culture: acknowledging the growing impact of globalization upon localities, while asserting the importance of those localities as sites of struggle and conflict, as well as of 'commonality'. (O'Byrne, 1997, p 75)

The choice of topic was partially prompted by the academic interests that I had developed during my undergraduate course in sociology and social policy. The 'underclass' debate was a highly topical and contentious arena of academic debate during the early to mid-1990s when I took my degree, and equally prominent in media and political critiques of the 'dependency culture'. The disparate yet interrelated debate surrounding the underclass captured a wide range of anxieties including welfare dependency and an erosion of the 'work ethic'; a more general decline in civility and morality and growth of lawlessness and antisocial behaviour; absent fathers and an increase in female-headed households – and the increasing spatial concentration of such phenomena. By the late 1990s, under the influence of New Labour, the same concerns were being addressed in terms of 'social exclusion'. This was accompanied by a concerted political will to reverse the polarisation of society that had occurred under the previous government through reintegrating the 'excluded' into society, and regenerating the communities where growing proportions of them lived. The remedies were predicated on a particular understanding of what constitutes 'social exclusion' and emphasise training, retraining and re-socialising the workless into paid formal work through a combination of incentives, persuasion and compulsion. This 'top-down' notion of social exclusion and the moral obligation to work that is an adjunct of those political definitions required a 'bottom-up' perspective in order to assess the relevance of such models at a situational level. The emphasis is on developing an understanding of social exclusion that locates the individual's perceptions of exclusion as central, and is able to comprehend the ways that social inclusion and regeneration policies operate within a specific locale and their outcomes for those affected by them.

With a few notable exceptions (Howe, 1990; Jordan et al, 1992; MacDonald, 1994), little of the literature on poverty and welfare in the 1980s/1990s said much about the actual lifestyles and practices of those classed as 'socially excluded'. Beresford, challenging the 'them' and 'us' of social policy research, pointed to the near exclusion of the groups deemed eligible for 'social inclusion' from recent debates and policy proposals. Consequently, people with experience of poverty have no control over how they are presented or the policy responses that are devised to deal with them (Beresford, 1996, p 51). This exclusion of the poor from debates on poverty and welfare is not new. The historical debate reveals that despite periodic changes in nomenclature, questions surrounding the causes of poverty and welfare dependency were still being fought on the same ideologically polarised terrain and with many of the same assumptions that have informed debates since the 19th century (Macnicol, 1987). Ideological preferences and theoretical orientations have tended to present either overly structural or individualistic accounts of human behaviour while the interactions between the two, as acted out and constructed in daily practices, have been largely neglected. Wacquant (1991, p 51) notes that:

> Class lies neither in structures nor in agency alone but in their relationship as it is historically produced, reproduced and transformed.... Class identities, practices, and 'lived experience' are not 'afterthoughts'.... They enter into the making of these classes.

These interests were also stimulated by my own experiences growing up on and around housing estates on the outer fringes of south London. Choice of research topic is often motivated by personal and biographical factors. Okely (1992) notes that in the 1970s, feminists were arguing that 'the personal is political'. For academics, she adds, the 'personal is theoretical' and this will have implications for both analysis and presentation of data. Yow (1994, p 1) argues that:

> Reflexivity requires recognising that ethnographic writing is not simply stating the 'facts' but is a cultural construction that emerges through the participant's interpretation of experience, and the role of the researcher who interjects themselves into this process.

Given the consensus in qualitative textbooks that the establishment of rapport and minimising social distance is vital for the quality of data, several commentators have pointed to the advantages of utilising personal experiences and insights in research. Bourdieu (1996, p 24) argues that social proximity and familiarity produce the social conditions necessary for 'non-hierarchical' communication since:

> The rationale for the questions is found in her dispositions, which are objectively attuned to those of the respondent herself. As certain female interviewers report, the affinities between women, enabled obstacles linked to differences in social conditions to be surmounted – in particular, the fear of patronising class attitudes which, when the sociologist is perceived as socially superior often adds itself to the very general, if not universal, fear of being made into an object.

My interest in the varied economic strategies employed by members of a locality under conditions of economic uncertainty and low pay, and the ways in which these are achieved, or otherwise, through people's social ties can be traced to the recession of the late 1980s and early 1990s. This resulted in a large growth of unemployment in London from 200,000 in 1985 to 464,000 in 1988 and also accelerated the long-term decline of London's manufacturing sector (Hamnett, 2003, p 73). In the mid-1960s, over one third of London's labour force were employed in manufacturing, falling by over 50% by 1981 until it stood at 19% of total employment. Between 1981 and 1999, manufacturing lost a further 350,000 jobs – 47% of the total in a single decade. Over the same period, construction also experienced a rapid drop, losing over a quarter of total jobs (Hamnett, 2003, p 32). Meanwhile, the expansion of banking, finance, insurance and business services has altered the class structure of London from one dominated by a large working class in the post-war era, towards one where affluent, middle-class managerial and professional groups are the ascendant social groups. In the UK the percentage share of these groups increased from 24% to 41% between 1979 and 2000, while in inner London its share increased by 26% to over 50%. Buck et al's analysis reveals that the main relative 'losers' in London have been those in mid-level occupations – clerical, sales and skilled manual work – while the share of unskilled service workers has remained stable in contrast to unskilled manual workers who have declined (Buck et al, 2002, pp 152-3). A result of these changes in London's occupational and class structure has been a large growth in inequality as household earnings at the top have risen significantly and fallen at the bottom end. The transformation from an industrial to a post-industrial city has been accompanied by a transformation from an industrial towards a post-industrial occupational structure, argues Hamnett, and that since the mid-1970s:

> While London has become a wealthier and more prosperous city during the last thirty years, with a much larger and prosperous middle class, it has also become a much more unequal city. There is a large and growing divide between the earnings, the incomes and the living conditions of the prosperous, expanded middle class, and those of the economically inactive, the less skilled, the low paid and unemployed who have fared far less well. (Hamnett, 2003, p 6)

Within this changing industrial and social climate, the collapse of the construction industry effectively ended my career as a bricklayer and later prompted a new 'career' as a mature student. The seemingly lucrative prospects compared to the burgeoning low-paid, 'feminised', entry-level service jobs that had enticed myself and many of my friends into the trade during the 'building boom' of the 1980s, had mostly disappeared by the early 1990s. The few small- to medium-sized building firms that were managing to survive the recession were engaging in drastic cost-cutting (that is, wage-cutting) strategies as they were inundated with requests for work, and too many firms chased too few contracts. The nature and structure of the construction industry has traditionally lent itself well to casual work, while 'cash-in-hand' labourers or skilled tradespeople have always had a presence on building sites. Increasingly prevalent was the practice of laying workers off, then re-employing them 'off the cards' and paying them less than the market wage, with welfare benefits tacitly operating as an illicit wage supplement. Unskilled manual work had not entirely disappeared and could still be found via the same local contacts as previously. The difference was that the availability of such work was becoming progressively dependent on those contacts and subsumed under informal working practices. Further, these and related income-generating practices were becoming central to the longer-term economic survival of many households, rather than a short-term solution to temporary bouts of unemployment and financial crisis.

These changes in the economic prospects of many residents coincided with an influx of drugs into the area from the late 1980s. This was not new – the anecdotal accounts of older residents suggest that drugs have been a prevalent feature of youth culture in the area since at least the late 1950s. However the scarcity of legitimate opportunities meant that the drug trade represented a readily available career option for some, rapidly appropriating local trading networks. Through the activities of a small minority of drug addicts, a vast localised market for stolen goods developed, meaning that previously marginal lifestyles and practices were brought closer to the everyday lives of the wider community. Campbell notes that the working-class taboo against "grassing" has long been sustained by an economic ethic that accommodated "respectable villainy" within the community (Campbell, 1993, p 170). From the late 1980s the expansion of the drugs market revived the area's historical links to organised crime that operated indirectly on the estate, through colonising the estate's channels of information and influence (see Chapter Four). This unsettled previously held notions of 'legitimate' behaviour as pursuing

5

'respectable' ends came increasingly to rely on morally dubious means. As Chapter Seven explores, many low-income residents suspended their abhorrence towards those involved in illegal activities in order to purchase goods and items that would have otherwise been unattainable. The empirical sections of this book testify that the ability to participate in localised lifestyles and forms of consumption represents a major subjective dimension of social inclusion. Consumption provides a means of differentiation from socially constructed notions of failure, through demonstrating the capacity for choice in a society where choice is a defining feature of citizenship (Taylor, 1998). Bauman (1998, p 41) observes that:

> The poorer are the poor, the higher and more whimsical are the patterns of life set in front of their eyes to adore, covet and wish to emulate. And so the 'subjective sense of insufficiency' with all the pain of stigma and humiliation, which accompany that feeling, is aggravated by a double pressure of decreasing living standards and increasing relative (comparative) deprivation.

The contingency of many households' fortunes at the bottom of a post-industrial labour market meant that maximising economic stability increasingly involved resorting to locally available and proven strategies for economic survival. Any study setting out to examine how residents of a locality develop collective solutions to economic marginality, needs to acknowledge the interrelationships that exist between different spheres of economic activity – in formal, informal and illegal economies – and how they generate localised dimensions of inclusion/exclusion. The underclass and social exclusion debates, through quantifying people into areas of extreme poverty and widespread unemployment "locate in the margins (where the excluded stand) what is happening in the centre (in the destruction of wage-earning society and of the welfare that was based upon it)" (Murard, 1996, p 3). The tendency to focus on the most deprived residents of the most poverty-stricken localities often misses the ways that wider structural changes are transforming and fragmenting working-class areas. Simultaneously, those same changes are increasing the importance of localised relationships based on reciprocal mutual advantage, which cut across and realign traditional notions of 'rough' and 'respectable'.

Research for the book was not conducted on a 'sink estate' of the type that has preoccupied commentators on the underclass and socially excluded but on a 'mixed' working-class locality containing a finely grained continuum, with deprivation and poverty existing in close proximity to relative (working-class) affluence. The lifestyles and consumption patterns of many residents failed to accord with a dichotomy between a demoralised, indigent 'excluded' and the rest. Neither did the residents' lifestyles correspond with policy proclamations concerning the causes of, and solutions to, 'social exclusion'. The reality was more complex and fluid, with some of the unemployed and economically inactive individuals and households having access to resources, which in turn provided lifestyles in excess of many of the 'working poor'. Other households relying on low-paid work topped up with in-work benefits were augmenting their incomes through a variety of innovative and entrepreneurial activities. Many of the unemployed and workless appeared to rely solely on state benefits. Although spatially close, they were socially distant and remained largely absent from the pubs, social clubs and houses of certain locals that acted as forums for the exchange and distribution of information and openings to make money. The disjuncture between much of the literature and my own observations shaped my research interests and the perspective that I applied to it, which was to understand how residents interpret social exclusion and how this understanding shaped the nature of the responses to exclusion through drawing on locally available resources.

The informal economy and social-structural change

The research interests discussed above are also pertinent to broader sociological debates concerning the future of work and over what constitutes 'work'. An increasingly diverse range of activities has been studied in connection with work over recent years in response to the limitations of much post-war sociology. This largely defined 'work' in terms of paid formal employment. These categories were developed within the framework of Fordist mass production and were premised on a 'rational' evolution of economic development from 'traditional' economies distinguished by a high level of small-scale, labour-intensive informal activity, towards 'advanced' economies. In the latter, labour and the provision of goods and services are progressively integrated into formal institutional structures within a regulatory framework supervised by the state (Rostow, 1960). As the economy becomes disembedded from society, institutional differentiation becomes a defining feature of modernity (Parsons and Smelser, 1956). Smith (1994) argues that the survey techniques and mass enquiries employed by industrial sociology were appropriate to an increasingly homogenised, industrial society. Other aspects of work, such as domestic labour, informal and 'street' economies, though acknowledged, were regarded as peripheral to the overall advance of modernity.

> The original studies of industrial society were based on the observation that people spent much of their waking hours in regimented work, which threw them together in concentrated spaces with other people, forcing them to share the same experience.... Out of such conditions arises a situation in which people begin to share an identity with one another, as well as a perception of the world: a particular consciousness. On this basis was built the political agenda of working-class parties of the early part of this century. (Smith, 1994, p 76)

This dualism was also reflected in the dichotomy between 'formal' and 'informal' economies, which originated in studies of urban development in the Third World. Field studies in Africa revealed that among the urbanising population people created their own income opportunities located within networks of self-employment and small enterprises. These were often more reliable and profitable than the scarce opportunities in the formal economy (Tripp, 1997). In the advanced economies the dominance of the large-scale, mass-production system was undermined by the 'realities' of the global economy and technological advances in communications and production techniques. The concepts that were developed to analyse work became increasingly redundant as they applied less and less to the empirical picture. Williams and Windebanck (1999) point out that while a relative formalisation of work has occurred over the long term, its end state – full employment – which defined its terms narrowly as *male* full-time employment, has never been achieved in the advanced economies. The rise of underemployment in the guise of part-time and temporary work, and the expansion of in-work benefits to subsidise low-wage jobs, means that societies are moving further away from full-time, permanent employment.

The advance of neo-liberalism through the 1980s and the state's retreat from economic and social intervention in order to stimulate market-led growth was assisted by a swathe of deregulatory policies, which promoted labour market flexibility. Small firms, once regarded as a marginal leftover from a traditional economy, were applauded as an entrepreneurial and innovative response to the crisis of Fordist mass production. The ideal type of 'flexible specialisation' was highlighted in studies of the 'Third Italy' where the term referred to new and decentralised means of production, performed by a distinct category of 'artisan' firms and underpinned by the principle of familialism and kinship relations (Piore and Sabel, 1984, pp 225-9). By the end of the 1980s, Castells and Portes were arguing that advanced industrial societies were witnessing the re-emergence of older forms of working relationship, which were expanding at the expense of previously formalised relationships:

> The process of institutionalization of economic activities is slowing down.... Subcontracting prevails over union contracts in various sectors. The cash economy is expanding in the microeconomic realm, while barter is becoming a crucial feature of economic exchange. New legions of would-be workers are entering a casual labour market, where a new breed of entrepreneurship is on the make.... And above all, there is the disenfranchisement of the institutionalized power conquered by labor, with much suffering, in a two-century-old struggle. (Castells and Portes, 1989, p 11)

Mingione (1991) claims that the 'main distorting factor' in the sociological tradition has been the strict division between a model of traditional society based on principles of reciprocity (collective before individual interests) and one of modern society based around principles of association (common interests defended by an organisational structure). This simplifies the complex reality of social arrangements, argues Mingione, since principles of reciprocity and of association have always coexisted in different combinations in particular historical contexts. What we are witnessing, he maintains, is the demise of the Fordist-Keynesian era of 'divided' societies and the dawn of 'fragmented' societies. By 'fragmented' he is referring to a shift in the institutional regulation of economic life away from 'associative' forms: horizontal interest groups, universal redistributive state policies, homogenisation and standardisation (which, he notes, were often overemphasised by social scientists). In 'fragmented' societies these tendencies are reversed and more complex combinations of reciprocal networks emerge. He argues that the reciprocal and social aspects that underpin economic life can illuminate the processes whereby the social division of labour is recomposed in order to provide viable, although highly unequal, economic strategies:

> Beyond the visible institutional and associative divisions (in other words, the class structure), a variety of micro-organisational differences, mainly based on various kinds of reciprocal institutions (from the internal division of labour within the nuclear family ... to kinship and informal practices in local communities or within ethnic groups), play a persistently important role. (Mingione, 1994, p 25)

The contemporary significance of informal working practices and support networks is that they are an important part of the different ways that societies, households, gender roles and working practices are changing in the face of broader patterns of socioeconomic change. Studies of informal working practices and reciprocal aid have revealed that they are inseparable from formal welfare and labour market institutions, providing an implicit and hidden contribution to their functioning. It is through closer knowledge of informal practices that a fuller understanding of the functioning of social institutions can be achieved (Henry, 1981, p 1). Despite the differing political slants that have been attached to such practices, argues Roberts (1994), what the various studies of informality share is the:

> ... belief that existing bureaucratic structures cannot adequately meet the economic need of the mass of the population. Household strategies suggest that people can choose and their choices make a difference, despite the economic and social constraints they face.... They become actors to get what they can out of the existing system. They thus shape politics, sometimes through social movements, but often by simply not supporting the *status quo* of established political parties. (Roberts, 1994, p 7).

This book is an empirical investigation of the varied ways that individuals and communities adapt to, and resist, the bureaucratic, welfare and labour market institutions that they face and the social relations that support those adaptions.

Research methods

Given these concerns it was felt that a qualitative and biographical approach would be the most appropriate. Quantitative data, through aggregating people into preconceived categories, fails to capture the ways in which intra–class processes of stratification are expressed and reproduced. In exploring the sources of community-based exclusion and the implications for the life chances of individuals and households, the focus was on the categories that people employ in their everyday lives and the reciprocal relations that sustain people's social links. Max Travers (1999), advocating the use of qualitative approaches to studies of class and status, cites Mathew Speier's observation that:

> The sociologist's lumping of people into various socio-economic categories of membership tells us very little about the structure and process of everyday life. *Rather it is the lumping that everyday participants do that tells us that* ... what we want to discover, so as to come out with news about society's workings, is precisely how members decide for themselves what social categories of membership they are in at any interactional moment. (cited by Travers, 1999; emphasis in original)

Chamberlayne and Rustin (1999, p 21) note that a biographical method, through contextualising statistical data and demonstrating what they mean for individual lives, contains implications for social policy since "individuals are not merely passive victims of fate and the strategies of response available to them, and the ways in which these are facilitated or otherwise by public policy, is relevant to outcomes". Furthermore, such an approach can highlight the 'network of existing relations' between the individual and others located within the constraints of the economic and social:

> The point is that people live their lives within the material and cultural boundaries of their time span, and so life histories are exceptionally effective historical sources because through the totality of lived experience they reveal *relations* between individuals and social forces, which are rarely apparent in other sources. (Lummis, 1987, pp 107-8; emphasis in original)

Gaining access to a sample involved two approaches and was guided according to the nature of the information sought. The first approach involved a 'snowball' or chain referral method, in which friends and associates on and around the estate introduced me to people to interview. Snowball sampling is especially appropriate where populations may be hidden and no sampling frame is available to define and randomly sample the population (Faugier and Sargeant, 1997). My interest in exploring the sources and structure of the local informal economy meant that many of the participants were engaged in illegal activities, albeit due to the circumstances in which work was performed. Therefore such research involves ethical concerns surrounding confidentiality and the potential consequences of publishing the research. Mann (1996, pp 66-7) has pointed out that social research findings rarely bring benefits to the group studied and may even be detrimental in that they may assist increased or new methods of policing and surveillance; more intrusive enquiries into specific groups, and an extension of the power of welfare professionals. Dean and Barret (1996, p 32) note that certain research subjects may induce a 'chilling effect' and become taboo areas for research or discussion. This can occur either because of the ideological arguments and policy prescriptions that they may unwittingly support, or because of the liberal academic establishment's standards of political correctness. Nevertheless, recent political endorsements of paid work as a panacea for the problems of exclusion and the policy of 'tough love' that has accompanied it, reveals that such proposals are made in the absence of knowledge of the lives of those affected by such policies. Oscar Lewis' (1968, p 20) 'culture of poverty' thesis attracted much criticism from liberal academics in the 1960s, which overlooked his emphasis on structural conditions in reproducing poverty, focusing instead on the cultural adaptions that, he argued, emerged in response. Lewis was aware that his research might endorse negative stereotypes of the poor, but maintained that any improvement in their lives could only be achieved through a close study of their lifestyles and the constraints that they live under.

Respondents were assured of anonymity in any publications and appear under pseudonyms, with aspects of their details altered to safeguard their identities. Dean and Barret (1996, p 26) note that the confidentiality of individuals would not prevent the group studied, or the locality in which research was undertaken, from adverse publicity or detrimental policy that may result from the research. In circumstances where the research may attract a wider readership than the confines of academic journals, it may be necessary to disguise the name of the area, as in W.F. Whyte's (1981) *Street corner society*. Not until the third edition, published 40 years after the research, did Whyte (1981, p viii) reveal that 'Cornerville' was an assumed name for Boston's North End. Whether to disguise the name of the area for the book or not proved to be a significant dilemma, but it was felt that masking the area's identity would make it impossible to discuss the history of the estate and how this has been shaped by decline and rejuvenation of the area's industrial profile; the housing policies and priorities of successive governments; and how these have combined to shape the social and demographic character of the estate today. This is vital in accounting for factors particular to the locality, and broader structural factors in understanding patterns of social relations. Further, the size of the estate, which covers over 825 acres across two London boroughs (Sutton and Merton) and houses over 40,000 inhabitants, minimises the potential of any adverse implications. The participants and their lives are not exceptional or uncommon and the experiences they recount will be recognisable to anybody who has ever lived on, or has experience of, life on any contemporary British housing estate.

The ability to utilise personal connections means that issues of trust are built into the process of snowball sampling as a result of the already existing personal ties between participants (Biernacki and Waldorf, 1981). This proved especially useful in the early stages of fieldwork where I relied heavily on such methods. I had known Steve for several years through his older brother who is a good friend from high school. Steve was a few years younger than us and, when younger, had hung around on the periphery of our group of friends. Later, during his adolescence he acquired a reputation as a prolific thief and for excessive displays of violence. Although this was a relatively short phase of his life the 'cultural capital' that he acquired stood him in good stead for his later 'career' as a cannabis dealer. My interest in Steve was not in his drug dealing but in the wide array of contacts that he had established from this, which has provided him with a steady supply of cash work and other sources of income ever since. Spradley (1979, p 23) proposed 'thorough enculturation' and current involvement in the scene being studied as two hallmarks of a 'good informant'. In a similar vein, Plummer (1983, p 101) observes that:

> A half dozen individuals with such knowledge constitute a far better 'representative sample' than a thousand individuals who may be involved in the action that is being formed but who are not knowledgeable about that formation.

Through the persuasion of his brother, Steve agreed to be interviewed and to introduce me to other people who might be of interest. He put me onto Darren, a car dealer/mechanic who runs his unregistered business largely on the estate. His insights into the economic ethics by which the informal economy operates proved extremely valuable, as did the people who he introduced me to. Another 'key informant' was Tina, the partner of one of the male respondents, Colin. Through her own experiences she was interested in the policy issues surrounding lone parents and was instrumental in providing me with leads to lone parents on the estate, which formed the basis of Chapter Six. Fieldwork took place between October 1998 and March 2000 with interviews usually taking place in people's homes and a few conducted in pubs, cars and a local café. Most of these were tape-recorded where this was felt appropriate. Most, although not all, agreed to the interviews being recorded. In such cases and during the interviews that took place in public the main themes were logged in a notebook and written up afterwards.

Research on the estate largely entailed spending three or four evenings a week sitting in people's houses. Steve and his girlfriend's house was particularly important since his involvement in informal work, and connections to the networks through which such work is found, meant that there was a steady stream of visitors who were likely to be of relevance to the study. Most of the sample on the estate were either working undeclared at the time of the interview or had previous experience of such work. Snowball sampling involves sampling within rather than across cases. As a consequence it tends to promote a sample that is homogeneous in its attributes, rather than providing linkages to groups whose social characteristics are different (Lee, 1993, p 67). This raises questions of representativeness and the extent of the income-generating strategies or lifestyles described, which will remain undetectable through such methods (and any other method). However, I would argue, following Plummer, that such methods yield more valid data. He argues (1983, p 102) that in any research there must always be a trade-off between reliability and validity and that:

> The problem ... is really being tackled from the wrong end: validity should come first, reliability second. There is no point being very precise about nothing! If the subjective story is what the researcher is after, the life history approach becomes the most valid.

Moreover, a homogeneous population was itself advantageous in exploring the nature of social networks; how the individual uses them in generating opportunities; the kinds of opportunities that informal methods provide; and the processes of social closure that reproduce those opportunities. Interviewing people with ties to other research participants can also act as a form of triangulation, through allowing for verification of details and events. To overcome problems of bias and to gain a more comprehensive view of life and labour on the estate, interviews were also conducted with the (formally) 'working poor', the unemployed, participants on employment training schemes and the New Deal, other residents and community workers.

Interviewing people involved in running or participating in employment training schemes and the New Deal involved negotiating access through formal channels. The process of making initial contact was frequently frustrating and took longer than anticipated. Introductory letters tended to go astray, messages were frequently not passed on and meetings were postponed. Eventually, I managed to gain access to Job Club – a compulsory 12-week programme for the unemployed that focused on increasing employability and assisting the participant's job search – and the New Deal for Young People, which was established in 1998. Given the setting, which inhibited many people from speaking freely, and the clear demarcation of our roles, it was initially difficult to conduct informal interviews. The maintenance of 'fronts' designed to impede the researcher's progress through concealment and deception is common where physical access has been gained, but social access has not (Lee, 1993, p 133). Many, although not all, respondents appeared uneasy being given open-ended questions and several commented afterwards that they had expected a more structured question and answer format. As Dingwall (1997, p 58) notes, during an interview respondents are required to demonstrate their competence in the role in which the interviewer places them. Some, but not all, will be part of the 'interview society' where the self is constructed as an object of narration. Others, such as the Pakistani women interviewed by Isabel Bowyer, had no experience of being interviewed and found it hard to talk about themselves or their experiences as mothers. She argues (1997, p 76) that:

> The ways of constructing the world that we take for granted, and the methods of exploring those constructs by asking for views and opinions from respondents, are not neutral but part of a particular social and cultural orientation. Data collection needs to be highly sensitive to differences, not just in the way questions are asked or topics raised, but also in the choice of methods themselves.

In light of these difficulties I decided to revise the approach and to use a semi-structured format. This focused on the main themes identified during the first six (unstructured) interviews and concentrated on work history, experience of and attitudes towards employment training schemes, perceptions of labour market opportunities, as well as social sources of support and information relating to work. Using this method yielded a good cross-section of Job Club participants, and I was able to conduct 36 interviews each lasting approximately one hour.

Conducting the research entailed collecting a mass of data, only a small proportion of which is presented in this book. However, many words of transcript are integrated into the research and, regardless of the extent to which the participant's perceptions and experiences inform the research findings, the decision over what data to include and in which sequence, rests with the author. Presenting a few hundred words of interview data from a 10,000-word transcript frequently struck me as an artificial and pernicious task, which failed to do justice to the actual sense of the actor's social world that a full reading of the text evokes. Considering the interview texts in their entirety dissolves the categories that are generated in order to impose a degree of internal consistency to the study. Raymond Williams noted the difficulty of capturing what he termed the 'structure of feeling', the "felt sense of the quality of life at a particular time and place" in his observation (1980, pp 63-4) that:

> We can learn a great deal of the life of other places and times, but certain elements, it seems to me, will always be irrecoverable. Even those that can be recovered are recovered in abstraction, and this is of crucial importance. We learn each element as a precipitate, but in the living existence of the time every element was in solution, an inseparable part of a complex whole.

The selection of quotations included in this book was guided by the research objectives, which sought to explore the experiences and consequences of living on the margins of the contemporary economy. The book does not claim to offer an exhaustive account of the participants' lives but focuses on the economic strategies that are deployed and the 'cultures of solidarity' that develop in response to crisis, and which require "a new repertoire of behaviour, associational ties and valuations" (Fantasia, 1988, p 14). The data provided represent those areas that I have been able to utilise most effectively in presenting important aspects of people's experiences of and responses to chronic economic uncertainty.

TWO

Globalisation and social exclusion

The processes that have expanded the scale of global capitalism have occurred in varying degrees across the globe and increased the generation of wealth, while polarising its distribution both within as well as between countries (Townsend, 1993). These processes, it has been claimed, have eroded the capacity of nation states to act independently of the global market and challenged the assumptions and principles on which the post-war state rests. In political, business and many academic circles it has become part of the conventional wisdom that governments, businesses and individuals have no choice but to adapt to these changes. Robert Reich, for example, in his introduction to *The work of nations* (1993, p 3), argues that:

> We are living through a transformation that will rearrange the politics and economy of the coming century. There will be no *national* products or technologies, no national corporations, no national industries. There will no longer be national economies at least as we have come to understand that concept. All that will remain rooted within national borders are the people who comprise a nation. Each nation's primary assets will be its citizens' skills and insights. Each nation's primary political task will be to cope with the centrifugal forces of the global economy, which tear at the ties binding citizens together – bestowing ever greater wealth on the most skilled and insightful, while consigning the less skilled to a declining standard of living.

As Reich notes, the accumulation of wealth and privilege on one hand, and deterioration in the life chances of the urban poor on the other, is only one aspect of the transformation of society within an increasingly interrelated 'globalised' economy. Despite differences of emphasis in the literature, the main causes of these changes are an expansion in the volume of world trade under heightened conditions of competitiveness and an increasing integration of previously protected national markets. These trends have been assisted by developments in communication technologies allowing economic activities to be decentralised. This spatial expansion has been accompanied by new methods of organising production and labour along with an accelerating mobility of capital, labour, goods and information. The capacity to coordinate economic activities over vast distances has resulted in the 'industrialisation' of parts of the 'developing' world and 'de-industrialisation' of industries and regions in the 'advanced' world. In the latter this has been accompanied by an expansion of the service sector, which has become the main source of employment in those economies and, in certain 'de-industrialised' areas that have failed to make the transition to a post-industrial economy, the re-emergence of mass structural unemployment.

These changes have resulted in a reappraisal of existing frameworks for analysing the course of capitalist development. While there is a consensus in social science that capitalism has entered a new phase since the mid-1970s, the origins and significance of those changes remain contested (Elam, 1995). Much social theory of recent decades has been characterised by scepticism concerning the ability of contemporary societies to analyse themselves, reflecting postmodern critiques of science. Postmodernity takes a dubious stance towards meta-narratives claiming that social theory can only be placed in local conceptualisations of situations and experiences. Featherstone (1991, p 116), for example, warns against:

> [The] danger of overestimating the significance of beliefs which are produced, classified and discussed by specialists and underestimating the significance of practical knowledge, common sense classificatory schemes, which ... are called upon as social life unfolds, practically by individuals held together in various shifting power balances and alliances.

An emphasis on fragmentation and diversity ultimately has implications for the ways that we think about poverty and exclusion and the potential to alleviate it. According to Stewart (2000, pp 57-8), one repercussion of a "dominant postmodern ethos" characterised by "the inescapability and relativism of all regimes of power and authority" has been a retreat from programmes of political and social reform and a fatalistic assumption that structured exclusion is unavoidable:

> Even among those committed to exploring and enacting projects of social inclusion, the dominant ethos has been such to lead to the abandonment of general models of social inclusion, such as those articulated around ideas of egalitarianism, in favour of much more limited arguments

concerning the disadvantaged situation of particular social
constituencies. (Stewart, 2000, p 57)

Allen and Macey (1994) note that acknowledging postmodern criticisms
of social scientific knowledge need not invalidate that knowledge, since it
is within local situations that wider processes of historical changes are
experienced. An analysis that moves beyond the local to consider the
relationship between structural forces and individual action must concede
the reality of social-structural location and the interplay of wider sets of
processes as central (Allen and Macey, 1994, pp 124-8). The fortunes of
individuals and households, therefore, need to be understood within the
framework of global economic restructuring as well as in terms of each
nation's particular set of institutional arrangements since these form the
conditions through which responses are generated and articulated. As Bill
Jordan et al (1992) note, 'strategies' pursued at the level of household or
individual are themselves framed by 'strategies' pursued at a higher level
by collective actors such as the state, corporations and other institutions.

The following sections will consider certain models, which have
sought to make sense of these broader changes, to show how the
'socially excluded' have been located in contemporary debates about
the changing industrial, occupational and class structures of 'post-
industrial' capitalism. In tracing the roots of the term 'social exclusion',
Silver (1994) notes that each period of social and economic upheaval
brings with it new concepts to categorise those groups most
disadvantaged by change. While previous periods brought concepts of
'poverty' and 'unemployment', so contemporary changes have given
rise to new conceptions: 'underclass', the 'new poverty' and 'social
exclusion' (Silver, 1994). Regardless of changes in terminology, the
reshaping of labour markets and welfare systems, and the role and
function of the state in relation to them, figure centrally in these debates.

Post-Fordism and post-industrialism: theoretical approaches

Contemporary attempts to grasp the nature and significance of
economic restructuring have been developed from notions of the
'Information Society' developed in the 1960s by theorists such as
Daniel Bell (1973) in *The coming of post-industrial society* and in the
various strands of post-Fordist theories that emerged in the 1980s.
The former maintains that in the advanced industrial nations the decline
of manufacturing and expansion of service industries, in particular
the information industries, amounts to a transformation in the 'axial

principle' of societies (Bell, 1973, p 12). In post-industrial societies, theoretical knowledge becomes paramount, as computers rather than machines drive the production process and become the key technologies. Knowledge becomes vital both as a strategic economic resource and for purposes of social control and planning. The guardians of this knowledge – the professional, scientific and technical groups – become the chief social group vital for economic growth, replacing the industrialists and manual-manufacturing workers of the industrial era. During the post-war period there was a rapid growth in administrative, technical and professional occupations and it is through the growth of this knowledge-based elite, that the transition to post-industrialism is analysed. Between 1959 and 1981 these groups grew by 130% in Britain, with similar increases in public sector professionals (Allen and Massey, 1988, p 99).

While Bell was optimistic about the future of post-industrial capitalism, other commentators have pointed to the polarisation of income and opportunities that has accompanied these changes. The 'advanced services' require a high level of specialised education, which in turn has driven the massive expansion of higher education and technical training and allowed for a considerable degree of upward mobility into the service class, whose economic basis lies in its 'cultural capital'. In 1972 only one third of professional, managerial and administrative employees had fathers from the service class compared to 46% whose fathers were from working-class backgrounds (Goldthorpe and Payne, 1986), although more recent research indicates that trends in intergenerational mobility have slowed over recent decades (Blanden et al, 2002). As the proportion of the low-educated population has declined and those with high levels of education have grown, income inequality has increased. In Britain, average incomes grew by around 40% between 1979 and 1994/95. For the richest tenth of the population, incomes rose by 60-68% while for the poorest tenth they rose by 10% representing a fall of 8% after housing costs (Hills, 1998).

Post-Fordist theorists emphasise the shift away from the Fordist 'regime of accumulation' based on mass production and consumption towards a post-Fordist model based on techniques of 'flexible specialisation'. Escalating rates of commercial, technological and organisational innovation and the fragmentation of mass consumer markets have emphasised shorter production runs based on a greater variety of product types. Harvey (1992, 1995, 2003) relates the emergence of new social and economic divisions and the rise of a consumerist post-modern culture to long-run tendencies of over-accumulation identified by Marx. Marx (1976) argued that because capitalist production requires a growing mass of machinery and an increasing composition of capital, it also requires a mass production of commodities on a mass scale. Because capitalism is given to periods of crisis, the issue is the ability of capitalist relations to stabilise and establish themselves around a set of institutions that facilitate a further period of economic growth. The most recent period of economic and social restructuring has witnessed the emergence of a globalised post-Fordist regime based on systems of 'flexible accumulation', meaning greater labour market and productive flexibility. Overcoming problems of accumulation requires a spatial and temporal restructuring, which creates new spaces within which capitalist production can proceed. Harvey (2003, p 98) understands globalisation as expressing our changing experience of time and space, termed a 'time-space' compression, which he relates to the post-Fordist tendencies of global capitalism:

> ... an incessant drive towards the reduction if not elimination of spatial barriers, coupled with equally incessant impulses towards acceleration in the turnover of capital.... The trend towards 'globalization' is inherent in this, and the evolution of the geographical landscape of capitalist activity is driven remorselessly by round after round of time-space compression.

Like Bell, Harvey stresses the pivotal role played by knowledge, which becomes a "key commodity to be produced and sold to the highest bidder, under conditions that are themselves increasingly organized on a competitive basis" and vital in coordinating decentralised organisational formations (Harvey, 1992, pp 159-160). Geographic expansion and dispersal may provide a short-run solution but overcoming recurrent crises of over-accumulation require a 'temporal displacement'. In order to accelerate turnover time, argues Harvey, it became necessary to transfer resources in order to explore future needs. An acceleration of globalisation has been most prominent in manufacturing and finance. The creation of a global financial system has created "for the first time the formation of a single world market for money and credit" and transformed the economy and employment structures in the global financial centres (Harvey, 1992, p 161). This shift to flexible accumulation has had a profound effect on the social composition, class structures and consumption practices in urban centres. De-industrialisation and increased levels of urban poverty have coincided with an influx of affluent professional and managerial workers as the financial, real estate and insurance sectors have expanded. Decentralisation of jobs and population from urban centres reversed the pattern of Fordist development, reducing the supply of middle-income jobs with the most dynamic sectors generating a high level of jobs at both extremes of the income distribution (Fainstein et al, 1992).

As spatial competition to attract economic development intensified, cities became compelled to compete to attract increasingly mobile companies and consumers, giving rise to policies emphasising territorial competition. Hamnett (2003, pp 16-17) argues that the pro-market policies pursued through the 1980s and 1990s attempted to set the parameters for London's role as a major financial sector and hastened its transition from an industrial to a post-industrial city. 'Public–private' partnerships often meant diverting funds away from 'collective consumption' needs towards providing subsidies and the infrastructure to attract consumers and corporations, as urban centres began to be reshaped around shopping malls, consumer and leisure activities. While such consumer-based innovations promote the transition to 'flexible accumulation', they also replace the notion of social citizenship and of the city as a public space, with one of the city as a privatised place of consumption (Christopherson, 1995). Buck et al (2002) note that the Mayor's report on *The state of London* in 2000 reflects the national government's concern with the relationship between competitiveness and social cohesion. The report emphasises the need to attract more investment to maintain the city's competitive edge and also to address the extremes of poverty and wealth, which undermines social cohesion and impedes economic competitiveness. The significance of city competitiveness is also reflected in the agenda-setting studies for the Greater London Authority. This includes a strategy to identify and promote competitive advantage; investing in knowledge and business-based institutions; upgrading the skills of the workforce; modernising business-related infrastructure; and making the city an attractive location for people and businesses (Buck et al, 2002, pp 4-6). For Harvey, the construction of places as 'symbolic spaces' provides a framework through which relations of class, gender and race can be analysed. The connection between place and social identity was central to the struggle between labour and capital within an overall patterning of uneven geographic development (Harvey, 1992, pp 303). Place-bound identity rests on the power of tradition, which becomes hard to maintain in the face of flux and transience. Tradition itself becomes commodified and marketed as such for the urban professionals who have come to dominate whole areas of previously working-class inner cities through a process of gentrification, and who command space through social mobility with money providing the route to membership of the community (Harvey, 1992, p 303). In London, the spatial expansion of gentrification has penetrated into the last refuges of working-class inner London, and been accompanied by a steady concentration of poorer and less-skilled residents into social housing. Between 1981 and 1991, inner London boroughs experienced an average rise of 38% in the size of professional and managerial groups, and outer London boroughs an average increase of 21%. Consequently the city is now less socially segregated at the borough level than it was during its industrial period, when a small middle-class residential area in the centre of the city was surrounded by solidly working-class districts, and more segregated at the local or micro level (Hamnett, 2003, pp 172-7). Buck et al (2002, p 29) observe that:

> In this spreading middle-class professional and managerial mass, corresponding to the transformations of London's economy, sit increasingly anomalous areas of public housing, the product of the great rebuilding of the 1950s and 1960s. The more desirable among them, meaning especially the low-rise LCC [London County Council] cottage estates, have largely been transformed into owner-occupier enclaves, especially attractive as starter homes for the aspiring middle-class, as have some of the better-designed tower blocks.

As residential segregation has diminished, social tensions have increased, which is exhibited in an obsession with physical and electronic security and surveillance systems. In 1995 the world's first police surveillance system in a residential area was launched in West End, Newcastle upon Tyne, one of the most socially deprived areas in Britain (*The Independent on Sunday*, 3 September 1995). London has witnessed the growth of private 'gated' estates over recent years, and at least four local authorities are considering the creation of private police forces to tackle the perceived upsurge in antisocial behaviour (Hamnett, 2003, p 209).

Harvey's account also emphasises how social divisions are maintained and strengthened through the culture of consumption and the status distinctions that they produce. The expansion of capitalism into previously uncommodified areas, argues Harvey, has to be viewed in relation to the promotion of a culture of consumption, which under conditions of 'flexible accumulation' places an increasing emphasis on symbolic capital. This gives a new lease of life to aesthetic innovation and experimentation, creating "aesthetic twists [which] become an expression of class power" (Harvey, 1992, p 114). Following Bourdieu,

Harvey argues that consumption is not merely about expressing differences that already exist, it also becomes a way of establishing differences that conceal, through culture and taste, the real basis of economic distinction (Harvey, 1995, p 374). The influx of global corporations into the major financial centres and the reshaping of urban centres around the lifestyles and consumption practices of an affluent service class are contrasted with the growth of poverty, homelessness and unemployment, the poor ignored in a world "cluttered with illusion, fantasy and pretence" (Harvey, 1992, p 335).

Varieties of exclusion

While Lash and Urry (1987) emphasise many of the processes previously mentioned, they also account for how global processes are filtered through national institutions and frameworks and how these generate socially excluded groups. Central to their analysis is the claim that the era of 'organised' capitalism that developed from the late 19th century is moving into an era of *disorganised* capitalism. The driving force behind this is the increasing scale of industrial, banking and commercial enterprises, which makes them increasingly autonomous from direct control and regulation by individual nation states. Other factors that reverse the characteristics of 'organised capitalism' are the development of an educationally based stratification system, continued growth of a distinctive service class and the emergence of 'new social movements' increasingly divorced from class-based politics. Likewise, previous decades have seen a decline in the class character of political parties, a reduction in the core working class and an increase in cultural fragmentation and pluralism. Work is increasingly characterised by flexible labour processes, feminisation and an increased 'mental' element (Lash and Urry, 1987, pp 5-6). They argue that the same set of processes that gives rise to an extensive service class has also created new socially excluded groups through exerting a structural downward mobility for large sections of the working class, along with a set of structural locations that are filled by large numbers of immigrants. These groups are at the base of a restructured stratification system comprising a mass advanced service class, a smaller and debilitated working class and the new lower class (Lash and Urry, 1994, pp 145-6). Particularly relevant is their contention that the degree to which an economy is 'disorganised' and its accompanying institutional frameworks will largely determine the composition of new lower-class groups. For example, German capitalism was organised on a corporate basis relatively early in its development: industry was concentrated and links between the major banks, industry and the state were forged; and also included the development of trades unions, working-class political parties and a welfare state. Germany remains a predominantly manufacturing economy employing 40% of its workforce in this sector, compared to between 20-25% in the US and UK, and also remains a more nationally based economy than Britain with lower levels of foreign investment and inward investment from abroad (Lash and Urry, 1994, p 191).[1] High value-added work in the manufacturing sector is heavily unionised, more gender segregated and excludes higher proportions of older men than jobs in the service sector, which is a less developed sector than in the US and UK. Employees in these jobs are paid a family wage, which enhances the 'male breadwinner' role and places the family in a central position (Lash, 1994, pp 166-168). The implication for German women is a lower participation rate in the labour market, as they lack the opportunities to work in the sectors that have largely absorbed female labour in other countries. First, argues Lash, the greater traditionalism of German life means that there is less demand for advanced consumer services such as law, estate agents and building societies while the consumer service sector is also less developed than in liberal regimes. Second, since transfer payments to the unemployed are high, welfare services play a less prominent role. Women in the domestic sphere generally provide these services, unlike in liberal and social-democratic regimes where they are provided via state agencies employing high proportions of women. Restrictions on immigrants' citizenship rights and on enterprise formation restrict opportunities for job creation in the lower echelons of the service sector and in downgraded manufacturing, which is a common feature of immigrant groups in France, the UK and US. Thus the nature of German corporatism, while preventing the downward mobility characteristic of the 'new lower class' in the UK and US, also allows for a different regime of lower-class formation through the institutional exclusion of women from the labour market and immigrants from citizenship rights (Lash and Urry, 1994, p 180). In liberal regimes such institutional regulation is lacking: mechanisms of exclusion reside not in corporate institutions including the state, unions, employers' associations and the welfare state but in 'markets', in particular housing and labour markets. Whereas in Germany such institutions operate functionally, in liberal regimes they tend to operate spatially (Lash and Urry, 1994, p 156). The consequences of these exclusionary mechanisms and of the social and spatial divisions that they produce are addressed below.

De-industrialisation and the post-industrial city

Following the crisis of the 1970s the mechanisms established under the post-war era of Fordist industrial strategies and Keynesian 'demand-side' policies gave way to a political and economic ideology that would place global markets at the centre of the historical stage. Hirst and Thompson point out that this was largely the consequence of a set of political decisions rather than an inexorable process to which governments were forced to respond. The expansion of global capitalism was stimulated by policies that emphasised privatisation and deregulation as governments pursued often short-term policy objectives (Hirst and Thompson, 1996, p 2). As mentioned, proponents of globalisation have been influential in setting the parameters for debate and have fostered the "pathology of diminished expectations" given the dominance of world markets (Hirst and Thompson, 1996, p 6). This was reflected in the 1980s by the emergence, most notably in the US, UK and New Zealand, of the New Right and the ascendancy of neo-liberal theories and remedies. Between the mid-1970s and mid-1980s, 18 million new jobs were created in the US, compared to a net loss of three million jobs in the European Union (EU). This was attributed to the highly flexible nature of the US labour market compared to the inflexible and over-regulated European labour markets (Nielsen, 1991, p 4). Globalisation, it was argued, would allow markets to develop on a scale that would allow them to escape the grasp of inefficient 'over-extended' states (Ohmae, 1990). Callaghan (1997, p 3) writes that:

> Throughout the 1980s ... the concept of flexibility emerged to sum up at once both the nature of changes in the labour market which had been caused by economic restructuring, and the change in the nature of labour market participants and their work, which would allow economies to capitalise on such restructuring.

The spatial significance of these changes was emphasised in W.J. Wilson's prominent account *The truly disadvantaged* (1987), where he relates the growth of a black urban underclass in the US to the geographic relocation of industry. This, combined with a historical process of discrimination, has concentrated large proportions of African Americans at the lower end of the labour market (Wilson, 1987, p 12). A relocation of manufacturing employment away from the urban centres to where black people had originally migrated to fill demand for manufacturing labour, towards the suburbs and the West and South of the US, has resulted in increased concentrations of poverty. Formerly industrial regions of the US such as Detroit and St. Louis suffered extensive de-industrialisation in the post-war period: the latter, for example, experiencing a decline in central city employment from 431,000 to 273,000 people between 1953 and 1986 (Lash and Urry, 1994, p 152). These factors have combined to exert a downward mobility to underclass status, which Wilson defines in terms of the behavioural characteristics attributed by conservatives such as Murray, although these are seen as a product of structural forces to which culture has adapted (Wilson, 1987, p 41). Wilson's key concepts are 'social isolation' – isolation from mainstream groups and institutions – and 'social concentration' – the increasing proportion of African Americans living in extreme poverty (Wilson, 1987, p 61). He relates these concepts to the spatial transformations and changing role of the ghetto. Previously, the ghetto had formed a complete community with community leaders and a parallel set of institutions to what were found outside. The lifting of restrictive covenants and an emphasis on equality of individual opportunity from the 1960s, allowed the exodus of higher-income black families from the inner city. Consequently, it became more difficult to sustain the community's institutions in the face of sustained joblessness and the flight of those who had largely sustained them. Wilson attaches a central role to black male joblessness and the collective behavioural responses that emerged in response to the collapse of inner-city manufacturing employment. This normative vacuum combined with the 'emptying out' of economic space provided the conditions for the disintegration of the black inner-city family, increased levels of urban poverty and the reproduction of social pathologies. To locate where these processes have been more prominent, Lash and Urry construct a typology of cities: the de-industrialised, the restructured and the post-industrial (Lash and Urry, 1994, pp 151-6). Post-industrial cities such as Los Angeles and Phoenix in the US and Bristol in the UK, which never had a large manufacturing base, tend to have lower rates of inequality, high rates of employment growth and an expanding population, although in the US this consists of proportionately few black households. De-industrialised cities are those that started from a large manufacturing base, have witnessed large falls in total employment and a corresponding decline in population. Restructured cities such as New York, Chicago and London are those that have managed to make the transition to a post-industrial economy. Within this category are many of the global financial centres, which as discussed tend to have higher levels of inequality than post-industrial and de-industrialised cities. The growth of socially excluded groups also carries spatial implications in the UK and it is on the peripheral and inner-city social housing estates where processes of social and spatial segregation largely culminate and where some of the greatest deprivation is to be found. The *Joseph Rowntree inquiry into income and wealth* (JRF, 1995) indicated an increase in the number of 'concentrated poverty' wards over recent decades with widening gaps between poverty and wealth occurring at an increasingly fine level. One of the factors contributing to this is the strong link between social housing and low income. The report notes that the proportion of social housing tenants in the poorest 40% of the population increased from under 50% in the early 1970s to 75% by 1991 (JRF, 1995, p 29). The Social Exclusion Unit's *National strategy for neighbourhood renewal* (SEU, 2000) reports that between 20% and 30% of electoral wards in the UK suffer from multiple forms of deprivation (SEU, 2000, p 20); and around half of social housing tenants live in households with below 60% of median income after housing costs (ONS, 2004).

Hamnett (2003, p 156) notes that in the London housing market, housing tenure is strongly related to labour market position and income. The large increases in affluent professional and managerial groups have significantly altered the nature of the housing market and fuelled the inflated house prices. Increasing pressure for housing has pushed downwards from the top end of the market, as demand for housing has meant progressive buyers have had to seek housing in less desirable areas. This places increasing strain on the lower end of the market and squeezes out lower- and middle-income groups who are only able to buy in marginal, outer London boroughs. The increase in home ownership has been accompanied by a long-term decline and residualisation of the council and social housing sectors due to the sale of much better-quality stock in the Right to Buy scheme and large declines in new building. Buck et al (1986) argue that in London only a small proportion of ward-level unemployment is explainable in terms of differing rates of employment change. Above average rates of unemployment reflect residential concentrations of groups in a weak competitive position in the labour market rather than spatial variations in labour market conditions, and is associated with areas of rented accommodation, high population density and large proportions of manual workers (Buck et al, 1986, p 101). The notion of neighbourhood polarisation has been a central plank informing New Labour's approach to tackling social exclusion. This was reflected in the 1998 publication of the Social Exclusion Unit's *Bringing Britain together: A national strategy for neighbourhood renewal*, which, through the

New Deal for Communities, aims to tackle the web of deprivation affecting the most blighted areas (SEU, 1998). The scheme initially provided £800 million over three years in 17 of the most deprived neighbourhoods and in 1999 regional development agencies were established, responsible for the £1.3 billion Single Regeneration Budget. These policies represent part of a comprehensive approach to social exclusion that also attempts to deal with the 'spatial mismatch' and relates employment supply to demand through the creation of Employment Zones. The policies have been combined with training and retraining programmes, in order for the unemployed to adjust to prevailing labour market conditions. Underlying the recent emphasis on supply-side measures is the view that workers need to be equipped with the necessary skills and training to allow them to adapt to the rapidly changing demands of a global economy. Accepting the limits to fiscal and monetary policy that these changes place on governments, enhancing human capital is seen to represent the best route to social inclusion. This reflects the current dominance of individualistic explanations for, and solutions to, the problems of deprived communities and of the people within them. However, critics have argued that the direction of labour market restructuring and areas of job growth at the lower end of contemporary labour markets place severe restrictions on the capacity of supply-side measures in tackling social exclusion in isolation from more fundamental changes.

Labour market restructuring and low-wage employment

The changing labour requirements of a post-industrial economy, with technology-driven job losses making the unskilled redundant, provided the context in which modern concern over an excluded 'underclass' arose (Myrdal, 1962). Dahrendorf (1987) questioned whether a modern economy needs everybody and, citing Germany as an example, questions the extent to which modern economies could cope with a significant proportion of their populations economically inactive and still achieve respectable growth rates. He argues that our values, which emphasise the need for work, no longer coincide with the economic requirements of our society and that the underclass may represent the "ultimate extrapolation of the fate of many" (Dahrendorf, 1987, pp 12-15). Bauman (1998) argues that consumer activity has replaced work as the mechanism linking individual motives, social integration and systemic reproduction. In tracing the passage from a 'society of producers' guided by the 'work ethic' towards a 'society of consumers' ruled by an 'aesthetic of consumption', he argues that the poor no longer have any potentially productive role to play in society. Economic growth and the 'rise of employment now stand in an opposing relationship to one another, as technological progress is measured by its displacement of workers (Bauman, 1998, p 65). Nelson (1995) argues that accounts like those previously cited that focus on broad processes of systemic change overlook the role of managerial and bureaucratic innovations and the ways in which the application of specialised knowledge has been employed in service industries. He takes issue with 'convergence theories' that stress the parallels between the labour market structures of the advanced and developing nations. In the former, low-level service jobs are not generally concentrated in informal or residual sectors as in the developing nations but are functionally integrated within industries in the core sectors of the economy (Nelson, 1995, p 39). The rationalisation and concentration of the service sector particularly in the leisure, retail and catering industries capitalise on changing gender roles, increasing affluence and consumer demand. This produces a glut of low-wage, routine service jobs and increases the demand for a highly educated and well-paid elite to control this workforce. Subsequently, management and specialised training programmes proliferate, markets expand, competition becomes more intense and transactions more complex. This fuels a cumulative process that places ever-more emphasis on advanced levels of education and training. The inequality resulting from increased earnings at the top, argues Nelson, reflects the structure of post-industrial capitalism that professionals and managers helped to create, and "the bridge forged between knowledge, income and wealth creates new men and women of power" (Nelson, 1995, p 42).

Similarly, Byrne (1999) contends that the 'excluded' play a vital function in the present phase of capitalist development that seeks to control labour through a twin strategy of development and underdevelopment. The former refers to the pursuit of high-skill, high-quality employment, while the latter refers to a competitive strategy based on 'numerically flexible' low-wage, low-skill employment. It is in this latter sphere that the poor play a vital role as a 'reserve army' as a means of depressing wage levels and instilling discipline on the employed, in a context that places the creation of low-wage jobs as the solution to unemployment and high inflation. This has resulted in both 'core' and 'periphery' firms, while central to the development of a 'flexible' labour market has been the distinction noted by Atkinson (1984) between 'functionally' and 'numerically' flexible workers. The former comprise the nucleus of the firm, the 'core' workers holding full-time, relatively secure and well-paid employment. The latter are either employed under conditions of insecurity (which is built into the structure of an increasingly precarious formal employment regime) or occupy temporary, part-time or casualised jobs (Allen and Henry, 1996). Rather than being consigned to the margins of a peripheral economy, the distinguishing feature of the working poor today is their role in relation to and in connection with industries in the core sector of the economy (Byrne, 1999, p 53).Post-Fordist accounts stress the change in the size distribution of firms as they have adopted more flexible techniques in smaller decentralised units. This marks a trend from the vertical integration of firms towards looser more horizontal linkages, or from 'hierarchies' towards 'markets', as tasks have been removed from the hierarchical structure of the firm and marketed or subcontracted beyond it (Granovetter, 1985).The move towards more flexible forms of accumulation has been marked by new forms of capital–labour relations and assisted by an increase in outsourcing, subcontracting with different labour systems coexisting in tiered layers of subcontractors. These developments have been made possible by advances in communications and information technology, allowing capitalism to become "more tightly organised through dispersal, geographic mobility and flexible responses in labour markets, labour processes and consumer markets" (Harvey, 1992, p 159).

The growth of self-employment and small-business enterprise has often been heralded as highlighting the centrality of the market and resilience of entrepreneurial values in the face of bureaucratic regulation (Maldonado, 1995). Other commentators view the shifts towards post-Fordist methods of production as increasing labour autonomy and potentially reviving craft production (Piore and Sabel, 1984, pp 258-80). While such changes allow profit-making goals to be realised, the associated costs are borne by those in working-class occupations. The division between a core and periphery workforce polarises the labour market into non-competing groups and dissolves internal labour markets, which had previously tied workers to firms. Underinvestment in training reduces the supply of skilled workers whose skills are transferable across firms, thus allowing them to increase their bargaining power at the expense of the peripheral workforce. Beck (1992) argues that these changes have profoundly affected the experience of work, which under Fordism with its large-scale manufacturing plants had fostered the development of class identities and class consciousness. Work is now experienced not as a unifying experience but as an individualised society of employees (Beck, 1992, pp 99-101, 146-8). Consequently, argue Castells and Portes (1989, p 31), the class structure becomes diluted, as "the experience of labour and the emergence of stable class positions do not correspond to each other". The burden of employment risk is shifted away from the employer and towards the employee and through extending the social division of labour, it becomes easier for firms to implement changes in the labour process.

Crook et al (1992, pp 121-2) argue that these changes represent an emerging pattern of inequality constructed around consumption as traditional class boundaries have been eroded. The changes have displaced the capitalist class with a service class and fragmented the working class, with each fragment attempting to secure its place in the distributive system. This has resulted in a more intensive differentiation of class positions, separating the working class from an underclass on the basis of access to extensive and increasingly privatised consumption. As Hopkins (1991, p 277) notes, these cleavages were intensified throughout the 1980s by a tirade of neo-liberal propaganda promoting individual enterprise, the supremacy of the market and demoralisation of state welfare:

> As long as the rent or mortgage repayments could be paid, the family fed, the car serviced and the holiday booked in Spain, all appeared to be well. Working class solidarity seemed increasingly to be a thing of the past. It became easy to suppose that unemployment was due, at least in part, to a failure to get on one's bike; or to the workings of the economic system, which had to be left to work out its own salvation.

Kumar (1995) points out that the division between a core and periphery workforce is most advanced not in 'leading edge' manufacturing firms (which forms the basis of many post-Fordist claims) but rather in service industries and the public sector. The relative economic success and low unemployment rates of the US and UK are inexplicable without taking into account the growth of low-wage service sector work that is largely lower paid, less skilled, less unionised and with less security than in manufacturing (Kumar, 1995, pp 58-9). The growth of financial and business services in the urban centres has not made the unskilled redundant, but has instead generated a high number of low-wage service jobs through the occupational structures of these sectors and through the consumption practices of the new high-income urban professionals. The growth of specialised consumption and market niches has seen the revival of 'sweatshops' in cities such as New York and London as the needs of the market require production to be close to demand (Phizacklea, 1990). Increasing numbers of adaptable and mobile low-wage migrants perform domestic services, construction, catering and 'sweatshop' manufacturing in First World urban centres as the demand for low-wage labour expands (Jordan and Duvell, 2002). London remains a major destination for international migration, which corresponds to its role as a 'world city' receiving a third of total immigration into the UK. Between 1975 and 2000, London received a net inflow of approximately 450,000 recorded migrants, increasing from 41,000 in the period 1990-94 to 216,000 in the period 1995-99 (Hamnett, 2003, pp 106-7).

Sassen (1996, p 70) argues that labour market restructuring is polarising the service sector between 'knowledge and information intensive' sectors and 'labour-intense low productivity sectors' with large increases in low-wage service jobs forecasted. Similarly Gorz (1989, p 5) views social and economic polarisation as part of the general direction of change, whereby a largely deskilled working class is forced into downgraded service work whose primary function is serving the affluent knowledge-based elite:

> The division of society into classes involved in intense economic activity on the one hand and a mass of people who are marginalised or excluded from the economic sphere on the other will allow a sub-system to develop, in which the economic elite will buy leisure time by getting their own personal tasks done for them, at low cost, by other people ... the leisure time of the economic elite provide jobs, which are in most cases insecure and underpaid, for a section of the masses excluded from the economic sphere.

Since the mid-1980s the majority of jobs created in the UK have been low-paid, part-time service work increasingly performed by women, whose employment rates have grown four times as fast as men's across the EU since 1994 (Employment and Social Affairs Directorate, 1999, p 16). The growth of flexible part-time work has been presented as especially suitable for women because it allows them to maintain a 'dual role' in the domestic and employment spheres. A consequence of the trend towards two-earner households has been an increasing inequality between 'work-rich' and 'work-poor' households, the latter accounting for 41.4% of all working-age households in London in 1993. Between 1979 and 1993 the median income of no-earner households in London increased by 25.3%, while the income of one-earner households grew by 37.6% and by 60.5% for two-earner households (Hamnett, 2003, pp 100-1). A further consequence has been an undermining of the notion of a 'family wage' as an assessment of what constitutes a 'fair' salary and 20% of all people of working age live in households with income below half the national average wage (Bardgett and Vidler, 2000, p 25). These trends have also assisted the growth of low-paid employment to men as well as women. The wages of the bottom 10% of male earners in the US and UK remained stagnant or declined between 1975 and 1995, eroding the relationship between standards of living, family and employment position (Marris, 1996, p 54).

Hamnett (2003) takes issue with the polarisation thesis that predicts increasing proportions of jobs at the top and bottom end of the labour market. While post-industrial labour markets may generate large numbers of unskilled, low-paid jobs, this does not indicate that such jobs form an increasing proportion of total employment. Evidence points to a growth of income inequality in London, with marked disparities in earnings growth between manual and non-manual workers in service occupations. Between 1979 and 1995 earnings of male managers in the UK grew by 60% compared to earnings in personal services, which grew by 24%. In London, the gap was wider, with earnings for managers rising by 75% while earnings in personal services rising by 30% (Hamnett, 2003, p 84). Evidence indicates an upgrading of the occupational and class structure and a decline in the number of less-skilled workers, which is fuelling the increase in inequality:

> What the results show is a massive upward shift in real earnings, particularly in London, away from all deciles except the bottom one, to the highest decile band. This shows limited polarisation in that there are more rich and more poor, but it is a very asymmetric form of polarisation, with an increase at the top end fifteen times that at the bottom. (Hamnett, 2003, p 85)

However, as Hamnett concedes, analysis of changes in occupational structures using aggregate and Census data excludes those groups who work undeclared and outside of formal employment either to supplement welfare benefits or because of their immigration status (Hamnett, 2003, p 62). As outlined above, the importance of informal economic activities may have increased as a consequence of changes in the occupational and industrial structures of post-industrial capitalism as the poor have come under increasing pressure to supplement welfare and/or low-paid insecure employment (Pahl, 1984; Williams and Windebanck, 1998). Tilly and Scott (1978) adopted the concept of 'family strategy' to describe the evolution from a 'family economy' to a 'family wage economy' and finally to a 'family consumer economy'. Each stage was accompanied by a reduction of the collective coordination of the family's economic behaviour until, at the 'family consumer' stage, coordination was unnecessary as the male 'breadwinner' model ensured the family's economic survival (Tilly and Scott, 1978). For many, the labour market trends that unfolded through the 1980s and 1990s profoundly weakened the 'family consumer economy' and revived the 'family wage economy' as a dual income has become necessary if consumption is to be maintained at a reasonable level.

Strategies to 'end welfare as we know it' in the US and UK in recent years have involved a shift away from a 'passive' benefit system towards 'active' labour market policies. These have included training and welfare-to-work measures such as the New Deal for the Unemployed and New Deal for Lone Parents, which reflect the influence of policy analysts such as Lawrence Mead and legislation such as President Clinton's 1996 Welfare Reform Act (Mead, 1986). New Labour's objective of tackling 'social exclusion' aims to remedy the 'skills mismatch' of the unemployed through training and work experience, and provide incentives to rejoin the labour market through the introduction of a minimum wage and the provision of tax credits for working families and for childcare. Simultaneously, access to the benefit system for the unemployed, lone parents and disabled people has become increasingly provisional as reintegrating those deemed capable back into the labour market and 'reforming welfare around the work ethic' has become a mantra of New Labour (Lister, 2001a). A key element in recent welfare reform has been the expanded role of in-work benefits such as Working Tax Credit, increasing flexibility and competitiveness by depressing wages further and allowing the market to respond by creating more low-wage labour (Grover and Stewart, 1999). Jessop (1995) argues that the shift towards post-Fordism has been accompanied by a redirection of economic and social regulation, away from a Keynesian welfare system and towards a 'Schumpeterian workfare state' and that:

> In abstract terms, its distinctive objectives in economic and social regulation are: to promote product, process, organizational and market innovation in open economies

in order to strengthen as far as possible the structural competitiveness of the national economy by intervening on the supply side; and to subordinate social policy to the needs of labour market flexibility and/or the constraints of international competition. (Jessop, 1995, p 263)

In 1998 when research for this book began, between 1.9 and 2.4 million employees over the age of 18 (between 8% and 10.4% of all employees) were earning less than the National Minimum Wage (Wilkinson, 1998). In 2001/02, 31% of low-income households had at least one household member in employment and 10% had all those of working age in employment (Palmer et al, 2003, p 34). Tackling social exclusion through reintegrating the low skilled into work obscures the issue of low pay and in-work poverty. A Family Budget Unit report (Parker, 1998), for example, estimated that at average female manual earnings, both lone-parent and two-parent families were below a 'low cost but acceptable' level and at average male earnings they were not far above it. The report also doubted that the imposition of a £3.60 per hour minimum wage (1998) would make much impact in reducing poverty (Parker, 1998). The growth of low-income employment, in combination with the widest income inequality in the EU, has led several commentators to question the basic premise that paid employment will assist social inclusion. Indeed, a report, *Making work pay in London*, reveals how the government's strategy to 'make work pay' disadvantages Londoners due partly to high housing and living costs, which lessen the incentive effects of in-work tax credits. The report reveals that after childcare costs a lone parent with two children outside London is better off working full time at the minimum hourly wage (£4.20) than on benefits. In London the same parent would need to earn £7.76 per hour to be better off in work. A married couple with children in London would need to earn 46% more than an equivalent couple outside London to have the same disposable income (Bivand et al, 2003).

Evidence also points to an increasing instability of employment over recent decades. Byrne (1997) notes that while between 1990 and 1994 nearly a third of economically active men were unemployed at least once in this period, only 6% were unemployed for more than two years. Spells of unemployment are strongly related to downward mobility and those who start off above the lower quartile of the occupational structure, where the risk of unemployment is higher, are likely to experience future employment at a lower level than previously. In the London region, 24% of those starting off above the lower quartile experienced some unemployment between 1990 and 1999 at an average of five weeks per year. Among those in the bottom quartile, 34% experienced some unemployment over the same period at an average of nine weeks per year (Buck et al, 2002, p 221). Rather than a socially excluded underclass, this is a picture of a reserve army, argues Byrne, with recent welfare reforms reinforcing the regulatory effect of the unemployed on the low paid (Byrne, 1997).

This chapter has attempted to highlight some of the contemporary theoretical approaches to global economic change and also the position of the socially excluded within those approaches. As Kumar (1978) notes, although these changes have been presented as representing 'new times', many of the concerns of earlier analysts of industrial society remain. These include alienation, dispossession, the impact of new technologies and the social consequences of the division of labour; increasing inequalities in the distribution of wealth and privilege and the associated consequences for social cohesion. He observes, "Were Marx, Tocqueville, Weber or Durkheim to return today what might give them cause for despondency would not be the insufficiency of their original analysis but its continuing relevance" (Kumar, 1978, p 231). Indeed, recent discussions surrounding the impact of large-scale industrial change on the working classes and the persistence of poverty amid rising prosperity have a long lineage and display much continuity with their historical antecedents. These are addressed in the next chapter.

Note
[1] By 2000, manufacturing employment had declined to 22.6% of total employment in Germany and 16.5% in the UK (OECD, 2003).

THREE

Poverty and social exclusion: theory and policy

The intention in this chapter is to show how the current 'social exclusion' concept has been deployed in the UK and the historical, institutional and political contexts that have influenced the debates surrounding the causes of poverty and social exclusion. The social exclusion concept originated in EU poverty programmes during the 1980s while in Britain and the US the same concerns were addressed in terms of the emergence of an urban 'underclass' (Silver, 1994). The concepts are not unrelated and both are concerned with the relative roles of agency and structural and/or institutional causes and both emerged together with debates surrounding the 'new poverty' associated with global economic changes (Burchardt et al, 2002). In Britain, the underclass concept arrived from the US and became popularised in academic, media and policy circles largely via Charles Murray (1990; 1994). Anthony Giddens had already used it in 1973 and the core concerns had been discussed under the 'cycle of deprivation' debate in the mid-1970s. Giddens had used the term generically, to describe the ethnic poor at the bottom of the American class structure. He argued that similar, albeit less pronounced developments were occurring among ethnic groups in Europe. Giddens located its cause, like Gunter Myrdal (1962) just over a decade earlier, to an increasing polarisation of labour market opportunities (Giddens, 1973, p 219). Murray contended that the post-war expansion of welfare programmes had paradoxically increased poverty, arguing that social policy was the primary causal mechanism behind the growth of an antisocial 'dependency culture'. While in Britain the underclass concept largely avoided the racial connotations that it acquired in the US, the emphasis on female-headed households and jobless young males remained. The term gained favour in the ideological and political climate of the era through justifying New Right critiques of state welfare and playing to middle-class fears of the 'yob' (Mann, 1991, p 3).

More historically minded observers noted that the term contained the same assumptions that had informed debates over poverty since at least the 19th century. Critics argued that such terms restricted discussions of poverty through directing attention away from the structural roots of the problem and onto the deficiencies of sub-groups of the poor. At the same time, the actions attributed to these groups are too diverse for a unified explanation. The underclass is an umbrella term, which involves the 'lumping together' of disparate categories of social misfortune (Kornblum, 1984). The emphasis on the behavioural and cultural aspects of poverty meant that the underclass was defined according to one's definition of deviant and antisocial lifestyles. Bagguley and Mann (1992, p 118) report that by the early 1990s:

> Vandalism, hooliganism, street crime, long term unemployment, joyriders, drug abuse, urban riots, a decline in family values, single mothers and a host of other 'social problems' have been pinned on the British underclass.

Dean notes that the term had no single definition but various applications relating to a range of economic, cultural and behavioural characteristics (Dean, 1994, p 35). Differences arose over the relative significance of these characteristics and the direction of causal processes. Much of the debate surrounding the underclass, and later attempts to identify the socially excluded, is derived from quantitative analysis that calculates the percentage of long-term welfare recipients living in areas of extreme poverty. Those areas contain high rates of unemployment, welfare dependency, crime, female-headed households and indicators such as educational achievement rates that are lower than average. While the empirical trends relating to changes in urban poverty and family structure have been questioned, it is the differing interpretations of those trends that have marked the debate. Howard Becker pointed out that social problems consist of both an objective condition and a subjective definition. The objective condition is a verifiable situation that can be checked as to its existence and magnitude. The subjective definition is the awareness that the condition is a threat to certain values (Becker, 1966, p 2). Morgan (1985, p 121), commenting on accounts that give an optimistic gloss to the decline of the nuclear family, observes that:

> It is clear that this is not simply a set of empirical observations but a reflection of a fundamental ethical and political orientation. It is, after all a matter of choice and judgement whether one sees variety and diversity or whether, more narrowly, one sees variations on a fundamental family theme.

The practical implications arise because the way a problem is defined often contains a proposal for solution. The solution often serves to determine the problem, insofar as the emergence of a 'successful' social problem is the availability of a promising policy solution (Manning, 1991). Throughout history the diverse issues that have crystallised around the predecessors of the underclass concept have tended to polarise around two ideal typical frameworks: one that stresses individual agency and another that emphasises structural conditions. Attempting to squeeze the complex processes that produce and reproduce poverty into these constructs, works to the detriment of a fuller understanding of how these processes interact. Sullivan (1993, pp 66-7) observes that:

> Too extreme an emphasis on individual causation ignores growing evidence of the proliferation of low-wage jobs and increasing joblessness in inner city labor markets. Too much emphasis on structural causation ignores evidence that postponing child bearing leads to greater occupational success even within inner city populations.

Despite the overlap in these positions in, for example, the work of W.J. Wilson (1987) or in the anthropological accounts of Oscar Lewis (1966; 1968), the political and policy implications of the structure–agency dichotomy have tended to overlook nuances in the arguments. The positions taken reveal more about the political preferences of their proponents than the phenomenon itself (Mann, 1994). In his review of the 'cycle of deprivation' debate of the 1970s, Coffield notes that the distinction between the 'deserving' and 'undeserving' poor reveals the most perfect 'cycle' in the whole debate. He refers to the 'cycle of official deprivation of the poor' whereby this distinction contains the latent function of legitimising state policies that stigmatise and deal punitively with the poor (Coffield et al, 1980, p 213).

Poverty and policy in Britain

Concern over the work ethic of the poor and classifying poor people according to 'deserving' and 'undeserving' categories has been a recurrent aspect of British social thought since at least the 16th century. King Henry VIII's 1531 Edict required a Census of the poor to be conducted. The vagrancy laws that Henry VIII passed sanctioned draconian measures against the 'able-bodied' beggar who was to be flogged and fines imposed on those who provided them with charity.

The 1563 Statute revealed an early 'welfare-to-work' measure, which sought to enforce work habits in order to reduce poverty. It required all unmarried men with a trade and those under the age of 30 without work to perform other work at wages agreed by Justices of the Peace. All men aged between 20 and 60 without a trade were to be placed, at the same wages as servants, in households of the land-owning gentry (Geremek, 1994).

The Elizabethan Poor Laws began a gradual centralisation in the administration of poor relief, giving a key role to churchwardens who were to levy a sum on the inhabitants of the parish to be distributed among the poor. The legislation defined three categories of poor people to be relieved: those without work, those unwilling to work and those unable to work. For those without employment, materials and tools to enable them to work were provided. Those who refused to work were sent to a house of correction while the 'deserving' poor – the sick, the elderly and the orphaned – were relieved in almshouses. The 1662 Laws of Settlement established the boundary of responsibility to neighbours and community. Those in need could only obtain poor relief if they were considered settled in a given location based upon birth, apprenticeship or residence. Outsiders were removed to their place of origin. The complexity of the law led to many legal disputes and limited geographic mobility, leading critics such as Adam Smith to criticise the law for restricting the free movement of labour. Reform of the Laws of Settlement was a major aim of the early 19th-century Poor Law reformers. In practice, the legal and emotional issues surrounding 'settlement' still continue in the US, in the resistance to national welfare standards and the hostility to outsiders allegedly drawn to states with relatively generous welfare benefits (Katz, 1989, p 12). In Europe, they find their contemporary equivalent in media-driven fears over immigration from Asia, Africa and Eastern Europe and the distinction between deserving 'political refugees' and undeserving 'economic migrants'.

During the early 19th century, rising expenditure on poor relief convinced many social commentators that poverty was the result of unsystematic poor relief. The target of their criticism was the 1795 'Speenhamland' policy of subsidising the low wages of agricultural labourers according to family size and the price of bread. It was argued that this policy, combined with a large volume of uncoordinated charitable relief, created 'dependency', encouraged fraudulent claims and distorted the mechanisms of a free market. These beliefs formed the basis of the 1834 Poor Law Amendment Act, which sought to re-moralise the poor through the principle of 'less eligibility' and establish dependency on the labour market through the promotion of 'self-help'. Those unable to work were to be assisted in 'workhouses', which supplied work and sustenance although provided a 'less eligible' standard of living than that of the lowest paid labourer. The aim was to re-establish the incentive mechanisms that would drive the idle and malingerers onto the labour market. The 'able-bodied' working poor were to make provision for bouts of unemployment and sickness through personal insurance via 'Friendly Societies', access to which was only feasible for the more affluent members of the working class. In this way, writes Mann (1991, p 150), "the language of self-help was translated into dependence on wage labour" that strengthened distinctions between the 'deserving' and 'undeserving' poor and clarified acceptable notions of dependency.

By the late 19th century, anxiety over the conditions and behaviour of the urban working classes was widespread in social commentary. These fears reflected a sense of social and moral disarray, which accompanied rapid urbanisation and industrialisation and unease that the class of outcasts may expand to infect the 'respectable' working classes and threaten the middle class. The growth of large working-class populations in south London and the East End, mass demonstrations of the unemployed and bread riots in the East End in the 1860s and 1870s resulted in a heightened sense of insecurity among middle-class liberals and commentators (Stedman Jones, 1971, pp 238-41). Poverty was viewed as a problem for the poor themselves as moral agents and for society as a legitimate social order. Henry Mayhew's study of mid-19th-century London street life showed how the problem was not a weak attachment to working habits, but the structural conditions of a highly casualised and irregular labour market, which undermined the capacity for 'self-help' and thrift. He also drew attention to the 'dishonest poor' who were distinguished from the 'poor' by their behaviour and values, and by their rejection of work. In concluding his exhaustive study of London's underworld, Mayhew (1969, pp 426-7) noted that:

> As animals have their habits, so there is a large class of mankind whose single cleverness is that of representing themselves as justly and naturally dependent on the assistance of others, who look paupers from their birth, who seek givers and forsake those who have given as naturally as a tree sends its roots into new soil and deserts the exhausted. It is the office of reason – reason improved by experience – to teach us not to waste our own interest

and our resources on beings that will never return a moral profit to our charitable industry.

Marx employed a similar distinction, separating the 'dangerous class' – "vagabonds, criminals, prostitutes, in short the lumpenproletariat" from the casualties of capitalism – the "unemployed, orphans, pauper children and the demoralised, the ragged and those unable to work" (Marx, 1976, p 797). The potential of urban deterioration being transmitted across generations gained legitimacy in the late 19th century with the rise of positivism and Social Darwinism, although the phrase 'vicious circle' to describe this process had been used as early as 1839 (Coffield et al, 1980, p 167). Scientists sympathetic to the early eugenics movement began to apply hereditary theories to the study of families, concluding that low mentality and pathological patterns of behaviour and family structure were transmitted through the generations.[1] Others emphasised environmental factors such as poor housing and overcrowding as providing the conditions for intergenerational decline of the urban masses, as rates of poverty were higher in districts where higher proportions of the population had been born in London (Stedman Jones, 1971, p 132). In 1858, the medical officer of the Strand in London reported:

> So long as twenty, thirty or even forty individuals are permitted – it might almost be said compelled to reside in houses originally built for the accommodation of a single family or at most of two families, so long will the evils of ignorance, of indecency, immorality, intemperance, prostitution and crime continue to exist almost unchecked. (cited by Burnett, 1986, p 144)

Macnicol (1987) has traced the history of 'social pathology' explanations of poverty and notes that by the late 19th century, the essence of the 'underclass' concept – based on the economic behaviour of young men and the reproductive behaviour of young women – had been formed. These core concerns have been periodically revived ever since. During the inter-war period these concerns were addressed in terms of a 'social problem' group. This stimulated a series of investigations into the hereditary roots of a variety of conditions including 'mental deficiency', criminality, unemployment and 'mild social inefficiency'. In the 1940s the same concerns were again revived as the 'problem family' concept. Several investigations that set out to prove the existence of these groups failed to find convincing evidence. Essentially, argues

Macnicol, the historical evolution of the 'underclass' debate demonstrates that it is a resource allocation problem – the underclass becomes a 'problem' when they consume state welfare. The concept is one element of a broader conservative view of the nature of social problems and tends to be supported by those opposed to the redistributive potential of state welfare (Macnicol, 1987, p 316). Despite the lack of convincing empirical evidence, the role of genetic and/or cultural transmission perpetuating poverty has exerted a powerful influence on debates concerning the causes of poverty and the appropriate policy responses. These would later resurface around the use of Oscar Lewis' 'culture of poverty' thesis.

Structure and agency in urban anthropology

Poverty received little attention in Britain and the US in the post-World War II era of economic growth until 1962 with the publication of Michael Harrington's *The other America*, which reawakened public consciousness in America over the continued existence of widespread poverty. His account anticipated later debates, which would stress the changing labour force requirements of a 'post-industrial' economy and he estimated that between 40 and 50 million Americans remained poor. Harrington argued that what distinguished them from the poor of previous eras was that they formed the first 'minority poor' in history (Harrington, 1962, p 2). These 'new poor' were a product of the same advances that had increased the standard of living for the rest of society. They were 'upside down' in the economy and for them greater productivity often means worse jobs; agricultural advance becomes hunger (Harrington, 1962, p 12). Likewise, Gunter Myrdal's (1962) *Challenge to affluence* pointed to the possibility of an increasingly polarised labour market and technology-inspired job losses, as providing the conditions for the emergence of an unskilled and redundant urban underclass in the US.

In Britain, Brian Abel-Smith and Peter Townsend's 1966 publication *The poor and the poorest* challenged the belief that economic growth and an expansion of welfare services had eradicated poverty. They argued that while the composition of the poor had changed, widespread poverty remained. Low wages and large families were a more significant determinant of poverty than in previous eras, when the elderly and the sick had formed the majority of the poor. They set out to reshape the principles guiding social policy and argued against a subsistence level of poverty, which had determined levels of state support since the 1834 Poor Law Amendment Act had enshrined the principle of 'less eligibility'. Through the concept of 'relative deprivation', Abel-Smith and Townsend redefined poverty to include a perceptual and relational dimension, which included standards of social convention. A key element of their definition was the ability to participate in normal social activities and they stressed the link between resources and social integration. A lack of resources is the condition of being poor, while lack of participation in conventional social activities is the process of being poor. Using a foundation of 40% above welfare benefit levels plus rent as providing a 'widely approved' standard of living, they argued that the numbers living in poverty in the UK had risen from 4 million in 1953/54 to 7.5 million by 1960 (Abel Smith and Townsend, 1966).[2]

Interpreting the persistence of poverty amid rising affluence was discussed in terms of a new concept: the 'culture of poverty' developed by anthropologist Oscar Lewis. Using participant observation and life history collections to study Latin American poverty, Lewis maintained that the culture of poverty was a series of "common adaptions to common problems" that arose in a variety of historical contexts but was more pronounced under free market capitalism (Lewis, 1966, p xlv). His central theme was that the poor who formed the culture of poverty totalled 20% of the American poor and were distinct in several respects. First, by a lack of integration in the major social institutions, which Lewis related to their critical and cynical attitudes towards the state, the legal system and religion. Second, the culture is distinguished by a minimum of organisation that gives the culture of poverty its anachronistic quality in complex, specialised and organised societies (Lewis, 1968, p 9). Third, family and sexual practices differ from those of mainstream society and include "the absence of childhood as a specially prolonged and protected stage in the lifecycle, early initiation into sex, free unions or consensual marriage, a relatively high incidence of the abandonment of wives and children" (Lewis, 1968, p 10). Finally, Lewis identified psychological factors: a lack of impulse and little ability to defer gratification or plan for the future. The culture of poverty represented an effort to adapt to feelings of hopelessness, which develop from the limited opportunities for success in terms of the values and goals of the larger society (Lewis, 1966, p xliii).

Lewis' main concern was the relationship between culture and personality, and his focus was on the family as the primary group in which adaptions to poverty are made. Poverty became self-perpetuating because slum children were socialised into the values and attitudes of the culture and remained psychologically unprepared to respond to changing conditions or increased opportunities. Improved economic conditions, he argued, are essential, but may not be enough to eliminate this culture once it has become established. It might be easier to eliminate poverty, he contended, than the culture of poverty (Lewis, 1966, p 29). Responding to criticisms that his studies might perpetuate negative images of the poor, he contended that he was not placing the basic causes of poverty in the culture itself. Rather, he was exploring a series of cultural adaptions within "part of the larger culture of capitalism, whose social and economic system channels wealth into the hands of a relatively small group, and creates the growth of sharp class divisions" (Lewis, 1968, p 20). Since it was the values of the culture that kept certain groups in poverty, he argued that the culture of poverty could be eradicated by a 'social work' solution, whereby the poor would be re-socialised by psychiatric social workers. He also believed in the possibility of self-emancipation, arguing that political mobilisation among the poor would eradicate the social and psychological core of the subculture. Lewis' prescriptions reflected a strand of liberal thought that viewed the poor as passive and requiring 'professional' intervention to assist them in breaking out of their self-defeating behaviour. Wootton noted that in the post-war era this was accompanied by a shift in the nature and function of social work, from dispensing charity towards a psychiatric approach:

> In a very few years practically the whole profession has succeeded in exchanging the garments of charity for a uniform borrowed from the practitioners of psychiatric medicine ... so we pass out of the frying-pan of charitable condescension into the no less condescending fire – or rather the cool detachment – of superior psychological insight. (Wootton, 1960, p 293)

The structural basis informing Lewis' study was frequently overlooked and it was used by a variety of writers from both sides of the political spectrum as it became infused with ideological motives. Edward Banfield was instrumental in attaching a conservative perspective to cultural interpretations of poverty, and raised many of the issues surrounding poverty and welfare that would be revived by neo-conservatives such as Charles Murray in the 1980s. Banfield defined classes as groups sharing a "distinct patterning of attitudes, values and modes of behaviour, not people who share a similar socio-economic location" (Banfield, 1970, p 2). As poverty had decreased among the majority of poor and minority groups, its persistence among a minority 'lower class' was a consequence of a distinctive lower-class culture that kept them in poverty. Banfield argued that liberal reforms aimed at improving the conditions of America's lower class through increased state intervention and an expansion of welfare programmes are pointless. Such measures may actually be counter-productive, he argued, through increasing discontent and heightening perceptions of relative deprivation. The problems of the lower class would continue to reproduce themselves on an ever-increasing scale because:

> The lower class forms of all problems are at bottom a single problem: the existence of an outlook and a style of life, which is radically present-oriented and therefore attaches no value to work, sacrifice, self improvement or service to family, friends or community. (Banfield, 1970, p 211)

The relative significance of cultural and structural factors also marked the polemical debates surrounding Daniel Moynihan's 1965 report, *The Negro family: The case for national action*. Critics frequently neglected Moynihan's emphasis on unemployment and low wages as the root of family breakdown among African Americans, instead focusing on the 'tangle of pathology' that he argued resulted from it. Moynihan (1967) argued that labour market disadvantage had undermined the stability of the black family, making it increasingly difficult for the black male to provide for his family. Pointing to high rates of broken marriages, illegitimacy, welfare dependency and female-headed households among urban black families, he argued that the black community had polarised between a stable middle class, and a disadvantaged lower class. The lower-class subculture was distinguished by its matriarchal structure, which in a patriarchal society such as the US resulted in its disadvantage. Moynihan stressed the causative role of the black American family structure and argued that reversing the exclusion of black people required specific attention. He argued for federal action to create employment for black males, thereby strengthening the stability and resources of the black American family and reinstating the male as head of the household.

Similarities were drawn between the liberal-oriented 'culture of poverty' theories and the more conservative theories of Banfield (1970). All located the perpetuation of poverty in the values and behaviour of sections of the poor. While cultural theories recognised the existence of social and economic determinants, they did not believe them to be directly causal once the culture had established itself. When discussed in terms of race, the idea that disadvantage may exist in cultural differences offended critics who, in the context of the Civil Rights

Movement, were pointing to the role of institutional racism and labour market discrimination. The culture of poverty was increasingly criticised for its negative portrayal of the poor, although few critics paid sufficient attention to the different policy implications raised by conservative and liberal perspectives of the theory. Valentine's critique locates Moynihan and Lewis' work in the 'pejorative tradition' of black family studies begun by the sociologist E. Franklin Frazier (Valentine, 1968, pp 20-4). Valentine criticises Frazier and Moynihan for their reliance on statistical data in order to interpret cultural patterns. Moynihan's presentation of empirical evidence was certainly open to interpretation and criticised as over-dramatic. The 'alarming' increase in black female-headed households represented a rise from 19% to 24% of all black households between 1949 and 1954 with no net increase between 1960 and 1964. Certain data such as the relative decline of black family incomes compared to white family incomes was neglected and data that ran contrary to Moynihan's findings were omitted (Franklin, 1997, p 164). The report's exclusive focus on the disintegration of the black family neglected wider trends occurring across the advanced industrial nations. Family patterns that were perceived as pathological when practised by black families were also becoming part of a wider pattern of social and cultural change (Peters and McAdoo, 1983).

Quantitative data can provide the outline of a demographic reality, argued Valentine, but is a "surface phenomenon that may have a wide variety of cultural designs for living underneath it" (Valentine, 1968, p 6). The distinction between family structure and process – the diversity of experiences in family life – remained unexplored, the assumption being that if a female heads a household it must be suffering from a 'tangle of pathology'. Many of the culture of poverty's central tenets were being explored through ethnographic fieldwork and demonstrated the importance of informal reciprocal networks of kin and friends. Where Moynihan and others had assumed disorganisation in the absence of a male 'breadwinner', these accounts highlighted the stability of family life and its continuity under adverse circumstances (Stack, 1974, pp 27-32). Valentine maintained that the alleged sub-cultural values are measured against a historically and culturally bound image of the family based on dominant middle-class values and found to be pathological. The hidden agenda behind such accounts "is not to illuminate human variety or to elucidate social reality. The purpose is rather to support a set of class bound pre-judgements about a troublesome element in our society" (Valentine, 1968, p 35).

Field studies among urban low-income districts found them governed by an internal order that was both connected to and distinct from the wider society. Ethnographic accounts, starting from the same point as Oscar Lewis, have examined how people have adapted collectively to different situational and historical conditions. Despite the differences of emphasis, cultural theories have generally focused around the theme of disorganisation and pathology and are largely tautologies. Values are implied from behaviour, the behaviour is then explained in terms of an alleged sub-cultural value system. "This lack of clearly specified independent variables," writes Katz, "leaves the reasoning circular. Most expositions of the culture of poverty leave cause and effect hopelessly tangled" (Katz, 1989, p 42). Studies conducted in areas of concentrated and widespread poverty have argued that situational constraints are essential to understanding the way of life of the poor. From this perspective many of the defining value systems of a 'culture of poverty' are viewed as responses to wider constraints. Rather than socialisation providing the causal link between intergenerational poverty, continuities in behavioural patterns are seen as a result of successive generations facing similar sets of opportunities. Among Liebow's study of 'street corner' black males in Washington DC, he noted that "the son experiences the same failures, in the same area and for much the same reasons as his father" (Liebow, 1967, p 223). Rutter and Madge (1976) raised the same point in the UK in their review of the 'cycle of deprivation' debate in the 1970s. While recognising that continuities exist between the generations, they argued that this was affected more by regional variations in unemployment, crime rates and in access to schools and services. Discontinuities were also strong with at least half of all children studied failing to repeat the pattern, and over half of all forms of disadvantage arising anew with each generation (Rutter and Madge, 1976, p 303).

Rodman (1971) argued that conditions among the poor shaped behaviour and values more than in other social classes, with the fragile economic base leading to cultural patterns that are widely shared. He used the concept of 'value stretch' to explain these patterns, arguing that the poor do not differ in their values but in their ability to conform to them as closely as other social groups. They may share the values of the wider society, but have stretched those values or developed alternatives that are more suited to their circumstances (Rodman, 1971, p 4). From this perspective, structure and individual behaviour cannot be separated because structure exists internally, since behavioural patterns are a response to objective circumstances. Greenstone (1990) argued that the weakness of many cultural accounts was that they treated culture and rationality as dichotomous. He defined rationality as a "calculated adaption to prevailing circumstances". Cultural accounts that emphasise pathology and disorganisation lack the basic elements of organisation, which define culture. This results in a restricted view of rationality that overlooks the adaptiveness of certain 'ghetto pathologies'. "To deny the presence of those elements of rationality", noted Greenstone, "is to deny the presence of culture. In sum, talk about a broadly irrational culture is incoherent" (Greenstone, 1990, p 404). Behind the apparently irrational behaviour of the 'underclass', argued Wright and Devine, is an inner logic. "If the elements of underclass sub-culture seem irrational, it is because they represent common behavioural responses to curiously grotesque conditions" (Wright and Devine, 1993, p 128).

Rational choice, the New Right and the 'failure' of welfare

One consequence of the negative application of cultural models of poverty was their application to the anti-poverty agenda of the 1960s. As discussed, liberals became increasingly averse to explanations that attributed a causal role to agency and cultural issues were marginalised from the field of poverty research (Jordan, 1996, pp 86-8). In Britain, reluctance to engage in cultural and behavioural aspects of poverty also reflected the supremacy of Marxism and empiricism. For the former the focus was largely upon the relationship between capitalism and the state, and the role and function of the welfare state within it. For the latter, working within the traditions of public administration research, the concern was more with the measurement and definition of poverty than with the attitudes and responses of the poor towards their situation (Mann, 1999). As the influence of sociology and anthropology declined, economics increasingly defined the framework in which debates about the relationship between poverty, family structure and welfare were conducted. The influence of neo-liberal economic theory complemented a political hegemony on both sides of the Atlantic, which shifted the focus away from structural analyses of poverty towards a discourse that would place individual agency at the centre of its explanations.

As Manning notes, the New Right was acutely aware that social problems are socially constructed and that the problems and solutions can be changed through an effective manipulation of public debate (Manning, 1991, p 17). The historical evolution of the underclass debate illustrates that maintaining a particular definition of reality is essentially a political process: a confrontation between competing definitions of reality, in which certain groups can impose their definition on others

(Box, 1981, pp 31-2). The role of 'primary definers' (those structurally dominant groups who can alert the media to a particular event or problem) played a crucial role in defining the new 'common sense' surrounding issues of welfare and poverty in the 1980s. Right-wing think tanks such as the Manhattan Institute in the US and the Adam Smith Institute and Institute for Economic Affairs in the UK were instrumental in funding and disseminating neo-liberal ideas on these matters. These were then presented to the general public through a mounting succession of 'moral panics' that united around the 'underclass' concept, and through generous media coverage given to commentators such as Charles Murray. This gave academic justification to political critiques concerning the corrosive effects of over-generous welfare systems and the need for a 'law and order' response to check the tide of rising crime and antisocial behaviour.

Restoring the traditional nuclear family, which it was felt had been undermined by a tide of permissiveness and moral decline, was central to the New Right project. Oppenheim and Lister identified two key influences on New Right ideology: first, laissez-faire individualism, with its emphasis on the minimal state and free-market; and second, conservatism, with its adherence to traditional patterns of family type, gender relations and values (Oppenheim and Lister, 1996, pp 64-71). These strands united in their criticism of the role of state welfare in undermining family stability and the will to work. For the former, state-provided welfare is inefficient and disrupts the efficient functioning of a market economy through altering incentive structures. This results in a devaluation of the work ethic through removing the penalties of irrational economic behaviour. The latter argues that the family has been weakened through state intervention. Divorce has become easier and by providing welfare payments to lone parents, the state has actively encouraged the breakdown of the nuclear family. In practice, the remedies of the economic and moral New Right complemented each other and the economic arguments for retrenching the welfare state were bolstered by conservative arguments surrounding the damaging moral and social effects of state welfare (King, 1987).

The influence of rational choice theory became a major influence in social science. It explains the functioning of the social and economic systems not at a systemic level but as the result of the aggregated actions of individuals who make up the system. Its emphasis on the 'utility-maximising individual' suggests that individuals evaluate their available options and select the course of action that optimises utility (Coleman, 1994). This perspective is then allied to a sub-cultural model as subsequently, with large concentrations of people adopting non-traditional modes of behaviour, adverse values develop, which reproduce dependency. It was from this position, that Charles Murray (1984) launched his critique of post-war social policy in *Losing ground*. His analysis was highly influential in debates surrounding the 'problem' of welfare dependency. The growth of welfare services and an expanding economy in the US since the mid-1960s, argued Murray, had been accompanied by an increase in welfare dependency and antisocial behaviour. Liberal reformers, in advocating more generous policies for the poor, failed to recognise the damaging consequences of their reforms. Social policy, although well intentioned, altered the rewards and penalties that constrain human behaviour and increased rather than reduced certain cultural tendencies.

> I begin with the proposition that all, poor and non-poor alike, use the same general calculus in arriving at decisions; only the exigencies are different. Poor people play with fewer chips and cannot wait as long for results.... The reformers of the 1960's were especially myopic about this, tending not only to assume that the poor and non-poor were alike in trying to maximise the goods in their lives (with which I agree), but also that, given the same package of benefits, the decision that seems reasonable to one would seem reasonable to the other. They failed to recognise that the behaviours that are 'rational' are different at different economic levels. (Murray, 1984, p 155)

Murray's final sentence reveals a fundamental area of consensus with liberal perspectives concerning the behavioural aspects of poverty. However, for Murray, the problem was not based in the labour market or the growth of structural unemployment but in the provision of state-provided welfare. By the early 1990s Murray was applying his analysis to Britain. Reviving the distinction between the 'deserving' and 'undeserving' poor he identified social behaviour as the defining feature of an underclass: "drug taking, illegitimacy, failure to hold down a job, truancy, and casual violence" (Murray, 1990, p 2). He suggested that illegitimacy is the best single indicator of underclass formation. Pointing to a correlation between illegitimacy and social class, he noted that the prevalence of out-of-wedlock births was significantly higher among the lower classes. His comparative analysis revealed that districts containing high proportions of Social Class V residents had illegitimacy rates of over 40%. Changes to the benefit and housing allocation systems have made it economically viable for lower-class young women to raise children without fathers. Crime has become relatively safer for the habitual criminal, the "classic member of an underclass" (Murray, 1990, p 3). Proof of the existence of an underclass is the high concentration of lower-class men who are 'voluntarily' unemployed. Murray returned to Britain 10 years after his original analysis and concluded that on all three of his indicators – males not in employment, crime rates and out-of-wedlock births – the British underclass had grown since 1989. "What had been a nascent underclass in 1989," wrote Murray in *The Sunday Times Review*, "had by 1999 become one that increasingly resembled, in behaviour and proportional size, the underclass in America" (Murray, 2000). As long-term welfare dependency is regarded as a process of calculating the utility of various options, the logical solution would be to make the benefit system less attractive. This would drive the 'workshy' onto the labour market and deter young women from having babies that they were unable to support. Engaging in a 'thought experiment', Murray envisaged a possible prescription for the US as:

> Scrapping the entire federal welfare and income-support structure for working-aged persons, including AFDC [Aid for Dependent Children], Medicaid, Food Stamps, Unemployment Insurance, Worker's Compensation, subsidized housing, disability insurance and the rest. It would leave the working-aged person with no recourse whatsoever except the job market, family members, friends, and public or private locally funded services. It is the Alexandrian solution: cut the knot, for there is no way to untie it. (Murray, 1984, pp 227-9)

The ideological and theoretical critiques of such constructions have been outlined previously and need not be repeated. Nevertheless, the empirical evidence provided by Murray has been subject to scrutiny. Bane and Ellwood note that the temporal pattern of welfare dependency in the US fails to correspond with changes in family structure. Benefits increased significantly between 1960 and 1972: Medicaid benefits were added and eligibility rules relaxed. In contrast, the level of welfare benefits fell 20% between 1972 and 1986. Despite an increase in lone-parent households by three million between 1972 and 1984 and the labour market contracting over the same period, the number of children on Aid For Dependent Children fell by over half a million (Bane and Ellwood, 1994, p 111). The relative advantages of welfare in relation to work decreased during the 1970s, contrary to

Murray's claims, which relied on evidence from Pennsylvania where benefit levels increased at double the national average throughout the period (Katz, 1989, p 154). In Britain and the US the growth of a 'dependency culture' through the 1980s and 1990s was occurring as benefit levels were falling and eligibility rules tightened. Murray's central claim concerning the implications for children raised by single mothers has been questioned by a host of empirical studies, which explored the attitudes and motivations of lone parents (see Chapter Six).

A series of publications for the Institute of Economic Affairs explored the central problem of underclass formation in similar terms. The thread of the argument was that low-income families have been penalised and weakened through changes to the tax and benefit systems. Lacking appropriate role models, the sons of single mothers tend to become involved in antisocial behaviour while the daughters grow up to repeat the process. Without the civilising force of marriage the unemployed fathers of these children achieve status through combat and sexual conquest. Trapped in a permanent adolescence they represent a 'warrior class' (Morgan, 1995, p 145). For 'ethical socialists' Dennis and Erdos, it is the liberal intelligentsia through advocating 'non-judgementalism' who have created the permissive moral climate and breakdown of social sanctions, which accelerated the rise of 'uncommitted fathers'. They reviewed a survey undertaken by the National Children's Bureau, which indicated a correlation between lone parenthood, deprivation and maladjustment in child behaviour. The child lacking a 'publicly committed father' would grow up to become more individualised and less willing or able to undertake social duties. Dependent upon state benefits they remain in a state of 'egoistic socialism' (Dennis and Erdos, 1992, p 73).[3]

Patricia Morgan's contribution built on similar premises to those in the Institute of Economic Affairs series and stressed the policy-induced dimension. However, she argued that the problem was not an increase in lone parenthood but the decline in the two-parent family structure. Penalising lone parents, she correctly pointed out, would not necessarily lead to a corresponding increase in two-parent families. Such proposals neglected changing employment trends and the decline in full-time, semi- and unskilled employment. Combined with the expansion of welfare services, which have moved in favour of lone parents, and a 'legal disestablishment' of family life reducing it to a "matter of personal taste without communal basis", the two-parent family has become more difficult to sustain (Morgan, 1995, p 89). The end of the 'breadwinner ideology' manifests itself in the rise of single-person households, the sharpest increase being among single men. Lacking familial obligations these men lose the incentive to work, Morgan maintains, noting that unemployment rates among widowed, divorced and separated men aged 16 to 64 were double the level for married men in the 1980s (Morgan, 1995, p 149). The antisocial consequences of these trends generate both a 'law and order' and a 'professional' response and a further extension of the state into the private sphere of the family. Morgan argued that the decline in two-parent families is not irreversible and that economic factors are the primary causal agent. The state, Morgan argued, "is making it abundantly clear that it is not prepared to support a man's efforts to provide for a family and does not recognise his costs when his wife cares for his children" (Morgan, 1995, p 107).

Notwithstanding the differences of emphasis, the core concerns surrounding poverty and welfare since the Poor Law remain as state dependency is again translated into a form of behavioural dependency. In this version its roots are identified not in the culture itself, but as the result of a permissive and over-extended state that undermines the work ethic and autonomy of the family structure. This inevitably leads towards further intergenerational dependency since:

> Social policies which make the role of the father redundant, or weaken the legitimate authority of parents in the socialisation of their children, is likely to create environments in which only exceptional children are capable of growing into genuinely mature and autonomous adults. The vast majority of children reared in broken or inadequate homes are headed for welfare dependency. (Segalman and Marsland, 1988, p 121)

From the underclass to social exclusion

By the late 1990s the underclass concept, its pejorative assumptions and ideological bias rejected by academic social science, had become largely redundant. 'Social exclusion' offered a more neutral alternative to the Anglo-American 'underclass' and despite variations attached to the term most definitions encompass two closely related sets of phenomena. Following restructuring of the advanced capitalist economies the first emphasises a process of exclusion from the labour market, which in turn has implications for other dimensions of exclusion such as in the spheres of consumption, savings and social activity. The second approach identifies the erosion of social citizenship of certain groups and emphasises equality of status over equality of income (Marshall and Bottomore, 1996, p 33). It was in this context that the term was originally used in French political discourse during the 1970s, to describe the excluded one tenth of the population unprotected by social insurance (Silver, 1994).

The explanatory focus of social exclusion is therefore wider than earlier discussions of 'poverty' discussed in distributional terms, or the underclass concept where behavioural and moral aspects are primary. What is at issue is the relationship between the distributional and relational aspects of social exclusion and the term therefore offers a more pluralistic view incorporating divisions based on gender, citizenship, ethnicity and age that relate less to class and labour market-based categories (Buck et al, 2002, p 9). Burchardt et al's definition is based on the notion of participation in five key areas – consumption, savings, production and political and social activity. Using data from the British Household Panel Survey (BHPS) for 1991 to 1998 their study discovered a significant degree of stability on each dimension of exclusion between 1991 and 1995. Between 20% and 25% of their sample experienced low income and the same proportion experienced low wealth. However, less than 1% of their sample was excluded on all dimensions in any year (Burchardt et al, 1999).

Procacci relates the concept of exclusion to the decline of class analysis. He argues that the emphasis on constructing 'typologies of exclusion' neglects the dynamic aspect of inequality addressed by the latter, which demonstrates that inequality is not created outside social space but within its institutions (Procacci, 1996, p 12). Townsend, who as discussed earlier, argued for a relational understanding through his concept of 'relative deprivation' cautioned that:

> Poverty has to be 'situated' through time in relation to social and institutional structure and not simply denoted by relatively low disposable income. ... Subjective (or collective sentiment about) deprivation is a valuable analytical and explanatory variable. However, it cannot be fully assessed independently of *actual* deprivation, and the latter could be argued to be primary in understanding a whole range of social and psychological phenomena. (Townsend, 1993, p 35; emphasis in original)

The meaning of social exclusion varies according to the national and ideological contexts in which it is employed, which will have important political and policy connotations. In Britain through the 1990s it was increasingly applied to describe the casualties of 18 years of Conservative government (Walker and Walker, 1997). For New Labour the term provided an organising concept around which their 'Third Way' ideal would deliver both social justice and economic efficiency. However, political definitions often endow the term with restrictive meanings that contain the potential for marginalising certain social groups under a new label and divert attention from the more general rise in inequality and labour market insecurity (Paugam, 1996, p 4). Levitas identifies three different discourses surrounding social exclusion in the UK, which have different policy implications to tackling exclusion. First she identifies the redistributionist discourse, which stresses the roots of exclusion in poverty and the erosion of citizenship rights. This tradition of empirical research into deprivation and poverty has long provided a forum for critically re-evaluating the dominant ideology of individualism and explanations of poverty couched in neo-classical economic terms (Rustin and Rix, 1996, p 13). The social integrationist discourse is rooted in a Durkheimian conception that stresses social inclusion through labour market activity. Finally, Levitas identifies the moral underclass discourse, which like its predecessor emphasises the cultural distinctiveness of the excluded (Levitas, 1998, p 7). Levitas argues that the dominant political discourse on social exclusion reflects an emphasis on social solidarity. This constructs exclusion as exclusion from paid work, with paid employment providing the route to social inclusion (Levitas, 1996).

While acknowledging the structural roots of exclusion, many of the assumptions that informed earlier debates remain. These focus on the detrimental effects of welfare dependency in transmitting modes of behaviour that have a corrosive impact on the work ethic of the poor, and build upon the policy recommendations imported from the US by policy analysts such as Lawrence Mead. For Mead (1992), the failure of state welfare in the 1970s and 1980s was not that it was overextended nor because it was too limited but because it was permissive. Welfare programmes were awarded as entitlements and failed to set behavioural standards for the recipients. This fault lies in the 'sociologism' that pervaded the liberal reformers of the 1960s and which viewed the poor as essentially passive:

> The poor are seen as inert, not active. They are spoken of in the passive voice. They are people who *are* or *have been* disadvantaged in multiple ways. They do not *do* things but rather have things *done* to them. They are the objects, not the subjects of action. (Mead, 1992, p 129; emphasis in original)

Mead took issue with rational choice theories, which assume that individuals respond on the basis of assessing various incentives and disincentives, since such theories are based upon a mistaken model of competence. Reforms aimed at altering incentives to work by either reducing the attractiveness of welfare benefits, or by offering voluntary training and education programmes are destined to fail, argued Mead:

> The poor do not face unusual obstacles to work, if one *assumes normal competence*, namely the confident maximising attitudes of the better off. Workers actually encounter more practical difficulties with employment than nonworkers, which shows that competence, not social fairness is the important variable. (Mead, 1992, pp 157-8; emphasis in original)

The problems of poverty have less to do with unemployment and more to do with the dysfunctional behaviour and passive attitudes of the poor. Overcoming this has become a major concern of policy makers and has given rise to a new 'dependency politics', which focuses, not on macroeconomic issues, but on social and personal concerns: "the question is how to deal with problems of basic functioning of the very poor. The social, more than the economic structure of society is at issue" (Mead, 1992, p 211). Since the poor cannot be relied upon to fill low-wage, low-status employment on their own initiative, work must become a duty, a condition of citizenship enforceable by the state. This should not be seen as coercive, argued Mead, but as a paternalistic policy, which joins the benefits that poor people require with conditions that they meet certain behavioural standards. Governments must seek to require poor adults to work more than they do, enforcing employment in the same way that it collects taxes or upholds the law (Mead, 1996, p 265).

New Labour's 'ethical socialism' is committed to social justice without challenging the existing social and economic order. The objectives of state welfare have been redefined from pursuing equality towards promoting opportunity, based on a contractual relationship between the state and its citizens. Frank Field, previously Minister for Welfare Reform, has been a leading critic of the top-down, rights-based, redistributive welfare state, arguing that it is unsustainable since "altruism alone is not a strong enough motivational force to sustain the sheer size of the welfare edifice as proposed by Titmuss" (cited by Lund, 1999, p 448). Central to Field's critique is the role of means-tested benefits that create 'poverty traps', reduce work incentives, encourage dishonesty and fraud and lead to the morally detrimental effects of welfare dependency.

> Almost half the population live in households dependent upon one of the major means tested benefits. Means tests penalise all those attributes – such as hard work, work being adequately rewarded, savings and honesty – which underpin a free, let alone a civilized society.... Lying, cheating and deceit are all rewarded handsomely by a welfare system which costs on average £15 a day in taxation from every working individual. Again it is difficult to estimate the destructive consequences welfare now has for our society. (Field, 1995, p 122)

Katz points out that advocates of 'welfare-to-work' frequently employ a contradictory definition of dependence. When applied to the poor, dependence erodes competence and encourages permissiveness. No similar equation is made when applied to state subsidies to agriculture, tax incentives to private industry and corporate bailouts that also provide shelter from market forces and distort incentive structures (Katz, 1989, pp 160-4). The emphasis on the relationship between rights and duties, notes Lund, reflects earlier concerns among 'New Liberals' at the turn of the century. Concerned to protect the development of social rights from claims that they corrode a sense of 'duty', the 'New Liberals' identified a social category deemed incapable of meeting the obligations of 'competent' citizens. These groups were then suitable for coercive policies of the kind advocated by Charles Booth (Lund, 1999, p 459).

As discussed in Chapter Two, other commentators have argued that the present emphasis in welfare reform contains an underlying strategy to expand the labour supply to meet the requirements of the new precarious and casualised end of the labour market (Smith and Macnicol, 2001). Lois Wacquant (1999) sees these trends as part of a 'new penal common sense', which, originating in America, is being internationalised – its aim being to criminalise poverty and to normalise insecure, low-paid employment:

> Mead has the merit of seeing and making us see that the generalization of precarious work ... rests in actuality on the direct use of political constraint aiming, not at the destruction of the state as such in order to substitute for it a kind of neoliberal Eden of the universal market, but at

> the *replacement of a 'maternalistic' welfare state with a 'paternalistic' punitive state,* which alone is capable of imposing desocialised wage labor as a societal norm and foundation of the new polarized class order. (Wacquant, 1999, pp 319-53; emphasis in original)

Despite attempts to dampen the effects of such policies and 'make work pay' through the introduction of a minimum wage and the extension of in-work benefits to supplement low pay, critics note that these policies cannot offer a long-term solution to extensive income inequality. The equation of poverty with unemployment and dependence is becoming redundant, as the composition of the poor has changed to reflect changes in occupational structures, income distribution and the impact of supply-side social policies:

> The greatest single group of poor people are already in work. 3.5 million poor people live in working-age households. There are more working poor than there are unemployed. There are more working poor than there are poor pensioners. As growing numbers of single mothers, people with disabilities and anybody else who possibly can is urged into work, it becomes ever clearer that most poor people are not the feckless/hopeless/helpless but people who work very hard for long hours and yet still fall below the poverty line. (Toynbee, 2003, p 9)

Later chapters will explore aspects of the current policy focus on employment and increasing employability from the perspective of the 'socially excluded'. For many, economic behaviour has adapted to cope with current labour market insecurities, which are further compounded by a welfare system geared towards the requirements of labour market flexibility. Such behaviour bears little resemblance to the notion of a work-shy, dependent and passive sub-culture that has formed the basis of many discussions of social exclusion in political and policy circles. The avoidance of destitution imposes the adoption of innovative and flexible patterns of activity on many of the 'excluded' although for reasons to be outlined, these are not always practised within the confines of formal structures. From the perspective of those adopting such practices they may represent a more rational, albeit imperfect, solution to economic marginality than those offered by more formal routes. The next chapter will explore the industrial history of the area where the research on which this book is based was undertaken and in tracing the development of the estate since its opening in the 1930s, consider how the economic fortunes of the residents have been affected by wider processes of industrial, demographic and social changes. Again, these issues display a considerable degree of continuity in the same way that themes identified in discussions on the extent and consequences of poverty on the estate in the 1930s, were repeated 60 years later.

Notes

[1] For a more recent version of this argument, see Hernstein and Murray (1994).

[2] Marx (1976) had previously argued for a relative definition of poverty. Commenting on Gladstone's remark to the House of Commons in 1834, on the tendency for growing prosperity at the top to be accompanied with increasing misery at the bottom, Marx noted that: "While the rich have been growing richer, the poor have been growing less poor.... How lame an anti-climax! If the working class has remained 'poor', only 'less poor' in proportion, as it produces for the wealthy class 'an intoxicating augmentation of wealth and power', then it has remained just as poor. If the extremes of poverty have not lessened, they have increased, because the extremes of wealth have" (Marx, 1976, p 806).

[3] John Hobcraft (1998), analysing data from the National Child Development Study, echoed Rutter and Madge's earlier conclusions (1976) that:

> Our review of the most extreme associations makes it tempting to propound a generational or life-course determinism, since so many of the most plausible linkages ... do appear quite regularly among the strongest predictors.... But it is essential to emphasise that all of these associations captured here are just aggregate tendencies and in no sense determinist.... Despite the general, but not complete, causal priority of our explanatory variables both in time, and in their measurement, we remain cautious about attaching causality to the associations observed, regardless of the plausibility of the links. (Hobcraft, 1998, pp 93-6)

FOUR

Life and labour on the St. Helier estate, 1930-2000[1]

The St. Helier estate was built between 1928 and 1936 as part of a broader response to the nation's housing problems in the inter-war period. Seebohm Rowntree's (1917) report *Housing in England and Wales* estimated that 300,000 houses a year needed to be built immediately after the First World War. Given the scale and costs of construction, the report argued that the private sector would be unable to meet demand, and the state or local authority should assume responsibility in providing affordable housing (Fraser, 1984, p 181). The scale of state involvement in housing increased rapidly and between 1914 and 1939, 14 housing Acts were passed. In 1914 local authorities owned 0.2% of the housing stock. State-funded housing contributed 1.5 million new homes built in the inter-war period, increasing the stock of public housing to nearly 10% by 1938 (Power, 1987, p 26). Housing shortages were acute in London with 750,000 families living in multiple-occupation housing in the inter-war period, the majority of whom were small families. Eradication of the slums and the improvement of working-class housing had long been a key priority of London's municipal authorities. The Metropolitan Board of Works had 16 slum clearance schemes in operation in the late 19th century, but it was under municipal reform leadership that its successor, the London County Council (LCC), would become a provider of a large amount of public housing.

Under the architectural influence of W.E. Riley and G. Topham Forest, the LCC acquired an innovative reputation based on cottage designs and favoured a policy of decentralisation through housing the working classes in 'cottages' based on traditional, low-density housing with gardens, trees and open spaces (Buder, 1990). The Labour Party was broadly in favour of an outer ring based on garden suburb principles although Herbert Morrison, Labour leader of the LCC from 1934, warned in 1918 that while the slums must go, "what is even more important is that new slums and social sores shall not be created in London's outer ring" (Yelling, 1992, p 32). Between 1919 and 1939 the LCC built 82,300 new houses, which included eight cottage estates, on the fringes of London. Cottage housing comprised 85% of the

LCC's total output between 1919 and 1927 and included the massive Becontree Estate in Essex, the largest municipal housing estate in the world. It was felt that a similar undertaking was required on the outskirts of south London to deal with its considerable housing problems. According to the 1931 Census over half a million Londoners were still living more than two persons to a room. Many of these were living in the city's 30,000 'basement dwellings' that stretched along the south bank of the River Thames from Wandsworth through Lambeth, Southwark and Bermondsey (Burnett, 1986, p 243).

The favoured site was 825 acres between Morden and the River Wandle, south of Mitcham and astride the Sutton Bypass and it was named the St. Helier estate after an alderman of London, Lady St. Helier. Transport links were vital because local industry could only incorporate a proportion of the new population, and it was assumed that the majority would commute to London. The County of London gave the LCC the compulsory purchase powers it needed in 1925, although the proposals met with opposition from local authorities who were often hostile to LCC initiatives in their areas and were concerned at the costs of providing services on the new estates (Parker, 1999). Owner-occupiers voiced fears at the impact of a large influx of working-class Londoners on property prices and attendant fears over the newcomers' standards of behaviour. The estate was developed in sections under the 1924 (Wheatley) Housing Act and built between 1928 and 1936. When completed the total accommodation numbered 9,068 dwellings, mostly three-, four- and five-room cottages along with over 500 flats. These dwellings housed approximately 40,000 people – the largest LCC estate south of the Thames – at a total cost of £4,078,500 (Hyder, 1977, p 33).

The first tenants moved onto the estate in spring 1930 and by the late 1930s the estate was largely occupied by young families rehoused from south London. Despite attempts to introduce 'Garden City' designs with ample greenery and open spaces, the estate was criticised for its drab appearance. Opinion was divided, with one journalist reporting in 1936 "seeing it for the first time in the golden sunlight of a beautiful autumn afternoon and I thought it the perfect garden city" (*The Sutton Guardian*, 1982b). Simple designs and standardisation were enforced by economic considerations and after 1925 economies were achieved on the cottage estates by building 'simplified dwellings'. These offered a lower standard of accommodation at lower rents and shaped the physical character of the estate as much of the housing built under more austere budgets was located on the Carshalton side of the estate, with the earlier better-quality housing on the Morden side. Social divisions were reinforced from the late 1920s as priorities changed from relieving overcrowding to slum clearance. This entailed a shift away from the high-quality programmes of the 1920s aimed at 'general needs' towards welfare housing targeted at the poorest (Power, 1987, p 27). Although the bulk of slum dwellers were housed in inner-city flats the number of such families housed on the estate numbered 1,105 by 1939, mostly in the later houses in Carshalton. Housing policy priorities had an enduring impact upon the social structure of the estate, which exists to the present day in demographic, socio-economic and tenure variations. They also shaped the reputation of different sections of the estate according to a hierarchical classification of when the houses were built, their standard of facilities and what sections of the working classes were housed in them (Pollack, 1993).

The LCC policy was that rents should shadow those in the private sector but even with subsidies rents remained high. Although cottage estates were largely 'one class' estates housing the artisan sections of the working class, the cost of living was considerably higher on these estates. This often placed a burden on family budgets as money had to be set aside for fares, a recurrent grievance among tenants who regarded the extra travel costs as an 'additional rent'. The limited capacity of local industry to absorb the increased population led to high levels of unemployment on the estate in the 1930s, which caused a severe drain on local charities' supplies in the winter of 1938 (*Merton & Morden News*, 1938). Average rates of turnover on the cottage estates between 1927 and 1936 were around 10% as many returned to London to seek work (Parker, 1999). High rates of turnover made it difficult to establish a sense of community, a situation compounded by the absence of well-established community structures.

In 1939 there was a debate in local newspapers about poverty and the quality of life on the new estate, following high rates of prosecution among tenants for non-payment of rates. The debate was sparked by a speech given in 1939 by Mrs Loveman, organiser of the St. Helier Communist Party. Addressing a meeting at the St. Helier Community Hall she told them that life on the estate had been reduced to a 'mere existence'. This was not solely due to unemployment but also the combination of high rents, travel costs and the lack of well-developed travel and welfare services to which, as Londoners, residents were accustomed (*Merton & Morden News*, 1939b). In the ensuing discussion local GP Dr Mary Barton pointed to the higher levels of poverty on the Carshalton side, arguing that residents in Carshalton were disadvantaged by the lack of transport connections into London. She noted the strain of extra commuting times and the exhaustion of the women who often had to work to supplement the father's wages and whose lives were "just prolonged nervous strains" (*Merton & Morden News*, 1939c).

Problems of adjusting to life on the new estates were well documented in studies of the period (Young, 1934; Glass, 1939). One of the most significant aspects was the dispersal of networks based around families and friends who remained in London. Family networks were weakened further as the adult children of tenants set up home in other areas due to the high cost of housing in the area. In spite of the superior accommodation the vast estates were a marked contrast to the crowded tenements from where most of the residents were drawn and were often perceived as cold and alienating. Since the early days of the LCC, reduction in the number of alcohol licences issued had been a main aim of the 'progressives' temperance policy. Banning inns or pubs on cottage estates prevented the high density of small pubs in the old working-class districts. Instead, there would be 'licensed refreshment houses' that "shall be *bona fide* refreshment houses and places of social intercourse and entertainment under proper conditions and under due control" (Gibbon and Bell, 1939, p 399). These 'refreshment houses' were often unpopular with working men, accustomed to the intimacy of the small 'local'. Opportunities for drinking were sparse and St. Helier, with a population of 40,000, had three pubs in 1939. The lack of 'local' pubs had implications for the development of the estates' social character and assisted the development of the 'privatised family' that Ferdinand Zweig (1961) would identify 20 years later in his study of industrial workers in the area. The additional costs and time of commuting later encouraged many workers to seek work locally, meaning that prosperity and poverty on the estate became increasingly linked to local economic conditions.

Industrial development in Merton and Sutton, 1920-81

The late development of south London meant that until the late 19th century there was little industrial development. Development of the Sutton area occurred after the opening of the Croydon to Epsom railway in 1847 and the population doubled between 1861-71, and doubled again over the next decade until it stood at 10,000 in 1883 (Charlesworth, 1983, p 10). Likewise Mitcham had preserved a 'rural' aspect well into the 20th century largely due to two influential families who blocked efforts to develop the town. The major industries were market gardening, and industries using the waterpower of the River Wandle such as snuff production and corn milling. These provided a base for later industrial growth by chemical and engineering works that would use the river's water as a coolant. Mitcham had long been among the poorest parishes in Surrey and was distinguished in the housing survey of Surrey in 1933 by having the worst housing conditions in the county as outward migration from London from the late 19th century had increased the population of poor and displaced residents. Many Irish labourers had been imported into the district for the building of the Wimbledon to Merton railway and formed a 'troublesome element' concentrated around the borders of Carshalton/ Mitcham (Hope, 1941). The area also contained a large gypsy population who had been attracted to the seasonal work and many settled in the area. *Nuffield College Reconstruction Survey* reports that Mitcham had the largest proportion of gypsy schoolchildren in Surrey, many of 'low mentality'. Most settled in a small area of South Mitcham known locally as 'The Rockies' or 'Redskin Village', which became notorious for the unruliness of its inhabitants (Michison, 1941b).

A surplus population of undesirable lower-class residents would, however, prove advantageous for attracting early industrial development. Following the 1845 Health Act many of the 'noxious' or dangerous waterside industries such as bone boiling, soap and chemical works, which had been located in the poorer districts of Lambeth and Southwark, relocated outside the County of London's administrative boundary. Its proximity to the River Wandle, the cheap value of land and a ready supply of casualised, poor labour made the area ideal for those industries and many relocated to the 'nuisance districts' of Mitcham and Carshalton (Martin, 1966). The varnish and paint industries became major local industries in addition to chemical, printing, dyeing and leather industries that established themselves along the River Wandle. The major period of development occurred between 1925 and 1940 with Merton an important site for the development of 'new industries' producing electrical and consumer goods. Many firms moved from cramped inner-city locations to the new 'industrial estates', which expanded rapidly in the 1930s. The majority of these new sites were located in Greater London and the South East, and several industrial estates were built within commuting distance from the estate. Although criticisms of the cost and expense of commuting to work were common on the estate, a substantial number of residents found local employment as industry decentralised from London and by 1941, 20% of St. Helier residents worked within a two-mile radius of the estate (Michison, 1941a).

The major employer in the area was Mullards, a producer of radio, and later television, valves, which employed a largely local workforce of over 3,000. Many employees lived on the nearby St. Helier estate, some streets containing so many Mullards' employees that they had their own social clubs for whist drives and other activities (Bruley and Edwards, 1997, p 19). Ferdinand Zweig interviewed 168 of the company's employees as part of a wider enquiry for his 1961 work *The worker in an affluent society*. The majority of workers from St. Helier were semi-skilled, shift workers, and (mostly unskilled) women, while the skilled workforce were more likely to own their own homes and live outside the area (Zweig, 1961, p 260). Workers at Mullards were well paid although there was a larger than average gap between the wages of skilled and semi-skilled workers, and the social distance between occupational groups was greater than in the other companies that Zweig studied. The 'new industries' required labour-intensive assembly work, which expanded the supply of jobs involving simple, repetitive tasks. When considering location, areas that contained large surplus populations of female and juvenile labour were favoured (Scott, 1999). St. Helier, with its high cost of living and young demographic profile provided an inexhaustible female and youth labour force. Often, two separate wage systems would exist: skilled workers were paid their own rates according to their trades, while the semi-skilled and especially women were paid using piece-rate systems to motivate output and link wages directly to productivity (Zweig, 1961, pp 251-2).

The decline of British light industry from the 1960s was reflected in the industrial structure of Merton, and many local employers followed a trend of relocation as production costs increased and the value of land rose due to demand for housing. The manufacturing sector still accounted for approximately 57% of employment in Merton in 1971. Sutton, which relied heavily on the distributive trades and retailing, had a manufacturing sector accounting for 30% of employment (Shepherd et al, 1974, p 71). De-industrialisation accelerated through the 1970s and Phillips, who had bought Mullards, halted production at Beddington in the late 1980s. Production was transferred to other sites around the UK and abroad and the Beddington site was demolished in 1993. Zweig's study concluded that his portrayal characterised the industrial worker in a fully-employed welfare state. He argued that 'security-mindedness' was a defining trait of the affluent worker as unemployment and poverty faded from memories. This was accompanied by a decline in class conflict as the 'revolution of rising expectations' and a rise in acquisitive orientations diluted class boundaries. In its place he identified an increasingly privatised and home-centred working class. Zweig argued that these trends marked a new and ascendant form of social organisation, where status distinctions superseded class divisions and traditional modes of living. Although subsequent changes have undermined Zweig's conclusions, he perceived that the final outcome depended upon the future of the economy and whether it could maintain full employment and prosperity (Zweig, 1961, pp 205-12). The industrial and labour market changes that intensified through the 1980s and 1990s would further destabilise the material basis of the 'affluent worker' identified at Mullards, and subsequently impact on the St. Helier estate from where many were drawn.

Industrial and occupational change in Merton and Sutton, 1981-2000

The economic fortunes of both boroughs over recent decades have reflected similar changes occurring at a national level, in the Greater London region and differences occurring within regions. There were marked differences between the two boroughs and a disparity, in the case of Merton, between regional data that gives an impression of a 'de-industrialising' North and a relatively unscathed South. In 1981 the manufacturing sector accounted for 36% of total employment in the borough compared to 19% for Greater London and 28% nationally. Merton de-industrialised earlier and faster than the rest of the nation, and by 1989 had lost over a third of its total manufacturing employment. By 1989 manufacturing accounted for 25% of employment, still slightly higher than the national figure of 23% and significantly higher than the 13% for Greater London (London Borough of Merton (LBM), 1994). Throughout the 1980s and 1990s the largest areas of economic growth in the two boroughs were in distribution and catering, retail, banking and finance, and public administration. These growth areas increased the supply of professional, managerial and unskilled manual work but failed to compensate for the decline in skilled manual work. By 1996 manufacturing employment had fallen to 15% in Merton and 6% in Sutton (London Research Centre, 1999a). The polarisation of income and opportunities that was occurring across the UK during this period was amplified in London and Greater London, where the ratio of the highest decile income to the lowest was the widest in the country (Lee and Townsend, 1993).

As service sector employment expanded and unemployment fell following the recession of the 1980s and early 1990s, a restructuring of the balance between full-time and part-time jobs and between men and women has occurred. Between 1991 and 1997 full-time male employment in Merton declined from 50% of the total workforce to

45% and in Sutton it fell from 43% to 39% (London Research Centre, 1999a). Full-time male employment is projected to decline further to 29% of total employment in Sutton by 2006 (Employment Service et al, 1997). Over the same period there was an increase in female full-time employment from 22% of all employees to 25% in Merton, and from 30% to 35% in Sutton. Female part-time employment experienced an aggregate decline in both boroughs although in hotel and catering work and in personal services, female part-time employment continued to rise (London Research Centre, 1999a). There were notable increases in female full-time employment in the hotel and catering sector and in the health, social work and community sectors. These changes are projected to continue as much job-growth has been low-grade service sector work. A report published by London Borough of Merton revealed that the borough's fast food sector grew 300% faster than the national average between 1993 and 1996, with employment in hotels and restaurants growing 30% faster than nationally over the same period. The report also noted the loss of diversity in the borough's sectoral pattern of employment as, in the context of a long-term decline in fulltime employment, its residents were becoming more dependent on fewer sectors (LBM, 1999).

Research conducted in 1997 by the Sutton Regeneration Partnership found that 44% of Sutton's employers were planning to recruit managerial/professional employees over the next year. Eighteen per cent were planning to recruit clerical or secretarial workers, 33% planned to recruit unskilled manual workers and 13% retail employees. This compares with just 7% planning to recruit skilled manual workers and 11% semi-skilled manual workers (Employment Service et al, 1997). These trends have contributed to an increasing gap in earnings, as the fastest growing sectors are those that pay above- and below-average local wages. While average incomes in Merton and Sutton are below the Greater London average there are large differences between sectors. In Merton, banking, financial and insurance employees earned 89% of the average income for Greater London. Those working in retail, distribution, hotels and restaurants earned just 59% of the average regional wage (Solotec, 1999). These figures only account for workers actually employed in the two boroughs and take no account of those who commute into London. However, there are marked occupational variations in travel to work patterns with professional and managerial groups more geographically mobile, while for the low paid and unskilled, labour market opportunities are often highly localised (Green and Owen, 1996). The following section examines how these changes in the industrial and occupational structure interact with the demographic and labour market characteristics of the estates' residents to produce locally bound patterns of deprivation, and the impact of these changes on the overall quality of life on the estate.

The social structure of St. Helier estate, 1981-2000

The larger part of the estate is located in the London Borough of Sutton, which was profiled in the 1998 Department of the Environment, Transport and the Regions Index of Local Deprivation as the least deprived borough in London with an official unemployment rate of 3.7% and 20% of its wards among the wealthiest 10% in England (DETR, 1998a). Borough-level data can disguise pockets of high deprivation, as poverty and social exclusion have become less uniformly distributed regionally and more concentrated within particular localities (DETR, 2000). As discussed later in this chapter, this presents problems in fostering community associations and targeting regeneration and employment programmes. As a local economic development officer commented:

> ★ "There are parts of the estate that are quite affluent with smaller pockets of poverty inside and poor parts with better off parts within them and that doesn't come through at Census level. It's hard to talk about the estate as if it's one place because it's split into countless small boundaries and any official ones are entirely arbitrary. There's a problem in developing a body that will further the interests of the estate. People are not worried about what's going on half a mile away on the other side of the estate. They're worried about what's going on in their own road."

As discussed, skilled manual, semi-skilled and unskilled workers have borne the brunt of industrial changes. Their adverse impacts are disproportionately experienced on the estate because of the large concentrations of those groups in the area (Table 1). The estate scores significantly higher on several indices of deprivation with the two northern wards falling within the most deprived 15% of wards in the country. Enumeration District (ED) data demonstrate concentrations of poverty occurring at extremely fine levels. Of the 28 EDs covering the two northern wards, 12% fall within the 10% of most deprived

Table 1: Social class of residents, by social class of household head, 1991: 10% sample (%)

	Professional/ managerial	Skilled non-manual	Skilled manual	Semi-skilled	Unskilled
Merton	45.6	17.5	23.4	10.1	3.4
St. Helier Merton	23.9	19.3	34.7	13.6	8.5
Sutton	43.8	16.8	27.4	8.7	3.3
St. Helier North	17.4	18.5	37.1	19.1	7.9
St. Helier South	17.5	14.0	40.4	18.4	9.7

Source: London Research Centre (1999a)

EDs and 31% fall within the 20% most deprived EDs. The remaining 57% of EDs are in the bottom 40% (London Research Centre, 1999b).

In June 1998, just before the fieldwork began, unemployment rates on the estate were around 11% compared to a borough average of 6%. Unemployment was largely concentrated among males in the 25-34 and 35-44 age brackets, who constituted 65% of the unemployed on the estate. The area also contained a higher proportion of long-term unemployed with 44% long-term unemployed against a borough average of 39% (LBS, 1998). A study conducted by the Basic Skills Agency in 1998 revealed that 22% of the estates' residents have low or very low literacy and numeracy skills compared to the borough average of 12% (Solotec, 1999). In 1981, 55% of the resident population of working age were economically active. This fell to 42% in 1991, despite a shift in the demographic structure of the estate, with an increase in working-age males and a rise in young families with children. By 2001, rates of economic activity stood at over 67% although many of these were employed in low-wage jobs. In 1999, over one third of the borough's Family Credit claimants were drawn from the estate indicating a concentration of low earners (LBS, 2001). There has also been a significant rise in lone parents on the estate from 2% of households in 1981 to 11% by 2001 – over double the borough average (LBS, 1981, 2001).

The estate has experienced a change in the age structure of the population since 1981, which is polarised between younger and older residents. Burrows argues that the increasingly bi-modal age structure of social housing tenants has occurred because the groups leaving social housing for owner occupation tend to be middle-aged, married and economically active. Fifty-six per cent of families who fill the vacant homes are economically inactive and 53% are lone-parent households (Burrows, 1999). Despite a decline in elderly residents on the estate, many of the still relatively high proportions derive from the original residents. A community worker on the Sutton Regeneration Partnership noted that these form a large, and frequently invisible, aspect of poverty on the estate:

> "When people talk about estates it's single mums, young blokes, drugs and crime. They forget there are lots of old people round here trying to make do on just a state pension. Because they're not out there in the street making problems for everybody else it goes unnoticed."

With families who have grown up and left home there is much under-occupancy on the estate. As these residents either die or vacate their premises they are replaced by young families housed by the local authority or else the houses are marketed as 'starter homes' and purchased as a first step onto the property ladder. These processes have increased rates of turnover on the estate, which in 1998 stood at 8% per year although in some streets it was as high as 12%. Many of the estate's longer-standing residents attribute the areas' problems to the demise of a 'settled' period that lasted until the 1980s. The 1977 Housing and Homeless Persons Act obliged local authorities to house those who had previously been largely excluded from public housing. The characteristics of those housed by the local authority since then, and the instrumental motivations of many who purchase houses on the estate are seen as undermining the area and contributing to its decline. One resident observed:

> "There's a fair amount of movement in and out of the estate but no mass exodus. The estate was stable for a long time but as the original generation dies off they're moving a new generation of people onto the estate and that's when the area started to decline."

In common with the national pattern, recent decades have witnessed increased rates of owner occupancy. Owner occupation increased from 22% in 1981 to 55% in 2001, with the proportion renting from the council falling from 75% to 38% over the same period. Although tenants of social housing are on average more deprived than owner-occupiers, differences between owner-occupied households within the lowest Council Tax band and the social rented sector are much smaller. In many cases this has resulted in the growth of mixed tenure estates meaning that access to housing is determined by both the market, and by the housing allocation policies of local authorities (Lee and Murie, 1999). Mixed tenure estates also contain the potential for fragmentation and social closure built around 'consumption sectors' that cut across class boundaries as the interests of homeowners and tenants diverge (Saunders, 1989). The most prominent example of residents' collective action in recent years has been organised by homeowners protesting against structural faults discovered in their homes, who demanded that the council either repurchase them or pay for repairs.[2]

Tenure divisions are particularly marked on the estate given the high property prices in the area. Many tenants regard it impossible to purchase their homes even with the discount offered to council tenants. The following tenant remarked at the 'public squalor' and decline of community institutions that have accompanied increasingly 'privatised affluence':

> "I've missed the boat. I should have bought this place a few years ago when they were going for 70 to 80 grand. Now they're double that and I'd need to be on over 25 grand a year to buy this place even with the discount (...) the houses are being tarted up but look outside the front doors. There's litter everywhere, dumped cars, the pubs have gone, the social club's been shut down, there's nothing for the kids to do and nobody gives a damn because they're too busy watching their houses go up and up in price."

The fragmentation of working-class communities was evident in the polarisation of views concerning the aesthetic changes that accompanied increasing rates of home ownership. Throughout the 1980s and 1990s the homogeneous, red-brick cottages that were once criticised for their conformity were being transformed as pebble dashing, plate glass windows, imitation timber frontages and extended porches were added to the original designs. This was an affront to conservationists and to many of the area's older residents who reacted to the changes with distaste. The discordant views were indicative of a more general splintering of interests on the estate as represented in the local newspaper in 1982. On one hand was the tenant who complained, "I don't like things changed. If people can afford to buy and redecorate their house they can afford to go elsewhere". On the other was the homeowner who retorted, "An Englishman's home is his castle – and I'll do what I like with mine" (*The Sutton Guardian*, 1982). These grievances reached a head after several complaints against the homeowners who added two Greek columns and a turret-like loft to their three-bedroom house (*The Guardian*, 1990). Following lobbying by a local conservation group and a small group of concerned residents, Sutton council mooted the idea of making the estate a conservation area to preserve its original features and consulted residents. Only 20 replies were received and the idea was dropped (*The Sutton & Cheam Herald*, 1992).

Patterns of housing tenure on the estate demonstrate significant differences across the three wards that reflect spatial concentrations of poverty and deprivation and the higher desirability of housing on the Merton side. As in the 1930s, indices of disadvantage are higher in the two Sutton wards of St. Helier North and South. Both wards contain higher proportions of council tenants, unemployment and economic inactivity, and accommodate more elderly and lone-parent households than on the Merton side (London Research Centre, 1999b). In health terms the two wards have the highest rates of death from heart disease in the borough while hospital admissions for mental illness, dementia and deaths by suicide are higher, markedly so in the case of St. Helier North. Hospital admissions for asthma for those under the age of 15 are double the borough rate as are admissions for childhood dental caries, which is strongly associated with poor diet (Merton and Sutton Health Authority, 1994). Reported incidents of drug and alcohol misuse are among the highest for the outer London boroughs, while St. Helier North has among the highest rates for violent and property crimes, criminal damage, sexual offences and robbery in the borough (Community Safety Unit, 1998).

The relationship between poverty, housing tenure and educational outcomes has been well established. Low income and living in council housing is strongly correlated to low educational attainment at all ages (Sparkes, 1999). Byrne and Rogers (1999) examine how the spatial separation of social classes creates their reproduction, through providing differential access to schools. For the affluent the independent sector remains an option or alternatively there are good high-performing state schools, which are largely grant maintained. Selection processes in those schools are increasingly geared towards the assessment of academic ability through entrance tests and interviews. Priority access also occurs through the designation of catchment areas or from designated primary schools, while area of residence may also be used as an indicator of the child's ability. The well-informed middle classes employ their reserves of 'cultural capital' (and the economic capital that underpins it in the form of private tuition and coaching for entrance tests) and through place of residence, monopolise places in the best schools. The choices of working-class parents are more localised. 'Under-performing' schools suffer compounding financial problems as they are filled with the most challenging children, and a non-academic ethos prevails inhibiting the development of bright children. Byrne and Rogers' analysis of Northumberland suggests that:

> What does matter is the construction of a landscape, which now has a stable form, with socio-spatial residential locations playing a key role in determining access to routes to schools which maximise the possibility of credential achievements. (Byrne and Rogers, 1999)

Processes of educational stratification operate acutely in Sutton, which contains several elite fee-paying day and boarding schools as well as high-performing grant maintained schools such as Nonsuch Girls in Cheam, one of the best-performing schools in the country and which regularly achieves 97% or more GCSE's at grades A*-C. Schools within the St. Helier catchment area consistently perform below the local education authority (LEA) and national averages. Watermeads on the Merton side of the estate has long been the worst-performing school in a borough where the average LEA score (37%) is already below the national average (45%) (DfEE, 1998a). Despite a change of name it was still judged as failing in a 1998 OFSTED report and an action plan produced by parents to save the school failed to prevent its closure. The school was closed at the end of 1998/99 and reopened at the start of 1999/2000 under the new name of Bishopsford Community School (*The Merton Guardian*, 1998).

Differences in educational access translate into the destinations of school leavers and reconstruct spatial patterns of labour market disadvantage. Thirty-five per cent of St. Helier's residents have no qualifications compared to 5% of residents in Merton and 4.2% in Sutton (LBS, 2001). School leavers from St. Helier tend to leave school and enter the labour market earlier, and experience higher rates of unemployment. Twenty-one per cent of school leavers from the estate enter employment or training at the age of 16, against a Sutton borough average of 9%. Of those who leave school at 16 to enter employment or training in the LEA area, 55% have five or more GCSE's at grades A*-C, compared to just 1.5% from the estate. A high level of fluidity between employment, training and unemployment was observed among this group. Forty-seven per cent of the estate's school leavers had been in the same job or training for over three months in July 1998. Twenty-nine per cent had left one job or placement, had experienced a period of unemployment and found another job, while 24% were in temporary employment and looking for another job (Luard, 1998, pp 6-7). The response of many local youths to labour market disadvantage and educational failure was acted out on the streets where they had grown up, which would stimulate increasing local concern at their activities and the overall quality of life on the estate.

Life on the estate, 1990-2000

In the standing of local housing estates St. Helier has not acquired the character of a 'sink estate' that characterises other nearby post-war estates due to the heterogeneity of the estate and its size, which has tended to disguise the extent of poverty. However, the image of the estate as an 'undesirable' area was established early in the estate's history as the presence of slum dwellers or a few well-known criminal families often suffices to label estates or areas within them. Later, the key event that reinforced the estate's image as a site of violent and serious criminal activity surrounded the St. Helier Arms, which achieved national infamy in the mid-1990s as the 'most dangerous pub in Britain' (*The Independent on Sunday*, 1994). Located in the centre of the estate this large LCC-style 'refreshment house' had long attracted police attention and in 1984 they went to court to prevent the transfer of the licence to a private landlord. They claimed that the pub had been used as a front for drug dealing and organised crime since the early 1970s, and that criminals had run the pub down by intimidating landlords in order to purchase it at a cheap price. The court refused to grant a licence to the pub, although an appeal by the prospective landlord overturned the refusal and the landlord was granted a licence.

Following several changes of landlord over the next five years the pub was closed for refurbishment at the beginning of 1989 and reopened later the same year. Despite claims that it had shed its previous image and transformed into a 'family pub', it attracted the custom of few locals, and quickly re-acquired its previous notoriety. In June 1992 Stephen Davis, a small-time local criminal, was shot inside the pub following an altercation with the pub's bouncers. One of the pub's bouncers received a life sentence for murder and the other two bouncers were jailed as accomplices. Following an attempted murder in the pub in November 1993 the police returned to court to have the licence revoked. The hearing was adjourned for the landlord to put her case forward (*The Sutton Guardian*, 1994). The pub's fate was sealed one week before the hearing when a victim was shot in the face in the pub car park and then had his throat cut. The police returned to court with a petition signed by 500 locals and the statements of former landlords, who testified to witnessing large-scale drug dealing and the sale of guns on the premises. The licence was revoked and the pub closed in March 1994 (*The Sutton Herald*, 1994). Plans to reopen it were opposed by the police, the local authority and various community organisations. In June 1995 magistrates refused to grant a licence and the pub was demolished in August 1996. Local community associations argued that the site's location made it ideal for redevelopment as a community/health centre complete with a small part-time police station, but the land was sold to private developers who built retirement flats on the site.

Although only a small minority of residents was involved in the pub's activities, it continues to form an important 'local legend' and cemented the association of the estate with criminality. Such narratives form an important aspect of the way that cultural identities are constructed and link those identities to place (Bird, 2002). The pub's closure also had more tangible consequences through altering the nature of crime in the area. The estate had provided an adjacent and ready market for large volumes of stolen consumer goods and drugs. These were distributed via the pub to their sycophantic agents on the estate who earned a percentage of sales. The removal of this major source of bargain-priced goods merged with the increase in serious drug use by ever-younger cohorts to create a burgeoning youthful criminal market, and focus a critical concern on the activities of the estate's youth. A community development worker commented:

> ★ "Since the pub's gone a lot of the more serious crime went with it, there were shootings and murders, the lot and you wouldn't just pop in for a quiet pint. I mean, with the pub you just avoided it but residents and shopkeepers these days are more worried about property crime, which is more random, cars getting broke into, burglary, vandalism, it's not at epidemic proportions but it is a big concern."

It was in this context that the 'Sutton High Street Burglary Posse' emerged to inflame the mid-1990s' political and media debate on the 'problem of youth'. This group of largely 12- to 15-year-olds, an alliance of kids from the estate and disaffected middle-class youths from the area, attracted national media attention following a vociferous spree of shoplifting raids and burglaries. The gang epitomised a brazen underclass of persistent teenage offenders. For the government, and to the frustration of local police, the 'Sutton Posse' highlighted the deficiencies of a criminal justice system, which was unable to prosecute the perpetrators because of their age and misguided social workers who often intervened on behalf of the children. Lady Olga Maitland, Conservative MP for Cheam, introduced a Ten Minute Rule Bill that attempted to enable magistrates to bypass the social services and send persistent young offenders to secure units (Norman, 1993). In the midst of this rise in youthful crime and drug use the police were criticised for their reluctance to combat crime in the area. This prompted a more proactive approach and through the mid to late 1990s, police action involved a succession of 'crackdowns' and dawn raids. Increased police presence on the estate did little to stem criminal activity despite initiatives such as the well-publicised 'Operation Teign', which targeted persistent offenders and drug dealers (*The Sutton Guardian*, 1994c).

The law and order response also had wider consequences for residents as the police were obliged to prevent misdemeanours that were previously overlooked. Successive 'blitzes' on untaxed cars were launched. The 60-year-old St. Helier Social Club was the only social club on the estate with a membership of 1,200 people, 40% of whom were pensioners. Following police pressure the club was closed in 1996 due to breaches of licensing regulations and hours (*The Sutton Guardian*, 1996). Plans for a £500,000 refurbishment were abandoned after the club was burnt down in 1998. Middleton Circle, a roundabout flanked by a parade of shops and the hub of the estate, had been the preferred meeting place for groups of teenagers for decades. Amid residents' complaints that the youths were an intimidating presence and claims that the Circle was a site for drug dealing, a CCTV was erected in the middle of the roundabout in 1998 and the groups dispersed. This contributed to a rise in vandalism and arson as large groups of teenagers took to wandering the streets, and renewed demands that the local authority take action to halt the rise in antisocial behaviour (*The Sutton Guardian*, 2001).

Although most residents emphasise that the estate's reputation is largely undeserved and the result of a small minority and a few high-profile events such as those described above, they have firmly entrenched themselves in the local consciousness. The chairperson of the tenants' association commented:

> "One myth I want to dispel is that this is a 'hard man' estate. If you call a load of kids hanging around on street

> corners shouting 'kill the pigs' at passing police cars and
> smashing the odd window, then maybe it is but you've got
> more chance of being hit by a zimmer frame than anything
> else. The real hard cases went with the pub and you've still
> got a few around but they tend to keep a low profile."

Nevertheless, the stigma directed towards the area is felt by residents
and may result in a self-fulfilling prophecy as legitimate options are
denied and improvised routes are found. Julie, a 28-year-old lone parent
recounted an episode that occurred shortly after she moved to the
estate, and which highlights the ways in which labelling operates to
confirm the assumptions of the labelling:

> "After I moved to the estate, I went out with my credit
> card and got a load of stuff on the card at my old address. I
> got caught by the police but they couldn't do anything
> because technically I'd done nothing illegal because I hadn't
> long moved. When they asked me why I did it I said, 'Do
> you think if I gave my real address that they'd give me
> credit?'. I had every intention of paying it but I couldn't
> use my real address. That's when I started to see the basis of
> living in a place like that (...) they tar you with the same
> brush and it's hard to get credit. The area's got a dodgy
> reputation so the people have as well, and in the end you
> have to take different directions to get what you want."

The estate's image was not only formed through a process of labelling
from outside, but reflected the concerns of residents who had long
complained at the reluctance to tackle adolescent crime and vandalism.
As discussed, the diversity of the estate's population – in particular the
high proportions of youths and elderly residents and the often contrary
interests of owner occupiers and council tenants, all living in close
proximity to each other – means that conflicts are commonplace. The
increased volume and visibility of street-level economic behaviour
adds to the perception of the area's decline and for many, indicates a
weakening of civic morality. A community worker resident on the
estate noted:

> ★ "A lot of people are poor but I wouldn't call the estate
> poverty stricken. The kids all wear designer clothes and get
> all the latest gadgets but the parents won't pay for their
> child to go on a school trip. It's the attitude of 'why should

I pay for something that I can get for free?' and in the end the trip's usually cancelled because not enough people contribute. It's the same with work. A lot of people would sooner not pay tax and keep their benefits so there's a lot of 'lads' round here: builders and car mechanics operating their businesses right out on the pavement. Nobody stops to consider that individual selfishness has consequences for everyone."

Studies indicate that estates with a more uniformly deprived population are more tolerant of lawbreaking and report fewer crimes than on mixed estates. Mistrust is directed at the police and social services with disputes usually settled informally (Burney, 1999, p 27). On the estate, extended networks are an important informal mechanism for protecting the interests of its members and in mediating between groups when tensions arise. Grievances can only be sorted out informally within and between networks possessing similar lifestyles, and where there is a degree of consensus concerning the legitimate method of sanction. The shift in the estate's social structure from a largely homogeneous 'one class' estate of young families towards a more diverse population has eroded the possibility for collective action based on a shared spatial location. As Burney notes, heterogeneity renders the term 'community' meaningless (Burney, 1999, p 57). Political rhetoric interprets this as a deficit of 'social capital'. As later chapters explore, there is an abundance of social capital on the estate but this circulates not on a neighbourhood basis, but among local networks based around particular forms of reciprocal aid. A sense of 'community' only exists within these networks of shared interests, and the informal processes through which disputes are settled do not extend to everybody. Research indicates that mixed tenure estates are not characterised by inclusive social networks and rates of mutual support between different tenure groups are low (Jupp, 1999). The distance between different sections of the estate means that there is no mutual way of arbitrating conflicts, or of defining commonly agreed problems (see Chapter Nine). Tensions between youths and older residents are the most common source of antagonism, as the following mother complained:

"It's a two-way thing. They moan at the noise and some of the old people really don't like the kids. They're always going 'don't play ball out there' as if it's wrong for boys to play football! So you've got young people being quite obnoxious to the old people because they're not very tolerant and the whole thing just escalates."

As the 'hoop iron' episode demonstrates, while sections of the estate will unite to promote their concerns there exists a pervasive indifference to the decline in the estate's overall quality of life. During a discussion of changes on the estate during her 13 years there, one resident observed:

> "The area isn't like Roundshaw, over there it's single mothers and unemployment but here the people are different, the culture's different. I can't explain it but there's no sense of belonging. The estate's so fragmented and it's like nobody feels anything for the people around them. People know who's selling drugs but nobody does anything because no one cares.... There's little social interaction between people here, no real community."

The regeneration of the estate

Two main approaches towards regenerating deprived communities have dominated recent policy approaches. First, boosting local labour markets through attracting inward business investment and encouraging small business formation. Second, is the belief that residents should be involved in defining the priorities that guide regeneration (SEU, 2000). The Single Regeneration Budget (SRB) Challenge Fund reflects the belief that a more efficient method of distributing funds is through the introduction of competition and citizen involvement. The bidding process for the SRB specifies two key criteria: the bid must represent a strategic response to local problems and it must have the agreement of a local partnership. Funded by the SRB, the Sutton Regeneration Partnership (SRP) had 45 projects in operation in the northern wards in 1998 concerned with employment, training and education, youth outreach services, community development, programmes relating to health promotion, parental support services, domestic violence and schemes to reduce crime and vandalism (Sutton Regeneration Partnership, 1999).

Noting that self-employment is lower in deprived areas, the government's Policy Action Team (PAT) recommend the promotion of self-employment and community enterprise schemes through offering advice, training and support grants to budding entrepreneurs (PAT, 1999). The SRP has schemes offering advice and support to small businesses, and was supporting several community enterprise schemes that had recently started during the fieldwork phase of the research. Evidence suggests, however, that failure rates among community enterprises are high unless supported by generous public subsidies (Taylor, 1998). There is no lack of entrepreneurial activity on the estate – indeed the estate's informal economy represents one of the few spheres of activity that transcends the fragmentary and often conflictual nature of the estate, connecting residents into a web of trading and exchange. Few residents appear willing to either risk trading housing and other benefits in return for a start-up grant and probable reliance on in-work benefits, or to surrender one of the few areas of their lives free from bureaucratic intervention to the guidance and supervision of 'professionals'.

The growth of tenant involvement has brought positive improvements in some projects but often the input of residents has been at the project and implementation level, rather than at the policy design level (Taylor, 1998). Apart from the determined efforts to involve residents by the SRP-funded Specialist Health Promotions, community workers active on the estate complain at a lack of local consultation prior to the SRP and the paucity of local jobs generated. A common, albeit partisan, grievance was that the SRP has usurped the services that have long been provided by those with a closer knowledge of the estate and its people. A member of a local church that organises several community-based services complained:

> "No real research on what was needed was conducted before the SRP and they bought in outsiders so where does the money go? To pay their salaries because I see very few residents in these new positions, so most of the money flows out of the community that it was intended to help. It's still the churches and voluntary organisations that are doing the real community work and not getting any recognition for it."

Lack of tenant involvement is aggravated by a lack of publicity surrounding the SRP and the lack of accessible information. As the chairperson of the tenants' association commented, "You'd need a degree in urban planning to understand some of the publications". A small minority of residents is active in community associations, which may actually increase tensions, as they tend to represent sectional interests (Reynolds, 1986). The youth outreach worker quoted earlier noted:

"On the Tenant's Forum participation started low and just
got lower. At present there are around 20 tenants that attend,
plus the 'great and the good'. Police spokesmen, community
workers, voluntary associations, but involvement in tenant's
associations, which is what we're trying to build, is abysmal."

A recent study noted that residents of deprived areas make clear
distinctions between those 'excluded' for reasons beyond their control,
and those excluded 'through choice'. Residents attempting to protect
often-tenuous neighbourhood conditions from further decline may
find it necessary to exclude disruptive elements (Richardson and Le
Grand, 2002). For example, a lack of youth facilities was recognised as
a major problem on the estate during consultation with residents.
Nevertheless, the tenants' association fiercely opposed plans to spend
£400,000 converting the community association into a youth club,
voicing concerns that it would become a centre for drug dealing and
disorder. This was in spite of the council's suggestion that it would be
made available for use by the wider community (*The Sutton Guardian*,
1994b).

At the time of the fieldwork it was too early to assess whether the
SRP would provide lasting benefits to the estate. The opening of an
employment/training office on the estate and programmes such as
NEWPIN (North Eastern Wards Parents in Need) have been well
utilised by residents. As many community workers recognised, it is the
size, fragmentation and widespread apathy on the estate that impairs
the development of a sense of community while the fractured and
adverse relations between residents possessing different lifestyles and
with different interests, may further distance those groups most 'socially
excluded'. Evaluation of the Scottish New Life Partnerships showed
that even with generous funding it took five years to nurture
community networks to a stage where all sections of the community
could engage in the consultation process (Taylor, 1998). Critics of the
SRB point to the short-lived nature of the funding and its diminishing
resource base making it unlikely that such programmes will bring
permanent benefits. Between 1995/96 and 1999/2000, the various
government expenditure funds, which influence the level of funding
for regeneration schemes, were subject to cuts of £2 billion or 30% in
real terms (Mawson, 1999). Finally, the political imperatives of
producing short-term, tangible improvements that can be quantifiably
demonstrated in reduced unemployment rates, increased levels of
economic activity and self-employment have concentrated largely on
developing individuals' 'human capital'. This is at the expense of longer-

term and more intangible improvements that include all sections of the community and may add to the decline of housing estates, by allowing the most capable to get jobs and move away. As one of the estate's employment and training advisors commented:

> "There's a fair deal more interest in training than in work. People don't want unskilled jobs where the pay is low, because they won't keep them for long (...) I ask what do they want to do in the future and the answer's always the same. Get a decent job and move away from here."

Notes

[1] Throughout this chapter, ★ indicates that a quotation has been transcribed from notes. In the quotations, (...) indicates that part of the text has been omitted.

[2] The problem was known as the 'curse of hoop iron'. In 1992 houses on the Carshalton side were found to be structurally unsound. A steel strip used to reinforce the brickwork had rusted, causing houses to crack and bow. Building societies were refusing to grant mortgages to potential buyers and property values plummeted by 20%. Residents formed the Hoop Iron Action Group and 150 locals marched on Downing Street to present a petition signed by 1,200 residents, demanding that the Department of the Environment provide funds for the local council to carry out necessary repairs. A report commissioned by Sutton Council on the affected homes concluded that the damage was cosmetic and not structural. The Department of the Environment argued that there was no evidence that the homes were defective under the Defective Housing Act, which would have required the council to buy back their homes for 95% of the market value. No help was made available to homeowners and building societies agreed to lend on properties again as long as 'remedial' repairs were undertaken at a cost of £700–£1,000 per house.

FIVE

Labour market opportunities and welfare-to-work[1]

> "I'd take a proper job if one came up but it'd have to be the right job and it'd have to pay the right money (...) this sort of thing's not what I intended doing and I've probably been doing it for too long. I mean it is an option but it's not one that I'd have seen myself doing when I was at school (...) I thought I'd fall into something, like when my dad left school he never had a clue ... but he got married and stuck at the same job for like over 30 years. I can't even picture that, you know, he's worked in the same job for nearly as long as I've been alive! My longest job's been about five years and that was around six years ago. Since then it's been bits and pieces really." (Ian, 31)

> "The only idea I had when I left school was to get a job for a few years, save up and get married at 20. I think in that respect I was pretty typical of most girls from my generation (...) I left school with no qualifications and was working the next week. I did factory work, some office work, worked in a shop (...) It was much easier to find work back then compared with now. So the idea of getting qualified never really entered our heads because it was like your life was mapped out and I just thought I'd grow up and be like my parents because they were married by the time they were 20." (Liz, 40)

Previous chapters have addressed the economic, social and political processes that have assisted the move towards increasing labour flexibility and 'non-standard' forms of employment and presented data, which have related the impact of those changes upon a local area. Several commentators have questioned the novelty of these 'new times', pointing to the similarity with dual labour market theories that emerged in the late 1960s. These portrayed a primary and secondary sector, which aided by exclusionary union practices and other institutional rules, tended to divide the labour market into non-competing industrial groups. Internal labour markets provided a route to upward mobility in the well-paid, secure, unionised primary sector. In the secondary sector, career advancement meant going outside the firm to find a better job (Doeringer and Piore, 1971; Bluestone et al, 1973). Pahl has argued that the unprecedented change in work patterns occurred not during the 1980s, but during the post-war 'boom' and that it is these historically specific features that have formed the standard against which contemporary changes have been measured (Pahl, 1984, p 313). The development, or revival, of a 'flexible' labour market may not be as novel as is sometimes claimed. However, this is a separate argument to one concerning the significance of these changes for the life chances of individuals, households and communities or how those most affected by these changes have responded and adapted to the structure of opportunities that they face.

Byrne (1997) argues that one consequence has been an important change in the structure of inequality. Under earlier conditions of full employment and universal welfare, patterns of inequality were continuous. This meant that a continuum existed between the poor and non-poor with a fair degree of movement between these two categories. The spatial and labour market transformations associated with the post-Fordist era have made incremental upward mobility harder to achieve and:

> There are really two sorts of lives, involving poverty and exclusion on the one hand and affluence and participation on the other. These two modes don't overlap. However, people and households can and do move between these positions. Indeed, the possibility of movement down is the key factor in the absence of feel-good associated with job insecurity. (Byrne, 1997, p 34)

Evidence reveals that occupational mobility has less impact in reducing inequality, as long-term inequality has increased and the relative position of the low paid has declined. In 1977 the top 10% of earners earned 2.75 times the amount of the bottom 10%. By 1997 this had risen to nearly four times the amount earned in the bottom 10% (McKnight, 2000, p I). Between 1990 and 1995 three out of four jobs entered from unemployment were temporary, part-time or low-skilled self-employment (White and Forth, 1998, p 39). Although women disproportionately fill these low-paid positions, 47% of men re-entering employment entered the lowest earnings quartile. There is also a significant persistence in low pay: 23% of men, and between 40 and 50% of all employees who remained in employment over a six-year period remained in the lowest quarter of the income distribution (McKnight, 2000, p 25).

These structural transformations in the nature and rewards of work have impacted on, and provided a framework through which, the life chances of individuals and households are experienced. The outcome of these changes at an individual level will be affected by a variety of economically relevant social and individual factors. When discussing labour market experiences and attitudes with people on the estate, certain features in each individual narrative emerged, in varying degrees, as playing a decisive role in influencing economic behaviour. Factors rooted in each individual's work history affected both current and future perceptions of work, such as work habits and the relationships with workmates and superiors established there. Status and pay levels of previous jobs were bound up with assessments of job market prospects, which were further influenced through lifecycle stages and domestic situations as well as 'human capital' factors such as educational attainment, training and work-related skills. Social milieu also plays a significant role in potentially increasing or lessening these individual characteristics and plays an important role in shaping occupational aspirations:

> Neighbourhoods are not just important because of the direct effect of local deprivation on the aspirations, but neighbourhood deprivation also affects school attainment which in turn has a powerful effect on the educational aspirations of boys and girls. (Furlong et al, 1996, p 561)

Strangleman (2001) suggests four interrelated ways in which neighbourhood influences impact on and shape economic behaviour and occupational aspirations. First, social networks based around the workplace and occupational identity have traditionally played an important role in fostering and reproducing social ties through the transmission of 'embedded knowledge' about work. These ties link work and extra-work spheres and condition work expectations between successive generations. Second is the local character of networks and the ways in which these are affected by industrial and economic changes. As capital becomes increasingly mobile, labour markets for the unskilled become more localised, placing more reliance on local networks. Third, Strangleman points to the manner in which networks are 'powerfully shaped' by class background and experience. In the context of depressed local labour market opportunities, reliance on a 'legacy of collective knowledge' increases. These forms of knowledge provide an "informed and sophisticated understanding of the local labour market" (Strangleman, 2001, p 261). Finally, networks are understood in relation to family, kin and generation with the importance of these networks enhanced due to the necessity of supporting and maximising a collective household income. Strangleman's article discusses the historical development of networks in the redundant coalfields of the North East where mining provided the main source of employment and identity, and is sensitive to the uniqueness of place and industrial history. The article also highlights the importance of understanding these networks in "combination situated within embedded historical events" in order to emphasise:

> A situation where working-class networks based around place and community still pertains and yet constrains actors and the range of choices open to them. But actors in such networks were at one and the same time still benefiting from the positive aspects of close-knit communities. (Strangleman, 2001, p 261)

As discussed in Chapter Three, labour market behaviour was the defining feature of efforts to identify a distinct underclass, and has dominated later debates surrounding the causes and responses to social exclusion. Using data sets from the Labour Force Survey from 1979 to 1986, Buck (1992) defined an underclass as those families and households that lack a stable relationship to legitimate employment. He distinguished between households that display a stable *lack* of employment and those that have an unstable relationship *to* employment. While the potential underclass grew from 5% to 10% of the working-age population between 1979 and 1986, the long-term unemployed of the 1980s, he argues, were not *stable* members of the underclass but *unstable* members of the working class. Their experience of unemployment was not as a normal condition, but as an interruption to stable work patterns (Buck, 1992, pp 11-19). Of greater relevance for the present discussion are the experiences of a largely unqualified cohort who entered the world of work between the early 1980s and mid-1990s and was socialised into the lower echelons of an emerging 'post-industrial' labour market. The reality of working lives in this section of the labour market has meant that bouts of unemployment are experienced not as an interruption to work, but as a normal feature of insecure and precarious employment. Evidence suggests that repeated spells of unemployment increased between 1991 and 1997, as half of all men starting a spell of unemployment in 1997 had left a previous spell within the previous six months (Dickens et al, 2000, p 98). As a Job Club attendee remarked, echoing the experiences of many others:

> "It's the way it goes these days, work for a few months, get laid off when the job's finished, sign on, get another job, sign off, it just goes on and on like that (...) It's difficult, really difficult, a lot of it's temporary contracts. I was working for Superdrug and they said they'll give me a three-month contract which they'd renew basically every three months so you haven't got any security."

Charlesworth observes that while working-class cultures have been over-determined by economic survival and dispossession throughout the industrial era, "new strains (are emerging) within working class culture that are the result of a rapid decay, within one or two generations, of an older culture" (Charlesworth, 2000, p 11). As the quotations at the beginning of this chapter suggest, social and industrial changes are experienced in a historically specific context and set of institutions: education, work, family and leisure that differ qualitatively from those of earlier generations. The 'life-stage principle' means that the impact of those changes will fall heaviest on those who are in a weak and dependent situation during the process of social change (Dewilde, 2003). The material presented in this and following chapters addresses how residents of the St. Helier estate in south London have experienced the disruption, within their lifetimes, to the class- and gender-specific routes that had provided the transition to adulthood. This requires an examination of the world as it was for the respondents and upon which their own future lives were premised, before structural changes in the economy and in working practices undermined for many the likelihood of achieving their early expectations.

Generations and labour market change

Charlesworth argues that the fragmentation of working class-cultures has been accompanied with a generational shift, as the earlier reference points in which lives were grounded and class solidarities sustained are replaced with insecurity, anomie and individualism (Charlesworth, 2000, p 2). Most of the respondents, who described their past and present experiences, stand on the cusp of these changes that were to impact profoundly upon working-class communities. Many were old enough to recall the diverging fortunes of their families and neighbours who experienced redundancies and large-scale unemployment through the substantial de-industrialisation of Merton in the 1980s and the decline of the area's older industries (Chapter Four). Others remember the prosperity in their families brought on by the 'building boom' of the 1980s, which would be reversed during the slump of the early 1990s. Those raised on and around the less desirable post-war estates would witness the process of residualisation as the stable sections of the population would leave to be replaced by single parents, the economically inactive and immigrants. Most report being vaguely aware that these changes occurring in their environment were partial aspects of a wider process of economic and social change. They were perceived, however, until directly impinging on their families and friends, as a distant threat, as Robert, now aged 32, remembers:

> "I remember watching the miners' strike on telly. I was still at school then, but I used to listen to my dad. He said you'd better sit up and take notice because it's them poor buggers today but it'll be us one day (...) then he said the same when it was all going off at Wapping with Murdoch and everyone used to go 'Shut up dad, will you?' (...) Then one day he come home and said that they were laying him off and that really brought home what all this was about."

The narratives recall childhoods largely spent growing up on local housing estates in the 1970s and 1980s. Their aspirations reflected those of their parents who had grown up in an era of full employment, expanding opportunities and a general increase in the standard of living for the working classes. Furlong et al (1996, p 562) note that:

> On a normative level ... as part of the process of socialisation, children come to share in the assumptive worlds of their parents, friends and neighbours and adopt similar outlooks on the world around them. Central to these normative orientations is a notion of the future socio-economic status: children learn about the occupational world in the home and the school and develop ideas about what to expect themselves."

Aspirations are also susceptible to changes in opportunity structures that will either provide the routes by which they are achieved, or block those routes. Between the mid-1980s and mid-1990s when most of the sample left full-time education, they were facing a set of labour market opportunities vastly different from that faced by their parents and elder siblings. School leavers entering the labour market during this period found that the jobs that they had grown up expecting were becoming increasingly scarce and replaced by entry-level work in the service sector, employment training schemes, unemployment and/or underemployment. In 1981, 89% of Sutton's economically active 16- to 20-year-olds were in full-time employment, 2.5% were employed part time and 9% were unemployed. By 1991, 61% were employed full time, 15% were working part time and 14% were unemployed (LBS, 1981, 1993).

While the restructuring of opportunity factors influences the degree to which cultural aspirations and lifestyles can be reached, the focal concerns often change slower (Gans, 1962, pp 248-50). Most of the sample from the estate left school at the earliest opportunity with either minimal or no qualifications, with the role of family contacts and local networks often providing alternative and more readily available routes into entry-level jobs. Having been promised a job for a removal company through a friend of his father's, Steve left school unqualified, confident that his future employment prospects were assured and looking forward to becoming an independent wage earner. The realities of manual labour quickly lost their appeal:

> "I was supposed to be getting a job through a mate of my dad's doing removals so I turned up on the first morning and the boss said he'd give me a week's trial (...) by the end of the first week I was too knackered to go back. I was carting furniture up and down stairs all day, the blokes just took the piss out of me all day and kept all the tips themselves and I think I got about 60 quid at the end of the week. I thought 'sod that' and never went back."

These early experiences were repeated until they modified job-seeking strategies and attitudes to employment. The direction those strategies would take, as later chapters discuss, would be influenced through the degree of access to locally based social ties, and an increasing awareness of their objective labour market location. A frequent theme was the different adjustment processes made between their aspirations and the potential of reaching them through their limited formal options. This often occurred at a crucial stage in the respondent's lifecycles at the point where cultural expectations, and the status passages followed by previous generations, had anticipated the passage to adulthood to occur. For many of the cohort that formed the basis of the interviews collected on and around the estate, this coincided with the closing off of employment opportunities during the deep recession of the early 1990s. As the number of low-wage and precarious jobs has increased following the recovery of the mid-to-late 1990s, working patterns have become steadily fragmented and many have never fully recovered. One Job Club respondent, whose early ambitions of running his own bakery were doomed by the closure of many small retail outlets in the area following the increasing monopoly of 'superstores', recalled:

> "I left school at 16 because I had a job lined up in a bakery (…) the job had been promised to me for years so I knew where I was going, work in a bakery, learn the ropes, get a loan and start up on my own. I soon found out there was no money in bread, all the little bakeries are closing down, being taken over by supermarkets else you've got chains buying up the family-run places and turning them into cafes (…) The business went under and all I knew was the bakery trade and the only jobs going were in supermarkets. [In] little places you get to learn everything: baking, ordering, doing the tills, icing, the lot. In a supermarket you just do the one job, baking the bread or serving and I didn't like the look of it."

Preferring the independence of self-employment to the close supervision and deskilled opportunities available in a supermarket, he built up a window-cleaning round with the aim of saving enough money to run his own bakery.

> "I built up my own round then bought another round off of somebody who'd fallen off a ladder. Then the same thing happened to me and I did my back in and had to give it up (…) after the accident they put me on the sick for six months then reviewed it and said I was fit to work. They put me on Job Seeker's Allowance and I was unemployed for six months so my advisor at the Job Centre advised me to come on this because I'd already turned down three jobs (…) She asked me what I do and I told her I'm a baker by trade so she came up with three jobs in catering. I said I'm a baker not a washer-upper so she sent me on this instead."

Practically all of those interviewed had considerable experience of working in entry-level jobs in the formal economy after leaving school. However, few of these early jobs resulted in stable, reasonably paid work, the typical trajectory being into work patterns increasingly characterised by short-term, low-paid jobs. Sheltered from the realities of their labour market location through the support of family and local networks that provided alternative sources of employment in the unregulated economy, their early work histories reveal a succession of short-term employment. Another Job Club respondent recalls:

> "When I left school (everybody) was going on about unemployment but I left school and expected it to be hard but it weren't really. I never took any of my jobs seriously and that was the problem. I just didn't have the attitude really I mean I was just out of school and all I wanted to do was to get out and enjoy myself (...) earning money was just a way of getting those things so I didn't care where it came from at the time."

While their employment prospects were framed by local labour market conditions and restricted by their lack of skills and qualifications, it is the peer group that, writes Gans (1962, p 37), "refracts these outside events and thus shapes his personality and culture". Peer group aspirations based on ties established in the neighbourhood and in school provided the more immediate goals and concerns that shaped early attitudes towards work. Twenty-nine-year-old Darren (see also Chapter Eight) recalled that:

> "We lived for cars and when I was 17 my only ambition was to have an XR3i with the wheels, the stereo the lot (...) I never gave work much thought. I mean I had to work to get money because I wanted a car and what work weren't important, it was just a way to get what I wanted and I got my first one when I was 20."

Working-class youth culture, writes Martin (1981, p 140) "is the expensive and mandatory self indulgence of the Wakes Week spiced with a touch of symbolic revolt against the adult world of work and responsibility" and a socially approved period of enjoyment and liberty before entry into that world. The difference for this generation is that the institutional underpinnings that had supported the transition to adulthood, and the secure jobs that had allowed earlier generations to move out of adolescence often failed to materialise. Chapters Seven and Eight examine the economic imperatives that, in the absence of regular work and the relationships established there, have provided a rationale for maintaining relationships established in adolescent peer groups. Commentators have long challenged the view that a present-time orientation is based in cultural variations in values and norms, regarding them as situational responses to the framework of opportunities that are encountered (Anderson et al, 1994, p 47). For Steve, bouts of relative affluence are sporadic in between searching for further opportunities, modifying his aspirations and income-seeking strategies towards the short term. This leaves little scope for the formulation of any attachment to the future, and has protracted the lifestyle of his adolescence into his thirties. Discussing his decision years earlier to drop out of the City and Guilds carpentry course he had attended at night school he laments:

> "I'd rather be chippying than what I'm doing now, which is not much really, just getting by. I mean I can make not bad money sometimes but I never know what's around the corner with this. I'd like it if it was regular then you know where you're going but like this, as soon as I get it [money] it's gone."

While poverty and disadvantage is often explained by a failure to defer gratification, debt financing has become a main engine of economic growth. Access to the loans and credit facilities required to obtain the symbols of social inclusion are frequently denied to those who are unable to demonstrate evidence of employment stability. One 25-year-old interviewed at the Job Club had dropped out of university in favour of six months in Thailand. Returning broke and unable to compete in the graduate job market he ended up in a series of temporary administrative posts, mostly in the public sector. Despite enjoying relatively constant and well-paid employment, the adverse aspects of this form of work are evident in the difficulty in forging any workplace relationships and in securing the finance required to make major purchases. Transience is the definitive feature of his working life and, for the irregular and low-paid workforce, constitutes an important facet of social exclusion:

> "It was OK in that the work was quite regular and the money wasn't bad but I didn't enjoy temping ... it's like you never know where you'll be from one week to the

next. You meet a lot of people but never get to know any of them, which is alright if you don't like the office or the people but when you're sent somewhere and the job's good, the people are nice and you wish you had a job like that too."

Q: "Because of the stability?"

"I don't know that a permanent job is more stable. They're getting rid of permanent jobs and filling them up with temps. I mean my income was pretty stable and the work was regular enough, because if you've got A levels, computer literate and the rest of it, you're never going to be out of work for long if you're prepared to temp. But how could I get finance as a temp? I wanted a car and went for a loan but I was turned down and I thought that'd never have happened if I'd had a proper job. So maybe it is stability in a way."

Work and exploitation in the service economy

By the time the respondents reached their mid–twenties, and finding it increasingly difficult to compete with school leavers for entry into the youth job market, many became steadily disillusioned with the jobs that they were able to compete for. As the income requirements of low-skilled workers change with the onset of family and other responsibilities, they are at a distinct disadvantage compared to younger workers and immigrants who often compete for the same jobs. Both qualifications and experience can act unfavourably at this end of the labour market. The old complaint about 'too much or too little experience' was repeated several times, and rings particularly true when competing for jobs whose workers are interchangeable with those with little experience and lower income requirements. As one 38-year-old unemployed gardener explained:

"I went for a job at the council last week. I'm a grade five groundsman and they told me you're too old. What they mean is that they don't want to pay me the money so what they do is give it to a 16-year-old train him up to grade five and still give him low money. They asked how much are you willing to work for and I said I'll do it for two fifty. I had four of them behind a desk asking me questions and

I answered every single one of them and I think that annoyed them. They're looking for somebody where they can go, 'We'll pay you a hundred and twenty a week' and they'll go, 'Oh yeah' because they're a kid living at home but I've got to be on two fifty a week because I've got bills and rent to pay."

Job tenure bears little relation to productivity, as upward career mobility at the bottom end of the service sector often entails a redefining of the job title and an increase in responsibilities with only a minimum rise in income. For the following 25-year-old lone parent, career advancement in the bar/catering sector proved to be a hollow promise:

"I worked in two pubs both for two-and-a-half years. The first one was one of my first jobs and the money was shit but it was part of the social life, which I didn't get from having kids so young. I worked there for two-and-a-half years then I moved down the road because where I was working in Young's they don't promote from within, you have to apply like everyone else. So all the time I was just bar staff my wages never went up. When I went up the road I was promoted to assistant manager, but saying that I was doing like 48 hours a week and still only bringing home a hundred and thirty quid a week which was terrible."

Flexible employment practices are highly stratified by age and gender with younger, older and female workers mostly experiencing these working patterns. Despite equal opportunities legislation, companies will avoid these rules so long as a 'flexible' pool of labour is a byword for cheap and submissive workers. As Caroline, who has several years' experience of supermarket work, explained:

"Where I worked I had the same job as three other men and one was on about eighteen thousand and one was on about sixteen and I was on eight. That's disgusting and I could have had them for that but they tried to talk their way round it saying it was their experience (...) I was offered a job up the Co-op and it was three seventy-five an hour. I said that's disgusting and she said I can offer you four twenty-five and I said that's still disgusting. It's not enough to live on and blokes would get more than that, it's discrimination."

Career advancement into a supervisory role can place the worker in an isolated position among workmates. Alienated from management who commands the workforce via supervisory staff, the supervisor can find themselves an outsider to the shop-floor staff that they had once worked alongside. For Caroline, the prospect of a higher-status job and imminent salary increase drove her harder to prove that she was capable of handling more responsibility. In the absence of any real opportunity for advancement a growing sense of disillusion and exploitation coloured her promotion, heightened by her growing estrangement from her former workmates, and she eventually quit her job:

> "When he told me they were making me up to managing my own department it really went to my head (...) then I ended up running everything, doing everything and starting at five in the morning, staying there till I was dropping dead. They just dump a whole lot more responsibility on you but your pay doesn't change (...) plus you have to give orders to the people you were working with before and that causes bad feeling and the real managers are never made up, they come from outside. You know, kids out of college, management trainees and they're the ones that are giving the orders to us to pass down so you're caught in the middle getting grief from above and below."

Scott (1985, pp 34–5) notes that the existing forms of labour control shape the nature of workplace resistance among subordinate groups. The absence of well-developed unions in the lower end of the service sector means that workers have no recourse to collective representation. Antipathy is often channelled, as with Caroline, towards their immediate superiors, fragmenting the workforce further. Borgois has pointed out that while academic research has comprehensively documented the erosion of income levels, union representation and the reduction in worker benefits that have accompanied the restructuring of economies around service employment, few have noted the "cultural dislocations of the new service economy" at a micro-level (Borgois, 1996, p 114). A fundamental difference in the nature of work in the service sector is that the worker's suitability no longer depends solely on competence but also relies on the acquisition of 'soft skills': the ability to project an element of self-identity and self-expression into the work. Finding the right candidate involves a more intensive selection process, psychological testing and evaluation of dress, modes of speech and attitude (MacDonald and Sirriani, 1996).

As the government attempts to reintegrate the unemployed into the expanding new opportunities, those charged with the task recognise that it will involve more than equipping workers with new skills. The skills that they lack are often not those acquired through education and training, but those related to the forms of conduct and disposition required in low-level service sector employment. Re-socialising them into the modes of behaviour required by many of the jobs on offer is harder to achieve among those for whom such behaviour is anathema. The manager of Job Club acknowledged this during a discussion of the sectoral pattern of job expansion in the area:

> ★ "There's around two thousand unemployed in the borough now and around two hundred of them are long-term unemployable. It doesn't matter how well the economy's doing you've always had those who either don't want to or can't work. The difference is that under the Tories they'd have signed them off as sick and they didn't have to bother with training. Now we get them coming through these schemes and it makes our job a lot harder. I mean can you see some of these blokes being told what to do by a 22-year-old girl? Because that's the type of job they're likely to be heading for (…) it's not just a matter of basic skills, which a lot of them haven't got, those things can always be taught. It's attitude as well, how you come across to people and that can't be taught so easily. With a lot of the jobs going you don't need many qualifications but they're looking for attitude a lot more now and whether your face fits."

Men approaching these jobs with a history of manual work in highly gender-stratified jobs may not bring the modes of behaviour and attitudes required. Paul had worked practically constantly since leaving school nine years earlier, with a work history comprising of grave digging, roofing and labouring. After being laid off from his previous job, he gained employment in a local supermarket while waiting for his next roofing job to start. He was unused to the working practices there and found it difficult to adjust to the intensive supervision favoured by the management, and seemingly accepted by the passive and largely female and student workforce.

"I got a job in a supermarket, which only lasted a couple of months. The people were alright but they let the bosses treat them terribly and they'd slag them off in the changing rooms but they'd never front them out to their face. The managers were all right wankers. It was worse than school, they were on our backs the whole time and you never got a 'well done' or nothing. It's not just that the money's crap but in those jobs people treat you like shit."

Jahoda has pointed to the personal impacts of working in such jobs, arguing that it is the nature of the work performed that reduces the attributes of the worker rather than the unskilled being unable to perform more challenging jobs (Jahoda, 1982, p 42). Liebow observed among his fieldwork that a succession of low-status jobs has a psychological cost to the worker, both in terms of self-image and in assessing present and future prospects:

Each man comes to the job with a long history characterised by his not being able to support himself and his family. Each man carries this knowledge, born of his experience with him. He comes to the job flat and stale, wearied by the sameness of it all, convinced of his own incompetence, terrified of responsibility of being tested still again and found wanting. (Liebow, 1967, p 42)

For these workers the opportunity to exercise any autonomy or control over the work process, to demonstrate any initiative or aptitude or to query any decisions made is severely restricted in this tightly controlled 'numerically flexible' end of the labour market. The skills that they bring to an employer are in abundant supply, and the workers are always made aware that they are instantly dispensable. Thirty-three-year-old unemployed respondent Tony had previously worked as a delivery driver for a local employment agency. He explained the manner in which the expansion of temporary employment is reshaping forms of worker compliance in the labour market, and the allocation of assignments is determined largely by attitude (Peck and Theodore, 1998):

"I didn't like the agency because they'll lie to you and say anything if they need you for a job (...) I wouldn't work with tachos [tachographs] because they can see exactly what you've been doing all day and it's like having your boss sitting next to you all day, so I said no tachos and the work stopped coming in. As long as you turn up to every job they send you to, never complain and do your job then the work will keep coming in. Turn down a few jobs or the slightest bit of lip to the client even if it is justified then that's it, the work will stop."

Despite the outwardly random and varied nature of the individual work histories, they display a pattern situated in the processes of structural changes in which their lives are located, and which were expressed through this network of broadly shared experiences. The end result for most was a descent into the margins of the low-wage, structurally precarious end of the job market. Insecurity and a common perception of exploitation in low-status jobs that are accorded little prestige by the workers themselves, or by social attitudes towards the jobs, frame their perceptions of work. As Sennet and Cobb (1972, p 264) noted, inequality and exclusion involves more than material inequality but concerns the relationship between individuals and between other social groups and the process of evaluation, through which individuals are measured according to their economic utility and labour market location. Thirty-six-year-old Stuart, who left school to enter a series of warehouse, trade counter and clerical work, found his working pattern following a downward spiral into more menial and sporadic jobs.

"All the time the jobs were getting worse because it was getting harder to get stuff out of the Job Centres and locals. When you're a kid, because you don't give a shit you'll just go for anything. Like you're at home so you're still going to get fed, have your washing done and the rest of it and you know that if you're really desperate you can always ponce a fiver off your mum so it gives you a whole different outlook about work."

This coincided with his girlfriend becoming pregnant in 1991 and a move out of the parental home. For the first time, work became a necessity, not something to be tolerated as a means of providing access to leisure pursuits. This resulted in a reappraisal of his labour market location in which his weak and perilous position became apparent. His growing awareness of this had a detrimental and cumulative impact as the interviews that he had once handled with ease became an ordeal, now that the pressure was on to become a breadwinner to a partner and child:

> "This was the first time I'd taken work seriously. I'd been doing agency work – driving, warehouse, labouring and it was too on and off. I needed something steady but when I went for anything there'd be blokes of 45 with 20 years' experience, people with A Levels and that. If I even got to an interview I'd get nervous (...) When I was a kid I'd just walk in and bullshit my way through the whole thing. Even the agencies didn't want to know anymore, not the decent ones anyway, and I kept trying until after about six months I ended up doing catering for an agency."

In an area of low unemployment and high job growth the complaint is not about the lack of work, but the lack of legitimate opportunities to attain a decent living from the jobs on offer. As discussed, the disincentive effects of low-wage work are especially acute in London where the cost of living is around 11–12% higher than for the rest of the UK, combined with the potential loss of Housing Benefit given the region's high housing costs (Buck et al, 2002, pp 153, 239). Many of the vacant jobs are commonly viewed as not designed to pay a 'family wage' and no longer a reasonable option at the major transitions that mark the passage to adulthood, as Stuart commented:

> "When I was at home I'd take anything because even if the money was crap I'd give my mum a bit and I'd still have 80 quid or so and this was pocket money: I had nothing to pay for. When you leave home and have kids it's a whole different ball game and you can't take those jobs anymore because they're designed for kids or women."

The trade-offs between the relative advantages of work and unemployment is a complex one that cannot be fully captured with a focus on economic incentives. Howe (1990, p 85) notes that "unemployment is a great financial, social and psychological burden but so too is work when it is low paid and has to be endured for long hours and in bad conditions". Indeed, the burden of unemployment may not be so heavy when compared to badly paid, and mentally stupefying work. Following the birth of his child, this respondent found it both economically rational and psychologically beneficial to give up work rather than pay the bulk of his wages on rent:

"Rent was 80 quid a week and we got a bit off but she couldn't work and I couldn't make enough to cover everything any more. The baby was ill and screamed all night, it really did my head in and the pressure was on to earn some money (...) I gave up the job because I couldn't look for a better one when I was at work and I thought I'm not paying out over half my wages for the place we were living in. So I packed up work till they got us a council place and it was hard on the dole but no harder than working. We weren't worse off and actually we were better off because I weren't paying out half my wages to live in a slum."

Employment insecurity and active labour market policies

A prominent feature of working lives in the low-wage, insecure end of contemporary labour markets is frequent and repeated contact with state agencies. As discussed in Chapter Three, 'Third Way' critiques of post-war social policy have argued that the emphasis on social rights was not accompanied by a corresponding stress on obligations. The government's approach borrows heavily from the US 'workfare' experience, not least in the consensus that welfare dependency is the primary cause of worklessness and the need for a compulsive strategy to enforce work habits (Daguerre, 2004). This 'work first' emphasis is tempered by a 'human capital' approach that extends the training and employment programmes initiated under the Manpower Services Commission (MSC) in the late 1970s and 1980s. The emphasis on training was continued under the Conservatives with the establishment of training and education councils (TECs) from 1990, and the introduction of compulsory youth training schemes (YTSs) for unemployed 16- to 18-year-olds. The replacement of Unemployment Benefit with Job Seekers' Allowance (JSA) in 1996 heralded the shift towards workfare and "was an important symbolic shift emphasising the clear expectation that claimants were to be supported only on the condition that they were looking for paid work" (Alcock, 2003, p 63). By reducing eligibility from twelve to six months and requiring claimants to prove they are 'actively seeking work' through signing agreements and attending periodic interviews, the JSA regime prepared the ground for the New Deal programmes through acting as a 'feeder programme' for the New Deal (Theodore and Peck, 1999).

What distinguishes the New Deal from supply-side measures

introduced under the Conservatives, argues Tonge (1999), is not the job creation measures but the extent of coercion that it employs. The original focus for the New Deal programme was 18- to 24-year-olds unemployed for six months or more. During the four-month 'gateway stage' participants are offered intensive job-search facilities, careers guidance and access to a personal adviser. Following this, participants are offered a subsidised job option, a placement with a voluntary agency, a place on an approved training course or on an environmental task force. By 1999 there were New Deal schemes for the long-term unemployed and for the over-fifties, for disabled people, lone parents and for partners of unemployed people. Attendance is compulsory for the 18-24 age groups, the long-term unemployed and the over-fifties. Under JSA and New Deal regulations an unemployed person will lose benefits if they are unavailable for work, fail to sign on or miss an interview with their adviser. If an individual leaves, is dismissed or refuses a job without good cause, they can lose benefits for up to 26 weeks, with non-attendance on employment training schemes also attracting benefit sanctions. Estimates from the New Deal for Young People (NDYP) suggest that 9% of those required to attend may incur a reduction in benefits during the gateway stage (Finn, 2003, p 73).

The process of downward mobility and chronic instability appears as a constant theme throughout the respondents' work histories. Increasing state surveillance to take low-wage jobs, and remain in them at the threat of forfeiting access to the benefit system intensifies the precariousness of their lives. Working lives are interspersed with frequent recourse to the Benefits Agency and Employment Service, where they are subject to the endless, complex form filling and suspicion that the respondents perceive as a common experience at the hands of front-line staff.[2] A key innovation of the New Deal is that it is delivered through local partnerships comprising TECs, local government, employers, community organisations and trades unions within a framework set by central government. It was anticipated that decentralisation would allow the New Deal programmes to adapt to local labour market conditions and encourage innovation and experimentation (Theodore and Peck, 1999). The work of the jobcentre and social security system is directed by regulations, which provide little scope for flexibility or an individual focus (Lian, 1999). The interviews with the participants and staff at Job Club frequently highlighted the tension between centralised bureaucratic regulations and individual circumstances. Despite the rhetoric of 'joined-up thinking', a local benefits officer Diane, who herself re-entered employment after several years as a lone parent observed:

"There are big flaws in the system and it's so frustrating. I had a woman in today and she'd been on Family Credit and for whatever reason, she'd given up work and gone back on Income Support. Because Family Credit's paid in advance and Income Support's paid in arrears she's left a week with no money and she was fuming. They say 'there's nothing we can do about it' and 'the law states' and the law might say one thing but when you're skint and you've got two kids you don't care what the law says, you care about where your kids' next meal is coming from."

Welfare reforms are presented as a 'partnership' between the participant and government and make the recipient an active participant in the training/job-seeking process. As a Child Poverty Action Group publication (CPAG, 1998, p 6) points out, the partnership is highly unbalanced:

It is clearly a contract between two unequal partners. If government fails to meet the promise of quality services and paid work, it is claimants who will suffer. If claimants renege on their side of the bargain, it is they who stand to lose out through the curtailment of benefit. This underlines the importance of provision being based on rights – the only hope of redress open to claimants.

Information relating to welfare regulations is complex and difficult to access, which results in a lack of power and self-confidence when dealing with welfare bureaucrats. Forty-year-old Liz spent months attempting to redress bureaucratic incompetence after her Housing Benefit was wrongly calculated once she started a part-time job:

"If you're trying to find anything out about the benefit system, trying to weave your way through it's so complicated and it's all vague, it's all about interpretation. I went to the library, looked through books, I went to Citizen's Advice, I went to Gingerbread who were very good, they obviously knew the law inside out (...) but it's time and energy sitting in the Citizen's Advice for three hours fighting something. They made the mistake and the temptation was to think, 'I'm not doing this, I'm quitting my job. You've messed me about and I'm 16 pounds a week better off, for going out to work for 16 hours and leaving my kids'."

Administrative capacity is a crucial - and often neglected – concern, as supply-side programmes increasingly require frontline staff to make discretionary judgements whether obligations have been met, and whether or not to impose sanctions (Handler, 2003). The far-reaching consequences of bureaucratic decisions for individual lives that are made by staff that the recipients have little confidence in, serve to erode any sense of autonomy and control that they retain over their lives. A key role of the personal adviser is to persuade the unemployed to re-evaluate their employment options. The priority given to placing clients in unsubsidised jobs driven by performance targets, means they are increasingly 'persuaded' to take any available job regardless of its suitability or channelled into compulsory job-related training. This further undermines the notion of a 'partnership' and generates adversarial relationships between welfare bureaucrats and their clients. The information technology tutor at Job Club remarked:

> ★ "People are really suspicious and they think they're being conned even when they're not ... the attitudes of the ES [Employment Service] front-desk workers aren't conducive to finding employment. It's like 'you will find work', and then they'll offer you the most impractical jobs – 'I can't get there', 'you will go', and the clients think 'fuck you' and it sets them up. The whole attitude is too confrontational and it doesn't build confidence, because of the way they see each other. You can't treat people like school kids and expect to get results."

Apart from the education option the opportunity for skills development is limited, and critics have noted that Britain's expenditure on labour market training is comparatively low (Dickens and Gregg, 2000; Daguerre, 2003). Subsequently, a significant degree of movement between training schemes and unemployment has been observed (Craine, 1997). Participants were rarely critical of Job Club or its staff but rather of the context that it operated within, which frustrates its stated aims of assisting social inclusion through labour market integration. Experience of a cycle of training schemes that failed to result in steady employment and a perception of being corralled onto them in order to massage unemployment statistics, was a viewpoint shared by many of the sample. One attendee at Job Club recalled the endless computer-based training courses he had been sent on over the past few years. None of these courses had resulted in a job or in his view, significantly increased his employability:

"The last few years I've been on and off of different courses
(...) I did the Training for Work, which is computers and
job skills and the Link Scheme. That was good but they
haven't helped me to get a job. They bring new packages
out then they have to set up new schemes to teach them. It
could go on forever, but in the end I'm long-term
unemployed and that's what an employer's looking at, not
whether I can use this or that computer package."

When applied to enforcing the obligation to work or to attend training
on those receiving state benefits the boundaries of obligation and
compulsion remain a sensitive one. It is here where the clients' lack of
power becomes apparent and the façade of working in partnership is
revealed. In his critique of Oscar Lewis, Valentine (1968, pp 118-20)
retorts that the hostility to institutions and centres of power that Lewis
cites as an indicative value trait of the 'culture of poverty' may be
consistent with objective situational factors. One Job Club attendee
commented:

"I think a lot of us here are a bit cynical of these schemes.
It's all too political and you feel like you're being pushed
onto them and from there into low-paid jobs that nobody
else wants just to keep the figures down. So it looks like
they're getting people back to work but they're not they're
forcing them, and that's the big difference."

When I interviewed 27-year-old Mark, he was working as a builder
as well as signing on and collecting the cheques for a friend who was
travelling abroad and did not want to interrupt his claim (Chapter
Seven). After leaving school, he had intended on following his father
in the building trade and becoming a plasterer. The decline of
apprenticeships in construction, and the increased emphasis on paper
qualifications meant that he needed to attend a formal course as a
means of entry into the trade:

"I went in the Job Centre and asked them to put me on a
plastering course. They said, 'There's no plastering courses'.
I said, 'I want to do a plastering course, I've had a go at it
and I like it'. They said, 'We can put you on a bricklaying
course'. I said, 'I don't want a bricklaying course, I want to
do plastering'. 'No you can't do it. There is a plastering

course but you've got to pay for it.' I said to her, 'What with my giro?'."

His contempt for the system is founded not in a distinctive set of values, but in his experiences dealing with an irrational bureaucratic system that purports to assist its clients but frequently frustrates their ambitions and erodes their self-confidence. His failure to gain formal qualifications and lack of confidence in formal routes altered his approach to work. His most feasible and readily available source of work was through the use of local contacts, where he has been able to find employment working largely undeclared as a labourer/plasterer.

"I couldn't be dealing with all their crap so anyway I could always find work through my dad's mates and people I knew. It pisses me off though because they don't pay me as much as blokes that are on the books but we're doing the same work and I'm always last in and first out."

The common complaint is that those formulating and administering policy appear oblivious to the situational constraints faced by the unemployed. This is illustrated through the *New Deal delivery plan*, which recognises part of its brief as being to "convince people that a 10 minute bus ride to connect with the Northern Line or a 20 minute bus ride to Wimbledon is not an insurmountable obstacle to job-hunting". In demarcating a 'local' labour market, most government agencies take it to mean a travel-to-work area (TTWA). Travel-to-work areas conceal spatial variations in the geography of unemployment through averaging unemployment rates for artificially large areas. As a result, they may overestimate the distances that the unemployed are able to travel to work and overlook occupational variations in job mobility (Turok and Webster, 1998). For the low-paid, unskilled, part-time workers and women with family commitments, labour market opportunities are often tied closely to the expansion or decline of opportunities within their immediate locality. In a vast area like the St. Helier estate, labour market opportunities vary according to location on the estate and are reflected in higher unemployment and economic inactivity rates on the Carshalton side. The insufficiency and expense of transport links into London has been a constant complaint since the 1930s (see Chapter Four). Intrinsic features of an area such as access to jobs, travel costs, housing tenure and the quality of local schools and services, combine with the acquired characteristics of who moves in and out of areas. As social groups suffering from greater disadvantage and less choice are housed in those areas, problems of deprivation accumulate (Power, 1999, p 37). As a community worker remarked:

> "Isolation and access to services is a problem the further you move towards Carshalton whereas on the Morden side you can be in central London in less than an hour. That goes a long way in explaining access to jobs because if you're bussing it to a minimum wage job you're pretty much tied to Sutton, Morden or Carshalton."

In the enthusiasm to reintegrate the unemployed back into work, these realities are often overlooked, and the target-driven strategy comes into frequent conflict with a 'client-centred' approach. Forty-five-year-old Roy had been without a full-time job for seven years, dividing his time between working part time and attending to his elderly parents with whom he lived. Unskilled and with minimal income capacity, he was sent for jobs that were both economically irrational and incompatible with his daily demands:

> "They haven't got a clue. They sent me for a job in a care home in Banstead. To get to Banstead and back takes about two hours a day for three hours work so after the fares there's no point. They made me go for it anyway so when I got there I told the manager interviewing me and he said it was stupid and he just phoned them and said I wasn't what he was looking for and he didn't even interview me."

Although the long-term benefits of education and training are widely acknowledged, it is competing and more immediate concerns that frequently compromise long-term ambitions. These daily concerns have serious implications given the current policy emphasis on increasing employability. Such a narrow focus overlooks research indicating that those who have a reasonable foundation of income are both more likely, and more able, to take up paid work (Oppenheim, 1999). A lack of resources impairs the ability to circulate in society and stay connected to potential job openings, and to possess the items necessary for entry into work. One 47-year-old respondent attending a local employment scheme pointed to his shabby clothing and commented:

"The Employment Service only look at unemployment in isolation (…) who's going to give me a job looking like this? But the Employment Service isn't going to give me a suit for interviews are they? To be eligible for work is expensive. You need a decent suit, clean shoes, a car that'll get you there on time. I get in my V-reg car in the morning and it won't start again and I think what hope is there of getting a job?"

Some are able to construct lines of action allowing them to bypass and negotiate their way through these institutional structures and retain a degree of command over their lives. For others, mistrust and anxiety pervade their encounters with state agencies, founded in their apparent powerlessness to resist their dictates. This point was made during the course of an interview conducted at Job Club:

"The Employment Service isn't reasonable, they put you on these schemes and they remind me of a rabbit run because once you're on them you can't get off (…), those administering it aren't up to much. You know what they say about paying peanuts and getting monkeys? They're generally mediocre bureaucrats really … (they) lack sensitivity and common sense – but it's frightening because their little power can be used to make judgements about you like making you go through the ritual of job applications and taking in the evidence. Most jobs don't even bother replying so you've got nothing apart from the odd rejection letter, but the onus is always on you and it's always assumed that you're lying. They've got an axe over us and you have to tow the line and take anything they offer no matter how banal and meaningless and easy to do, because let's say you've got £600 pounds in savings and they stop your benefit. Within three months you'll be destitute."

When accompanied by a rigid adherence to regulations, too strong an emphasis on compulsion and draconian penalties for non-compliance, the results may be counterproductive to the principle of 'empowerment' that current reforms are designed to encourage. The lives of the unemployed are sandwiched between low-paid and irregular employment on the one hand, and institutions that are regarded as coercive adversaries on the other. Cynicism based in first-hand knowledge of what the labour market has to offer and their treatment by bureaucratic staff remain major obstacles to the government's New Deal scheme and increased emphasis on training for work. Ultimately, scepticism and suspicion breed mutual mistrust and make a necessity of malfeasance. As Neil remarked when discussing the introduction of the New Deal programme:

> "I'll give this New Deal a go when they call me for it, which they haven't done yet (...) but I'm not going to look too eager or they'll go, 'Right if you're alright to do a course and run a business you're alright for a job', and kick me off the sick onto the dole. It's getting harder as it is and they don't give you no choice but to play it sneaky."

Coercing them into a low-wage 'flexible' labour market will fail to tackle social exclusion in the absence of jobs that pay a 'decent' wage that allow full independence from the benefit system. Although many participants were adamant that work should provide a 'living wage' free from in-work benefits, expectations of work were relatively modest and tailored to a realistic assessment of local labour demand, and the quality of jobs that their experience and training will provide. While it may be possible to move the unemployed into work, moving them out of low-wage work backed up by benefits may be harder to achieve as research indicates that among families leaving Family Credit only 5% moved off due to salary increases (Ford, 1999). Scott was 31 years old and had not held a stable job for the previous four years. He had recently embarked on a training course to improve his employment prospects and commented:

> "If this training gets me a decent job then it's going to be a good thing but if not it's a waste of time because if the jobs aren't there then what's the point? People are going to expect something out of this and if I'm still signing on and they're still sending me for interviews in Homebase in six months, I'm going to be pretty pissed off. In the end it comes down to attitude because if you want a job you'll get one but a lot of the blokes here won't work for the wages they're paying."

A survey of local employers undertaken for the *New Deal delivery plan* answering what level of gross pay they would intend paying participants under the Welfare-to-Work scheme, revealed that most would offer between £5,000 and £8,000 gross (Employment Service et al, 1997, p 46). Despite increasing differentials between in-work and unemployment benefits, the low returns on entering employment and the fact that wages are so low that they require a wage top-up are unlikely to remove suspicions that tackling social exclusion is a justification for policies that will push people into the low-wage periphery of the labour market. The same survey reports the strong feelings expressed about 'dead-end jobs' and the income requirements sufficient to live on in what is an affluent/high-cost area, but fails to address these more fundamental concerns. The economic incentives, as well as the quality and stability of the jobs that the 'socially excluded' are being persuaded to take up, is the issue that will determine the success of welfare-to work programmes for those participating in them. Otherwise, the cycle of intermittent spells of work and recurrent recourse to public funds is likely to continue. The government's *New Deal Core performance tables* indicate that in the unit of delivery covering the area, 50% of participants moved into unsubsidised jobs and 6% into subsidised jobs between October and December 1999. Of these, 35% retained the job for less than 13 weeks (www.dfee.gov.uk/ndimprove/xls/2000/). Diane's own experience, as a lone parent as well as a benefits officer, had given her a more sober assessment of welfare-to-work than political endorsements:

> "That Alistair Darling, he's on TV going: 'I've spoken to loads of lone parents and they're all enthusiastic'. I think well I don't know who you've been talking to, because the realities of it are that people might go back for a short time, because we get lots of people that have gone on Family Credit and then come off it again. Most of them are going into dead-end jobs and thinking 'Why am I leaving my kids to do this?'. Juggling that and childminders is a lot to take on, and I don't think you can just wave a magic wand and say 'we'll do this and that and your life will be better'."

This chapter has attempted to highlight the impact that the transition to a service-based, 'post-industrial' labour market has had for many of the people who recounted their experiences of work. Social exclusion is a multidimensional and dynamic process that is not captured solely through a focus on the determinants of labour market location and experiences. These have set the coordinates within which lives are experienced and provide the starting point, but in themselves they explain little about the practices and lifestyles that have emerged in response to social and economic marginalisation. These practices allow some to maintain a modicum of control over their lives and a measure of social inclusion as understood in its social context, while also constituting a further and significant dimension of community-based exclusion. Dismissing the emphasis on the resigned and passive psychological traits in culturally transmitted theories of poverty, Glasgow defined the 'survival culture' that emerged among black inner-city youth as a "very active, at times devious, innovative and extremely resistive – response to rejection and destruction" (Glasgow, 1980, p 25). However, neither are they free to implement paths of action free from structural constraints. The key to understanding the relation between individual action and structural location, argued Willis (1977, p 171), is:

> How structures become sources of meaning and determinants of behaviour in the cultural milieu at its own level. Just because there are what we call structural and economic determinants it does not mean that people will unproblematically obey them.

These issues are addressed in the remainder of the book. The next chapter explores the lives and motivations of a sample of lone parents, another group that, as discussed in Chapter Three, have featured prominently in the 'underclass' debate and have recently been the focus of policies to tackle social exclusion.

Notes

[1] Throughout this chapter, ★ indicates that a quotation has been transcribed from notes. In the quotations, (...) indicates that part of the text has been omitted.

[2] Since the fieldwork was undertaken, the Employment Service and Benefits Agency have been merged into a single service, 'Jobcentre Plus', combining job-search facilities and benefit administration.

SIX

Lone-parent households[1]

Lone-parent families have been a recurrent topic of public debate in Britain in the context of significant changes in family structure and the challenges to social policy that such changes pose. Married couples with children fell from 80% of all families in 1990 to 68% in 1997 (Matheson and Babb, 2002, p 43). Over the same period the number of lone parents increased by approximately 50%, from 1.15 million to 1.73 million. Lone-parent households comprise 24% of all families with dependent children in the UK, the highest proportion in the EU and over three times the proportion of 1971 (Moss et al, 1999). Studies have consistently demonstrated that lone-parent status has major economic and social consequences and the growth of such households constitutes an increasingly prominent, and largely gendered, aspect of social exclusion. For a large proportion of lone parents across the EU their status is a strong indicator of poverty and disadvantage. The gap in standard of living is widest in Britain, where lone-parent families' standard of living is 62% of that of all families with children and one third live below the poverty threshold (Chambaz, 2001, p 565). Two thirds of lone parents in Britain rely on Income Support and five in every six claim a means-tested benefit. They are more likely to suffer from long-term illness and are overwhelmingly concentrated in social housing (Ford and Millar, 1998, p 13). Standing (1999) notes the contrast between the employment rates of British lone parents with Sweden where 70% of lone parents are in paid employment, and only 3% have incomes below the national average. Sweden's high rates of lone-parent employment is supported by a comprehensive package that includes a state-funded system of childcare, long parental leave, paid leave for the care of sick children and shorter working days for parents. She adds (1999, p 485) that:

> In the UK poverty is not the prerogative of lone mother families but, rather, related to women's structurally disadvantaged position in the labour market and welfare state. Poverty organises lone mothers into a particular dependent status within the welfare state, in which they

become positioned as either 'welfare scroungers' or 'victims' of their economic status.

Recent decades have also seen a change in the composition of lone parents as steadily increasing proportions of births have occurred outside marriage. By 1997 never-married single mothers formed 42% of all lone parents, the fastest growing and largest sub-group of lone parents (Moss et al, 1999). Against a long-term trend of rising proportions of married women entering the labour market, the proportion of working lone parents fell from 50% in 1980 to around 40% in 1994 (Haskey, 1998, p 30). The rise in births to unmarried young mothers and the potential for long-term benefit dependency among this group has aroused most attention, making them the target of a frequently stigmatising and derogatory discourse in media and political debates. In this chapter, an ethnographic and life history approach is used to highlight how the choices of lone parents are shaped by the interaction between social policies, labour markets and family structures; their assessment of labour market and training opportunities; and the social support networks that they are able to draw upon.

Lone parents and New Labour

Against this background, recent decades have witnessed a political struggle to become 'the party of the family' and reconcile the growth of individual rights with a stronger sense of personal, familial and community responsibility (Rodgers, 1996). Like their Conservative predecessors, these concerns have placed New Labour in something of a dilemma, as Deacon and Mann (1999, p 5) point out:

> There is then a central paradox in New Labour rhetoric on welfare. It expresses the commitment of the new moralists to family values and to personal responsibility, but also echoes the emphasis placed by post-traditionalists upon difference and diversity and the irreversibility of the social changes wrought by modernity.

The family has moved to the centre of the government's agenda, with the establishment of a Family Policy Unit to coordinate family policy across departments. At the core of New Labour's efforts to find a 'Third Way' on the family, is a critique of both Thatcherite neo-liberalism and post-war social democracy. The former, it is argued, denigrated families, communities and the notion of social responsibility through their championing of economic individualism and the free market. The latter, through advocating a non-judgemental view on the family, in combination with the intellectual affinity between feminism and socialism in the 1970s and 1980s, gave a distinctly 'anti-family' stance to the Left (Driver and Martell, 2002). These provided a platform for New Right attacks on non-traditional family forms and a growing critique of the role of state agencies whose increasing intervention in the private sphere of the family, it was argued, had undermined the stability and viability of traditional family structures (Mount, 1982).

More influential in uniting the economic and moral objections to the post-war welfare state, were the causal connections made by influential US academics such as Charles Murray and Lawrence Mead (see Chapter Three). As discussed in Chapter Five, the basic premises informing Mead's 'work-fare' solution have become part of the new orthodoxy concerning the role and function of state welfare. Frank Field, previously Minister for Welfare Reform, conceives that the goal of social policy is the shaping of certain character traits and modes of conduct, of which welfare can play a vital role. In 1997 he outlined the new government's approach to lone parents, with the assertion that:

> The expectation that single mothers should remain on benefit until their children have left secondary school must be transformed. Income Support has to be changed from a safe long-term resting-place into a launch pad back into the mainstream of Great Britain Limited. (Field, 1997, p 31)

Grover and Stewart (2000) note that requiring the unemployed to actively seek work in return for receiving state benefits is not new. What is new is the extension of this requirement to previously economically inactive groups, such as lone parents and the disabled. The 'active society', notes Walters, seeks to dissolve the division between worker/non-worker on which the 'welfare society' was based, and to promote work for all as a remedy to social exclusion (Walters, 1997). This shift in policy objectives was initiated under the Conservative government, and marks a considerable departure from the long-standing predicament in social policy over whether a lone parent's primary duty should be to work or to care for his/her children. Until the mid-1990s, governments had accepted the recommendations of the 1974 Finer Committee's *Report of the Committee on one-parent families*. This argued for parity in the treatment of all parents with dependent children regardless of their economic status (Finer, 1974).

As discussed in Chapter Three, lone parenthood was at the centre of debates concerning the link between benefit dependency and the growth of a lawless 'underclass' throughout the late 1980s and early 1990s. The 1991 Child Support Act clearly revealed the influence of 'underclass' discourses on policy development. Amid Charles Murray's focus on the 'absent male', surveys revealed that only 30% of lone parents received regular maintenance from an absent partner and that over half of lone parents receiving maintenance received less than £25 per week (Ford et al, 1998, p 39). The Act required absent fathers to provide for their offspring and to maintain the parent (to the value of Income Support allowance for an adult). The 1991 Act also sought to increase part-time work among lone parents through reducing eligibility for Family Credit (FC) from 24 hours a week to 16 hours. The first £15 of maintenance paid by the absent parent was disregarded for working lone parents. Those in receipt of Income Support would gain no financial advantage from any maintenance received since it was deducted from benefits. This represented a conscious effort to reduce the two key factors that had aroused the concern of politicians and policy makers: the growing economic inactivity of lone parents and the transmission of values that sanction such behaviour. The Act also requires all lone parents in receipt of means-tested benefits to register with the Child Support Agency (CSA) and to name the absent father. Failure to comply without 'good reason' incurs a 20% cut in benefits. Criticism was levelled at the CSA for making no allowance for any 'non-biological' children that the absent parent may support. Given that around one million children live in stepfamilies, strict application of the rule is likely to result in convoluted sets of financial obligations across households (Millar, 1997, p 158).

The 'welfare-to-work' approach contains several elements that enable lone parents to become economically independent and extends the range of opportunities to do so. The New Deal aims to 'make work pay' through manipulating and integrating the tax and benefit systems, making employment more financially attractive in relation to benefits. One Parent Benefit, introduced after the 1974 Finer Report, was abolished in 1998. Child Benefit for the oldest child has been increased, while Income Support rates for children under 11 have received a 72% incremental increase. National Insurance contributions for the low paid have been reduced and aligned with the starting rate of tax, which was reduced to 10 pence in the 1999 Budget. The introduction of the National Minimum Wage (NMW) has mostly assisted women, due to their concentration in low-paid and/or part-time work. Of the 1.5 million people whose wages increased after the NMW was introduced, two thirds are women, of whom two thirds are employed part time (Rake, 2001). Working Families' Tax Credit (WFTC) was introduced in 1999 and is the centrepiece of the government's aim to increase the economic benefits of work. Around 1.5 million families are entitled to WFTC. The benefit is paid at higher levels than its predecessor, FC, and it is estimated that families will be an average of £24 a week better off compared to FC (CPAG, 1999).

The government has also recognised the scarcity of affordable childcare as a serious impediment to lone parents' employment and introduced Childcare Tax Credit (CCTC). This covers up to £100 of childcare costs for the first child and £150 for subsequent children but is only payable if the parent uses registered childcare. CCTC will be of little assistance to the many parents who rely on informal childcare (Wheelock and Jones, 2002). Furthermore, the parent's contribution of 30% of childcare costs may represent a heavy burden to lone parents given that their average hourly pay is 12% less than for all working women (Gray, 2001). Nationally, take-up of CCTC has been low with just 11% of WFTC recipients receiving the credit. Scott et al (2001) attribute this to the low levels of provision in low-income areas because childcare providers have little financial incentive to set up, as well as the discrepancy between the average costs of care and the maximum credit that can be claimed. They also question the objective of training 50,000 unemployed 18- to 25-year-olds to provide additional childcare through the New Deal, pointing out that the commodification of childcare is likely to reinforce care work as low-paid, insecure and gendered employment.

The 'welfare-to-work' approach also contains an authoritarian element in the threat of compulsion and possibility of financial penalties for non-compliance. The New Deal for Lone Parents (NDLP) avoids the degree of compulsion that characterises the New Deal for Young People (NDYP) and New Deal for the Long Term Unemployed (NDLTU) as participation is optional. Lone parents are required to attend a compulsory job-focused interview once their youngest child reaches school age, and will incur reductions in their benefits if they fail to attend. Gray (2001, p 191) notes that the 1999 Welfare and Pensions Reform Act allows 'availability for work' requirements to apply to all claimants at some future time. She continues that if the persuasive elements of the government's strategy fail, lone parents could, in theory, be required to seek work before their youngest child is 16. The lone parents interviewed for this study made it clear that the perennial media and political debates surrounding lone parents and benefit dependency did have a negative impact on their self-esteem. Popularised research findings claiming that the children of lone-parent families are emotionally and educationally disadvantaged compound the doubts surrounding their own parenting abilities. When these are presented alongside the exhortation of paid work as a moral duty of the citizen, these dual pressures denigrate the lone parent's role as a carer and may heighten their sense of isolation from mainstream society.

The education/training option in the New Deal is especially important for lone parents, since three quarters left school at 16 and 41% have no qualifications (Finlayson and Marsh, 1998, p 47). Findings from a study of NDLP indicate that those with no qualifications and lacking basic skills were the least likely to participate. The same survey reveals that it was those already seeking work who demonstrated higher participation rates and 62% of participants who entered employment said that they would have found work anyway (Hales et al, 1999). As suggested in Chapter Four, a paradox of measures to increase individuals' 'human capital' is that they may actually increase patterns of intra-class inequalities through assisting those who are more likely to have found employment of their own accord, and failing to offer a 'hand up, not a hand out' to those with the worst employment prospects. Employment rates of lone parents are strongly associated with training, qualifications and higher potential earnings. Ford et al's (1998, p 60) findings suggest that:

> What discriminated between those who got jobs and those who didn't was training and qualifications, not any underlying work orientation. This is an important finding, it assigns little role to 'benefit dependency' for example, in explaining lone parents' position in the labour market.

A more fundamental question concerns the quality of the jobs that lone parents are entering and the potential for long-term dependence on in-work benefits. The concentration of lone parents in part-time and/or low-skilled jobs rarely allows full independence from the benefit system. Moreover, as the interviews testified, the daily contingencies and problems faced by lone-parent households make stable employment difficult. Hale et al's (1999) evaluation shows that 25% of those parents who entered employment returned to claiming Income Support over the survey period. Of those who remained in work, most were employed in unskilled or low-skilled personal and protective services, sales or routine clerical work. The majority worked between 16 and

30 hours a week, one third earned less than the NMW of £3.60 per week (April 1999) with a median wage of £4.00 per hour (Hales et al, 1999, pp 216-21). Gray (2001) notes that currently, the NDLP only supports training up to NVQ Level 2 and for a maximum of 12 months. She raises the important point that unless lone parents are assisted in training beyond basic courses to meet existing skill shortages they will merely compete for entry-level jobs with the unemployed, which could paradoxically increase unemployment (Gray, 2001, p 194). While this may expand the labour supply of low-paid workers, it will do little to ameliorate the economic difficulties facing lone parents or improve the incentives to do so.

Changing policy priorities, and the expectation that lone parents should, where possible, engage in paid employment, provided the context to the interviews. The following section is based on fieldwork and interviews conducted with 19 lone mothers living on the estate, and others contacted via the local Gingerbread association. The interviews traced the mother's major lifecycle transitions and explored the situation in which family formation occurred. A central aim was to discover the extent to which informal systems of welfare based in the locality and in social ties are utilised by these parents, and the factors that shape decisions over work and welfare. This approach gives priority to the perspectives of lone parents, whose views may provide a corrective to the assumptions of policy makers and whose voices, note Edin and Lein (1997, p 13), are too frequently submerged by statistical interpretations and academic discourses.

Transitions to motherhood and labour market orientations

The lone mothers interviewed gave birth to their first child between the ages of 15 and 27, with only three having a child either outside of marriage or without a cohabiting partner. Despite individual variations most biographies followed broadly analogous courses, with the majority having left school with minimal qualifications and working in entry-level jobs prior to establishing a steady relationship around their late teens or early twenties. One divorced 27-year-old parent of two children voiced a familiar recollection:

> "I always did well at school till I got into high school and then maybe it was my friends, but I didn't attend many classes and you couldn't learn anything useful anyway because the kids ran the school and the teachers had given

up. Nobody really pushed me to work and I mean none of us thought about exams or careers. I left school with a few GCSEs, really low grades and worked in a sewing machine shop until I met Tim [ex-husband]."

Julie, a 28-year-old divorced lone parent recalls that her adolescent aspirations were focused on enjoying herself as a prerequisite to having a baby and settling down. This represented a prevailing theme among the biographies, as the girls pursued traditional and culturally acceptable passages to adulthood.

> "It's a big issue you know, teenage girls getting pregnant but that's the way things are nowadays so should you blame them or blame the parents or the schools? I don't know but look at me. I don't blame myself but at 18 I felt I'd done so much already that there wasn't much left to do and at that age you think, 'Oh about time I had a baby' and now I'm a bit older I think why did I think like that?"

Scholarly debates surrounding the relationship between adolescent pregnancies and welfare dependency have centred on cultural and situational explanations. In the former, teenage pregnancies are influenced through inherited cultural dispositions. Once established through socialisation, cultural values and behaviour ensure the continuation of poverty through legitimising alternative family forms and joblessness (see Chapter Three). The situational perspective stresses social and economic factors, which limit the options facing low-qualified young women. In the absence of reasonable employment prospects or routes to upward mobility, motherhood represents the most available and feasible entry into adulthood and the most realistic chance of establishing an independent household. Certainly, a lack of education and poor work prospects restrict the range of options, as Julie recognises with the benefit of 10 years' hindsight. However, the causal relationships proposed by situational accounts build on a similar model of human behaviour to that offered by cultural perspectives. Both versions rest on opposite sequences of causation, but both concede that individuals choose from the range of options available and act in accordance with the one that brings the greatest utility (Fernandez-Kelly, 1994).

Situational accounts offer more plausible explanations of human behaviour, particularly when viewed through the prism of ethnographic and qualitative research. However, the causal connections posited between early motherhood and restricted opportunities often overlook the differing temporal frames in which the reshaping of opportunity structures, and the development of cultural aspirations occur. Subsequently, insufficient attention is paid to the cultural norms through which early aspirations are formed, and the likelihood of achieving them when their material base becomes increasingly untenable (see Chapter Five). This would suggest that reproductive behaviour and family formation patterns have changed less than the context within which they occur. Rather than choosing early motherhood and welfare dependency as an alternative to low-waged menial work, their occupational horizons were conditioned by their expectations of establishing a nuclear family. Julie commented that:

> "It was really the thought that you're going to get married and have kids and stay at home maybe because that's what my mum and dad did and it influenced me. But at that point my main interest was having a good time because I knew that I'd need to get married soon and have a baby because I dread to think where I might have gone if I hadn't had a baby at 19."

The testimonies of these lone parents point to the not insignificant role that social and cultural milieu played in influencing their perceptions of motherhood. Most had been born to parents who had married relatively young and grown up in two-parent families, often on local housing estates that contained high proportions of such families. Three had grown up in lone-parent households themselves: two as a result of divorce and one of an unmarried mother. Three were raised in stepfamilies and two with unmarried cohabiting parents, leaving 11 who grew up in a household comprising of two married parents. Pathology and family breakdown were evident in their social environments, which tempered any sentimentalised view of family life. These families were marginal compared to the dominant two-parent norm that existed on the housing estates where they grew up in the 1970s and 1980s, and before they became occupied by increasing concentrations of the poorest and most disadvantaged sections of society. Thirty-one-year-old Nicky had grown up on the estate and moved to Brighton to live with her boyfriend at 21. The relationship finished after five years and she moved back to her sister's with her one-year-old son, while waiting to be rehoused by the council. After 18 months she was offered a house back on the estate where she had spent her childhood:

> "You've always had your crooks round here and the place
> is notorious for it. There'd be blokes bashing up their kids
> and wives, fights, mothers on their own with kids, it's always
> been here. But they weren't like my family or most of my
> friends and as kids those people frightened us and they
> were like how not to be (…) when I moved back here, the
> first thing I noticed was that there were a lot more of those
> kinds of people."

Pauline, a 32-year-old separated mother of two children, gave birth to
her first child at 18. The initial reaction of her family was moderated
by the fact that she was following a family pattern preceded by her
grandmother, mother and older sister, whereby pregnancy prefigured
family formation:

> "When I got pregnant I said I was keeping it and my mum
> and dad went mad but they came round pretty quickly.
> My mum had me at 20 and my big sister had her first baby
> at 21. I think my mum was looking forward to it more
> than me. We're a young family, and I suppose I was just
> following the family tradition (…) my boyfriend worked
> for Telecom at the time and we moved in with his family
> while we were waiting for a council place."

This is not a picture of deprived girls becoming pregnant because
their impoverished environments offered a lack of alternative passages
to adulthood. Neither does it give much credence to perspectives that
stress the intergenerational transmission of dependent modes of
behaviour. Instead, they were aspiring to join the ranks of the more
affluent and 'respectable' working classes from where most originated.
This was before a combination of individual circumstances, structural
economic processes and the historical changes that are transforming
families made this possibility increasingly remote. Divorce or separation
was the route by which most arrived at their current status, as one
observes:

> "After the divorce my life took a definite turn because
> before that I was aspiring to a normal life – a house, a
> child, a husband, a job, I mean that was where I'd always
> assumed I'd end up. Being on my own with a kid on 'social'
> and living in a council place hadn't entered into the picture
> at all."

The breaking up of relationships inevitably involved a traumatic period of domestic upheaval. This was compounded not only by the change and uncertainty in their material circumstances but in the realignment of their priorities surrounding the relationship between work, welfare and childcare. Dawson et al's survey suggests that for many lone parents, disruption in their domestic lives had made them especially protective towards, and reluctant to leave, their children (Dawson et al, 2000, p 35). It also entailed descent into a status that many had regarded negatively – disorienting previously held, and culturally grounded, notions of acceptable behaviour and respectability. As 23-year-old Jenny notes, these contradictory concerns were a source of further anxiety as she struggled to come to terms with her new identity and set of circumstances:

> "I'd always worked since I left school. After we split up I wasn't up to working, the whole thing had been awful and my nerves were all over the place (...) I felt that Sophie needed me around more than I needed the money because it had rubbed off on her. We were in a half-way house waiting to be rehoused and I just felt like 'where's my life going?' I hated queuing up at the post office with all the other single mums and I just dreaded an old school friend or whoever walking in and seeing me standing there."

Many studies have stressed that the economic behaviour of lone parents is framed by the tension between their roles as both the main carer and the main provider for their children. Schein's (1995, p 42) ethnographic studies found that:

> They view the world through the lens of motherhood. Work and all decisions related to it are placed within the context of their role and responsibility as a mother. They do not see themselves as providers, struggling to be the parent within that context. Rather, they view themselves as mothers, and struggle to be providers within that context.

All but two of the lone mothers among the sample had worked either prior to giving birth, or at some point after having their children. At the time of interview four were working full time, three were employed part time and four were in receipt of undeclared income. However, this snapshot cannot account for the degree of changes in their employment status over time. Twelve of the sample had engaged in some form of paid work since having their children, often spells of cash work that could be fitted around the care of children. Babysitting, cleaning, home working, income from lodgers or from delivery work were the most common sources of additional income. Few were able to transform these opportunities into more permanent sources of income as the same practical obstacles that apply to legitimate employment, also apply to cash work. Their previous experiences of work, their social contacts and the nature of the localised labour market that they could compete in, affected decisions over work and assessment of their current prospects. Twenty-eight-year-old Jacky, the parent of a five-year-old boy, was paid cash for working three mornings a week in a café. As she remarked, her options were restricted through her previous experience, which made her unable to legally earn enough to keep a family:

> "Before I had him I worked in a nursing home for a few years, then worked in a cinema. Basically, I'm unskilled and the only jobs I'm likely to get round here are similar ones to what I did before, which were alright when I only had number one to look out for, but they're not much good for me now."

Many lone parents feel that their children are entitled to a full-time carer particularly given the absence of a full-time father and the emotional disturbances that many have experienced. Those same mothers also spoke of their guilt at being unable to provide adequately for their children, highlighting an important source of conflict within their lives. As the requirements of consumer capitalism reaches into ever-younger cohorts, infusing children with increasingly materialistic attitudes, participation in prevailing fads and fashions becomes a crucial marker of inclusion into peer groups. A repeated theme was the sense of inadequacy that many feel at their difficulty in providing these items, or through having to rely on the goodwill of their family. Jacky's sister has been raising her two children alone, since her boyfriend left her shortly after the birth of their second child six years previously. It is not the personal privations that were hardest to adjust to, she explained, but witnessing the effect on her children:

> "The hardest thing about living on benefits is the guilt. Our lives are always 'you can't have that' and 'you can't do this' and 'we can't go there' and that's the hardest thing really, with children. They're so fashion conscious these

days and they've got to have all the gear just to fit in. I'm lucky my parents help out and his [ex-partner's] family are good, but sometimes I wish it could be me who spoilt them."

None are exempt from public debates surrounding lone parenthood and their negative portrayal in media and political rhetoric, which drives many public policies. All support the NDLP's objective of creating more avenues into work and increasing the provision of training for lone parents, although many chose to defer those opportunities until their children were older. However, as Jacky noted, it is the elevation of paid work as a moral duty and the accompanying condemnation of 'welfare culture' that leads many to conclude that their role as mothers and commitment to their children are devalued and unrecognised.

"It's rubbish all this 'we've got to get lone parents back to work'. We're doing an important job raising the next generation (...) you don't get any gratitude for being a parent but its bloody hard work especially when you're on your own. It's crazy, there's still no real childcare and nothing's changed. They're pushing us to work but the reason we don't go back is because we can't afford to."

Others argued that lone parents offended public sensibilities regardless of their status in relation to work and benefits and felt that they would continue to receive criticism whether they worked or received benefits. In practical terms, the concentration of lone parents in certain localities and a shortage of affordable childcare or after-school clubs in those areas does, as Jenny recognises, raise the potential for large numbers of 'latchkey kids' to pose significant social order problems.

"You're in a catch-22 situation because people expect you to work because they think you're just sponging and then you go back to work and your children are up to something, getting into trouble, then what are you? Then you're irresponsible for leaving them. Imagine if all the single mums were out at work, in areas like this you'd have hordes of 11-year-olds roaming about till their mums got back from work. I mean is that such a good thing for society?"

Although childcare costs and a lack of access remain well-documented barriers to lone parents' employment, many are averse to leaving their children with strangers in the formal childcare sector regardless of its availability. Family-based childcare is overwhelmingly favoured, as Wheelock and Jones' (2002) study found, pointing to the important role of family support in assisting lone parents to return to work. The current media focus surrounding the risks of child abuse and paedophilia also enter into judgements over the most appropriate form of childcare, and undermine trust in childcare workers. These fears represent perceptions that are commonly held, as one lone parent observed:

> "You get such mixed messages in the media. On one page you're reading that single mums can go back to work because the government are setting up all these wonderful childcare schemes (...) the next page tells you that there's probably half a dozen perverts living in your street. So everybody's paranoid and I mean, what mother in her right mind is going to hand her kid over to a bunch of strangers that could be rapists?"

The NDLP is targeted towards lone parents with children of school age and founded on the assumption that working becomes easier as children grow older. After initially considering going back to work, Pat discovered that childcare costs for her daughter would only be available until she was 11 years old. She contacted social services to enquire whether she was allowed to leave her children unattended and was informed that if her daughter came to any harm in her absence, social services would conduct an investigation to determine whether she was negligent. She delayed working until her son was older and able to look after his sister. A major, and related, concern is that working reduces the parent's supervision over their children and increases the influence of local peer groups. Attempting to transcend these influences requires participation in hobbies and leisure activities that place an infeasible financial burden on working lone parents. Many are working for an income so low that they are restricted by the same frugal consumption levels that state benefits provide. This means that they are unable to provide these, and their children have to create their own entertainment within the locality:

> "He doesn't go out drinking or anything but he's into golf and cricket and that costs a lot of money. Well, I do want

him to have those things because I don't want him hanging round on the streets but I have to say, 'Well, sorry, you'll have to make your own amusement', and it's a real dilemma. There's a problem on the estate with kids drinking and breaking into shops and when I'm not there I'm worried sick what he's doing."

Given these sentiments the overriding ambition is to provide adequately for their children's needs. However, these concerns are balanced against an assessment of the economic gains through work, along with a widely held view over the lack of any intrinsic satisfaction or chances for career advancement from the jobs on offer. As outlined in Chapter Four, trends indicate an increasing 'feminisation' of the labour force in the area over recent decades, due to an overall growth in the numbers of women employed full time. Although there is a glut of low-skilled part-time work, jobs in the hotel/catering, personal services and care sectors feature prominently among the 'hard-to-fill' vacancies. Time constraints and travel costs limit the employment possibilities of lone parents to certain periods of the day within the immediate locality. Despite the abundance of entry-level service jobs, there was a high local demand for jobs that fitted such a narrow set of criteria. Wage expectations were relatively modest and based on a pragmatic awareness of their economic worth in such a highly localised labour market, although all maintained that work should make a visible difference to their lives.

Among Finlayson and Marsh's sample of lone parents, the average 'reservation wage' (the gap between their target wage and the wage that they would accept) was £132 per week. Their report comments that, "Whatever it was keeping so many lone parents out of the labour market it was not unrealistic wage expectations" (Finlayson and Marsh, 1998, p 23). Structural features of the local labour market combined with the added difficulties that work imposes, were frequently cited in the current research as insufficient in compensating for lost time with children. Another parent remarked that she would consider herself irresponsible if she took a low-paid job, adding that:

"There's work there; I could go back tomorrow working in a shop, or stacking shelves, but why? I'd rather look after my kids properly. I mean it might be different if I was earning good money or even if it was something that I liked because you've got to balance up the pros and cons, but for what I'd make it's not worth it because for a mother you lose a lot for that."

Recent policy has been geared towards inducing lone parents into part-time work through increasing the generosity of in-work benefits, and extending eligibility by reducing the number of hours people need to work to receive such benefits, from 24 to 16. Widespread aversion towards a welfare state perceived as oppressive and unresponsive to their needs, means that the preference was for work that provided complete independence from the benefit system. In the absence of a second income, the majority of jobs in the area would entail in-work poverty and continuing reliance on state benefits. Indeed, evidence reveals that the continuing reliance of lone parents on in-work benefits once in full-time work actually increased from 20% of lone parents in 1991 to 32% in 1995 (Ford et al, 1998, p 71). As Nicky remarked:

> "What can a woman earn if she's on her own and she's got to be back by three o'clock? A part-time job's all she can do and it's never going to be enough so she'll be forced to take alternative routes (…) They say that if you go to work in a shit job they'll still pay some of your rent and you won't be worse off. No you won't but you won't be better off and at the end of the day, why should you have to leave your kid with someone else all day for no reason?"

In assessing the benefits of working, financial calculations and the likelihood of work allowing self-sufficiency feature prominently. However, these concerns are eclipsed by the need to maximise security in their economic environment and few were willing to jeopardise the relative stability of state benefits with the uncertainty of work. The expendability of workers in low-paid 'flexible' jobs, which represent the only feasible sector that most can enter in the short term, makes working a highly risky venture. The demands that sick children, school holidays and arranging childcare impose on working lone parents make the threat of dismissal ever present. Thirty-four-year-old Debby had worked in a miscellaneous assortment of legal and undeclared part-time jobs during her 12 years as a single parent.

> "I worked mornings as a receptionist in an accountant's office (…) Normally my mum looked after my daughter in the holidays but this time she'd gone on holiday and I was stuck so I phoned in and said I couldn't make it. He

said get something sorted out by tomorrow or don't bother coming back. Well, I couldn't get anything arranged in time so that was the end of that."

This was followed shortly afterwards by a move into a house on the estate. A frequent theme of this study has been the revelation of labour market marginality and the re-evaluation of labour market opportunities that accompanied the transition to adulthood (see Chapter Five). These concerns made undeclared work a financially rational and, when underpinned by benefits, a more secure option than opportunities in the formal labour market. As Debby explained:

> "What changed for me totally is that when I moved onto the estate I had my own home to provide for. I worked it out that I'd have to be earning quite a large sum to live to a certain standard. Even if I was earning £250 a week and where am I going to earn that sort of money? I still wouldn't be much better off and the option of earning more money and having my overheads covered became more viable at the time."

Calculating the earnings from her current job on top of her benefit allowance, she estimates a disposable income of approximately £140 a week for herself and her daughter, which she sees as unattainable in the formal labour market even with the incentives of in-work benefits. Duncan and Edwards argue that the economic rationality of lone parents needs to be located within a different model of rationality that emphasises 'socially negotiated, non-economic understandings' about what is morally right and socially acceptable (Duncan and Edwards, 1999, pp 118-19). Seen from this perspective, the distinction between 'rights' and 'responsibilities' is not as straightforward as the version currently driving the programme of welfare reform. The notion of responsibility is couched more in terms of the most responsible course of action for herself and her daughter. Working under these arrangements also minimises the ever-present psychological burdens of work, since fears of dismissal are lessened when it does not involve the possibility of destitution. The most pressing fear among those in the 'numerically flexible' sector of the labour market and living in an area of high property values and rents is the loss of access to the Housing Benefit system and the implications that this entails. As Julie explained:

"I'm scared to give up the 'social' and it's not so much the money it's the rent because once you're getting your rent paid it'd be awful if they stopped it and that's why I won't sign off because if I can't manage my rent I'll be evicted. Unless you've got a good job that's totally and utterly reliable, like where you've got a written contract and you're not going to be thrown out of work and they've got to give you notice, then and only then, would I think, right, I don't need your assistance any more."

Informal support and household finances

A major aim of this study has been to explore the ways in which people develop collective solutions to low income levels and economic uncertainty. For lone parents, it became clear that localised networks and the practical and financial support of kin are crucial sources of economic and emotional support. Among the sample of lone parents, the support of fathers and family was the major source of additional financial and material support. The image of the 'absent male' is derived from administrative accounts of the numbers of fathers who fail to pay maintenance or maintain contact with their children, once the relationship with their mother has ended. Official interpretations drawn from statistical records may not accord with reality, and certainly did not reflect the experiences of this sample of lone parents. Twelve of the lone parents interviewed reported that absent partners maintained contact with their children. The financial and practical assistance that those fathers provided was often a major, although frequently irregular, source of support. These arrangements are frequently negotiated between the partners themselves and bypass the Child Support Agency (CSA). The administrative criteria of the CSA and benefit system (discussed above) make it economically irrational to report any maintenance received or to name the 'absent' partner. Many of the mothers acknowledged the financial instability of their ex-partners, which made regular maintenance payments difficult. Consequently, more informal and flexible arrangements are developed, more suited to the economic realities that many of the fathers face. These arrangements are also regarded as fostering better relationships between the separated parents, and sustain closer ties between the father and his children, as one mother remarked:

"I would rather he came round here and gave me the money himself than getting it through an order book or whatever.

We're finished but he's still got a role to play with the kids. It's better for them if he takes them out and buys their clothes himself and then he knows I'm not blowing it all going out."

Such considerations also feature prominently in influencing the labour market behaviour of many fathers as Colin (see also Chapter Eight) notes. After a lengthy period of working cash in hand and signing on, he felt increasingly frustrated that he was 'going nowhere' and considered seeking a legitimate job. His decision to remain working outside of the formal labour market was based on his limited earnings capacity in legal employment, which would compromise the previous agreements he had made with his ex-partner over the support of his daughter:

"My place was 70 quid a week and the 'social' were paying that so if I was going to be legit I'd need to earn a decent wage and it just weren't there. I didn't want the child agency on my back and neither did she. When I left I said I'd give her 30 quid a week and sometimes I'd give her a bit more and if there was no money there was nothing for her but that's the way it always was. Now if I worked they'd make me pay her more and they'd pay her less and we'd all be worse off so it didn't make sense."

The CSA is viewed as a draconian instrument that is solely concerned with reducing welfare expenditure, paying scant regard to the needs of either parents or their children. Pat divorced her husband 10 years ago and neither she nor her children have had any contact with him since. Three years after her divorce she met a boyfriend who moved in with her. Although this relationship broke down after four years the two remain close friends, and the ex-partner visits her children, providing a regular financial contribution to the household. After being contacted by the CSA, she refused to name the biological father of her children. She argued that as he had paid her a lump-sum 'clean break' settlement he had no further obligation to her family. The family considered her ex-partner as the father of the children and he was prepared to help towards their maintenance. Despite these objections she was drawn into a protracted struggle with the CSA, and was finally forced to claim that she did not know the father:

"They insisted that I go for an interview with them, and I said no I wouldn't go for an interview. I don't know who the father is and do as you please. So they wrote back to me and said 'as you do not know who the father of your child is'. It was more on principle, it could have messed my life up and I thought you're not changing the rules halfway through. That was despicable what they did, people had made agreements and they said 'sorry we've changed it' and they made it worse because these men went 'well, up yours, I'm not going to work then', so what did they achieve by that?"

Following the introduction of NDLP, the media campaign, promotional literature and political endorsements that surrounded its launch emphasised the 'partnership' that would exist between the welfare system and its clients. The clients' responsibilities would be balanced by the state's responsibility to make employment financially attractive, and to remove the obstacles to independence that the cumbersome welfare system placed in the paths of its clients. Speaking to the three parents that had joined NDLP, it became apparent that participation sets in motion a bureaucratic process that is equally as antithetical to their interests as previously. Joining NDLP means the mother is moved off Income Support and onto Job Seeker's Allowance, which in turn attracts the attention of the CSA, as 27-year-old Mandy discovered:

"Their dad sees them once a fortnight and gives me a little bit of money which nobody knows about, which is better than going through the CSA because at least I've got a little bit above what I would have. I never had any dealings with the CSA because when I first started claiming they asked me a bit about her dad and it was 'do you want us to chase him?' whereas now it's 'you have to give us this information'. So I went on a course and to do it I had to change from Income Support to Jobseeker's Allowance, which I really didn't want to do but to do the course you had to. I gave them a lot of bullshit basically and just told them I didn't know who the father was. I had to or I would have lost money."

While critiques of state welfare bemoan the passive and dependent attitudes that the system instils in welfare recipients, the perspectives offered by these lone parents tell of an active and ongoing relationship of confrontational encounters with the welfare system. Many have developed an intricate knowledge of the maze of bureaucratic regulations, gained through endless hours in social security offices, local authority housing and Housing Benefit departments, Citizens' Advice Bureaux and through the examples and anecdotes that circulate through their personal networks. Feminist critiques of social policy have long highlighted the paternalistic nature of welfare provision, which attempts to impose patriarchal power relations through ensuring women's financial dependence on men. The women in this study were engaged in various struggles to preserve and extend the limited liberty they had in their lives, against institutions that are often perceived as a fundamental opponent to their interests. Cooperating with bureaucratic regulations is perceived as not only financially irrational, but also involves surrendering the limited autonomy that many had achieved by breaking their previous relationships.

Similarly, cohabitation rules are bypassed not only because of the loss of money that claiming as a couple incurs, or the loss of benefit if the partner is employed. A more salient point emphasised by the seven lone parents who were either unofficially cohabiting at the time of interview or had done at some point, was that it channels income to their male partner. It therefore entails a corresponding loss of economic independence and security. Maintaining a family on benefits and avoiding financial catastrophe remained the major daily preoccupation. Through necessity and experience most could make ends meet through utilising the resources of their kin-based and personal networks, through extreme financial astuteness and by refining the skill of economising. Few were willing to relinquish control of their finances and the limited security that control provides, to the possible unpredictability of a boyfriend. Mark (see also Chapter Five) lived officially with his father and slept at his girlfriend Mandy's house. This arrangement was based on her wish to preserve her own financial autonomy.

> "I can't move in properly because if I do they'll stop her money and give it to me so I become in charge of the giro for me, her and the kids, then what I do with it is down to me. She won't have it so what I have to do is leave my stuff at my dad's and just stay here at night. So it's not me who don't want to move in full time, it's her because it's not doing her any favours."

Campbell's (1993, p 174) depiction of the parasitic 'parochial itinerants' who "go(ing) home to change, or to eat, or to collect a Giro, while nesting in other women's houses" provides only a partial picture of the ways in which weakening of the material basis underpinning family life is transforming relationships between men and women. Studies have demonstrated that these processes have weakened the male 'breadwinner' model upon which both the nuclear family and the post-war welfare state was based. Ritchie's longitudinal study of 30 unemployed families in the late 1980s highlighted the psychological consequences of unemployment, and the strain that material hardship imposed on marital relationships (Ritchie, 1990). Lampard's analysis for the 1986 Social Change and Economic Life Initiative found that periods of unemployment and/or insecure work demonstrated a strong association with an increased risk of marital breakdown (Lampard, 1994). Ethnographic studies have long recognised that employment insecurity remains a serious obstacle to the formation of stable family patterns and more flexible arrangements may be adopted. Within these households, more malleable and less binding financial arrangements that minimise the risk of exploitation are in greater consonance with their economic situation (Liebow, 1967; Rodman, 1971). Financial arrangements in Mandy's household were similar to the other cohabiting households, with income kept separately and both partners paying for different weekly expenses. As she noted, the living standards of her household have improved since her boyfriend (partly) moved in with her, while the separation of finances allowed her to preserve economic independence and gave more scope for negotiating the terms of their relationship:

> "He's alright with money but I don't trust any bloke enough to give up control of my money to them. I mean the cheque's to pay for food and bills, so it should always go to the woman. No, I said we'll keep it like this, you can stay here but as far as the 'social' are concerned I'm on my own."

Lone parents and networks of support

Evidence suggests a significant gender aspect in the quantity and types of support available through social networks, as the increasing labour force participation of women has altered the forms of support available through both kin and friendship networks. The lone parents and unemployed females among the sample were more connected through localised neighbourhood networks than the sample of unemployed men or cash workers, whose networks tended to be based around their common position in respect of the labour market. For the women interviewed, this resulted in a high level of mutual support and the sharing of resources such as transportation and childcare. Informational resources on job vacancies are low, due to the shared life experiences of those who comprise these networks. Thirty-two-year-old Pauline commented that:

> "Most of my friends aren't working because they're at home looking after children so they're not much good as far as knowing where to find jobs goes. Some are working part time but we're all in pretty much the same situation financially (...) I'll pop round my friends' houses for a chat and we always have the same crap going on: money problems, trouble with the kids or from boyfriends."

Outside of daily lending, levels of material support are minimal. As discussed, more substantial forms of material assistance are provided through family support and/or absent partners. Although this can provide a structured system of support, it is also vulnerable to disruption through external factors (Wall, 2001). After 26-year-old Claire's separation from her partner, she moved in with her divorced father. He provided the care for her child, which enabled her to work part time while attending a beauty therapy course at college. Her father's increasing alcohol problems resulted in the repossession of his house, and dissolved the family support mechanisms that had assisted her ambitions of becoming a beauty therapist:

> "I decided to put myself through college and I went to college for three years and worked weekends and evenings. I was living with my dad at the time so he looked after Louise a lot, and that's why I was able to do those things ... everything changed after he started drinking and lost the house and I ended up on the estate (...) the family home had gone, which was where everyone would meet and talk and the family were still quite a unit but that had gone. I'd lost my babysitter and everything needed a lot more planning, plus I was spending so much time sorting my dad out that in the end all the things I'd been working towards just slipped away."

The changing structure of the family, restructuring of the labour force and increasing geographic mobility have altered the forms of support available through kin. As the proportion of working women has increased, many of the lone parents' mothers were themselves in employment and lacked the time to provide childminding and other types of daily support. Accordingly, financial and material maintenance has become a more prominent facet of kin support as the following lone parent reported:

> "If I'm stuck for money I'll tend to ask my mum first or my sister second. They're both working so they don't mind helping me out. My family don't live locally anymore, so they're not exactly around to lend a hand. I think they're a bit guilty about that so they try to make it up by making sure that we don't go short."

Forms of support are closely tied to women's domestic role and can occasionally develop into openings to earn a regular income through the provision of informally organised childcare. This was common on the estate on both an ad-hoc and more organised basis and does not represent a straightforward process of commodification, but is based on relations of trust and shared beliefs surrounding childrearing (Wheelock and Jones, 2002). As Tina described, for those who make use of such arrangements they serve to make formal employment a viable option in the near absence of affordable childcare, while containing financial resources within their network of friends:

> "I look after a couple of kids for some friends who work after I was talking to a friend across the road. She had a chance of a job and she'd be taking home over £200 a week, but her childminding would have cost her a fortune. I said I'd do it for £40 a week then they give me £5 a week for food and extras. So I looked after her Luke for a while then I got to look after her sister's little girl (…) I'm looking after another friend's so that's three and I make about £120 a week at the moment."

A central theme in the literature surrounding exchange relationships is that they operate on the basis of reciprocity. Nelson's study suggests that the single mothers in her sample distinguished different 'logic's of reciprocity'. Those with similar needs operate on the basis of 'balanced reciprocity', where it is assumed that equivalent levels of support will be exchanged. The second logic of reciprocity operates in exchanges with those assumed to be more affluent and the women "retain the norm and language of balanced reciprocity while freeing themselves from the obligation to make returns of equivalent material goods and services" (Nelson, 2000, p 298). Forms of exchange among members of a social network are legitimated by accompanying expressions such as balanced forms of reciprocity and rest upon criteria such as length of friendship and common position. Distinctions were frequently made according to notions of 'respectability' with those lone parents who arrived at their current position as a result of divorce or separation, at pains to distinguish themselves from the media stereotype of the teenage mother, as one 27-year-old remarked:

> "Lone parents don't get a fair hearing. Whenever you see them on Kilroy or something they always pick the youngest and it's like we all went out and got pregnant so we could go out and get a wonderful council place and live the high life on benefits."

Likewise a 38-year-old divorced lone parent voluntarily attending Job Club, contrasted lone parents' who are divorced/separated with the young single mothers who get pregnant, housed by the local authority and "settle down to a life on benefits until their kids leave school and do the same themselves". Her distaste was not directed at the young mothers due to her own experiences of the exigencies of lone parenthood, but that herself and her children are similarly labelled and stigmatised:

> "You're always going to get a group of people that want money for whatever reason and you're not going to change that by any policy. But people look at you and see you're on your own with kids and think 'oh well you live on that council estate' (…) I'd heard people in the playground say things like 'those kids on the estate they don't really stand a chance'. I'd seen it first hand and not for me, for them [children]. I thought it was awful that they're good kids and they're well behaved but they've got this stigma attached to them."

As later chapters explore, these distinctions manifest themselves in patterns of association and in the closure of informal support systems among those sharing similar lifestyles and lifecourses. While these bring positive benefits, for those who experience a change in status the principle of 'balanced reciprocity' is disrupted and the demands of friends can impose a significant burden on those who are only marginally better off than their unemployed friends. Socioeconomic homogeneity and shared location in respect of the labour market and welfare system underpin reciprocal relations. For low-paid workers such as Donna, the expectations of her unemployed friends for cash-based reciprocity exacerbated her problems as she lacks the money to recompense them.

> "I have trouble with baby-sitting because I can never get anyone. I haven't got any money to pay anyone to pick them up and it's just for an hour after school then I'm home but I can't expect someone to pick them up five days a week and not pay them, which has been the case lately. My brother's been doing it but now he's got a job, so at the end of the day I just think well fuck the job even though that's the thing that keeps me going, getting up in the morning, going to work. I enjoy what I do and I enjoy working with the people I work with."

These problems are exacerbated through the withdrawal of housing and Council Tax benefits in line with increased earnings, and the removal of benefits in kind such as free school meals. Donna secured a full-time, fixed-term position for the local authority after several years raising her children and working in low-paid catering and bar jobs. Despite needing assistance with material resources herself, her network of mainly unemployed friends and lone parents are unable to provide such aid and are a drain on her already meagre resources:

> "Like I've only got my mum and my brother. I haven't got any family, all my mates are bums sitting on the 'social' with no money and I can't borrow from anybody. Everyone borrows from me and I mean, the time I've paid my rent and my bills I'm left with £100 a month, which is absolutely fucking ridiculous. You know yourself there's no way you can feed an adult and two children. I have to pay school dinners and that's £12 a week. It's ridiculous."

For many lone parents formal employment is regarded as severely restricting the degree of control they maintain over their lives. Material hardship, the offerings of the local job market and responsibilities to their children bind their choices, but the limited autonomy that they possess is highly valued. Income from welfare benefits alone is insufficient in meeting weekly expenses and most women have developed an array of strategies to meet consumption levels. This involves a combination of aid supplied by family and from absent partners, income from cash work, purchasing items from catalogues and spreading the payments and through borrowing and bartering. Suffice to say, most have greater faith in their own capabilities in providing for their household than the uncertainty of formal opportunities in a low-wage, flexible labour market. These understandings, as Jacky argued, in conjunction with a social security system that makes it increasingly difficult to leave a job without being penalised through the suspension of benefits, means that working is regarded as detrimental to the exercise of agency.

> "I'm always worried that they'll phone me up and stick me on a till at Tesco's for £4 an hour. There's only so long you can do those jobs because they do your head in … with what I'm doing now at least I can jack it in if I get too fed up. If I upped and walked out of Tesco's then they wouldn't pay my Income Support and my rent, so I'd have no choice, I'd be trapped."

The final two chapters of this book explore in greater detail some of the themes that have been touched upon in this and the previous chapter. Current social inclusion policies have emphasised formal labour market participation and/or the enhancement of work-based skills through formal training. As demonstrated, the financial gains through formal work are often viewed as insufficient in meeting household expenses. Despite the progress of policies to enhance the financial attraction of work, the loss of benefits-in-kind, travelling and childcare expenses, and an array of other costs associated with work means that many consider that they would be little better off in formal full-time work. For lone parents these considerations were also made in the context of lost time with their children and the potential outcomes of this. The major problem, however, is not merely an economic one. The erosion of autonomy that the combination of an unstable job market and an increasingly conditional and coercive welfare system creates plays an equally significant role in modifying attitudes and beliefs surrounding work. Formal structures of work and welfare are not the only 'opportunity structures' open to people, and locally based informal systems play an important function in offsetting these structural and institutional pressures. The final chapters will examine the role of undeclared income and other forms of provision that are available through informal support mechanisms, and the role that these mechanisms play in reproducing patterns of solidarity and division on the estate.

Note
[1] Throughout this chapter, ★ indicates that a quotation has been transcribed from notes. In the quotations, (...) indicates that part of the text has been omitted.

SEVEN

Informal opportunities and social divisions

Investigating the magnitude of paid informal work has proven extremely problematic. Estimates of its scale have remained relatively constant since the early 1980s, ranging from 6% to 8% of GDP, despite fundamental changes in the economy and labour market over this period (Cook, 1998). Harding and Jenkins point out that a lack of regulation has been the historical norm, and changes in institutional boundaries and regulations will cause a corresponding realignment of formal/informal relationships. Defining an informal 'sector' is further complicated because of the different sources of labour and distinct spheres in which 'informal' activities occur, and they distinguish the 'household', 'communal' and 'underground' economies (Harding and Jenkins, 1989). Despite their differences, they all involve economic activities and monetary transactions that are outside bureaucratic state control and are not recorded by the Inland Revenue or in official data. This is the definition adopted for the present discussion. The present government has made the reduction of benefit fraud a top priority in the reformulation of welfare around the notion of responsibility. Although tax, National Insurance and VAT evasion form a far larger loss to the Treasury, it is the relation between undeclared working and the social security system that has received most attention among policy makers and in the media. Policies to reduce the former types of fraud have been marginal, compared to the resources aimed at detecting social security fraud (Cook, 1989).

The New Right critique of the welfare state continues to provide the framework in which debates about the connections between work, welfare and fraud have been conducted. Benefit fraud epitomises all that is wrong with a 'permissive' social security system, which penalises honesty while encouraging cheating and deceit. According to the Department of Social Security (DSS), working while claiming social security benefits accounts for 40% of all benefit fraud, with 120,000 people estimated to be working while claiming at any one time. The total value of fraudulent claims is said to range from £2 billion to £5 billion a year (DSS, 2000). For New Labour, the supposed growth of the informal economy is also proof of the failure of the previous government's policy of deregulation and these concerns were reflected in Lord Grabiner QC's report on the informal economy in 2000. Reporting that billions of pounds are lost each year to the informal economy, Grabiner recommended an 'environment of deterrence'. His proposals were adopted in the March 2000 Budget, and included more rigorous identity checks on claimants and a confidential phone line to advise people working in the 'hidden economy' how to formalise their activities. Grabiner advises publicity as a tool for changing public perceptions and a high-profile media campaign against benefit fraud has been launched (Grabiner, 2000).[1] He recommended a more stringent approach towards offenders, and in December 2000 it was announced that people convicted twice of making a false claim for social security benefits would have their benefit withdrawn for over three months. In recent years, resources directed at tackling benefit fraud have increased drastically. The powers of the Secretary of State were extended in the 1997 Social Security Administration (Fraud) Act, a Benefit Fraud Inspectorate was established with the duty of inspecting the efficiency of anti-fraud drives in local benefit offices and targets for reducing fraud have been increased annually (Sainsbury, 1998).

Such broad-brush approaches to social security fraud are unable to distinguish the extent to which the unemployed take part in undeclared work or the factors that will influence the extent of such work. Neither do they recognise the role of such practices in supplementing inadequate wages and/or welfare benefits, or the implications of such practices for the assumptions on which current social inclusion policies are based. If undeclared working is widespread among the unemployed, this contradicts claims concerning the reluctance to work that current policies of 'tough love' are designed to eradicate (Smith, 2000). Qualitative locality-based studies have offered contradictory pictures of the extent of paid informal work and the degree to which the unemployed participate. Pahl's (1984) Isle of Sheppey study found that the unemployed participated very little and remained largely excluded from formal and informal opportunities. He argued that the distribution of all forms of work was becoming unbalanced and that a polarisation between dual-earning 'work rich' and no-earner 'work poor' households was occurring. A lack of skills, work experience and relevant social contacts excluded the unemployed and, Pahl argued, have a significant bearing on class analysis since this division was becoming more significant than conventional manual/non-manual distinctions (Pahl, 1984, p 314). More recently, a study conducted by Williams of two low-income neighbourhoods revealed that out of a sample of 400, the 16% of benefit claimants among his sample performed just 4% of cash work (Williams, 2000). Of the 87 unemployed and economically inactive men interviewed by Macmillan (2003), 10 had worked undeclared at some point and only four were doing so at the time of interview (Macmillan, 2003). Jordan et al's (1992) study in Exeter, however, found that two thirds of their sample had either worked while claiming benefits or supplemented low wages with undeclared work. MacDonald's (1994) study in Cleveland reported that many of its sample of 214 had occasional recourse to 'fiddly jobs' (MacDonald, 1994) and Leonard's (1998) research in Belfast found that 49% of the unemployed men, and 27% of the economically inactive women interviewed also had some type of informal work (Leonard, 1998).

The fieldwork based on the St. Helier estate and surrounding area was largely conducted among an extended network of friends and their associates. All had a tenuous relationship with the formal labour market and of the 46 respondents, 21 were either working for cash at the time of interview or had done so at some point. For most this was intermittent and short term, although for a significant minority undeclared earnings were an important or major element of their total income. The sample was located through a 'snowball' method, which tends to promote a sample similar in its attributes. Although such a method can make no claims for representativeness, it is particularly well suited to exploring networks of distribution and exchange and their patterning in social relations. The choice of methodology, the circumstances of such work, its short duration, and the fluidity with which many move in and out of such work all hinder any reliable estimate of its size.

Although many residents of the estate were emphatic that informal activities in the area were rife, MacDonald (1994) has cautioned against taking such accounts at face value. First, the activities of the state may perpetuate the notion that undeclared work is widespread. The interviews were conducted against the backdrop of a new government determined to reform the welfare system around paid (formal) work, and one of the most intensive campaigns against benefit fraud in recent years. The political and media discourses surrounding abuse of the welfare system, feed into residents' common-sense perceptions to confirm their beliefs that abuse of the system is widespread. Also, some forms of cash work are highly visible such as the few residents who run car repair operations from their front gardens, and these are regularly used as indicative of the extent of undeclared work. Further, if a resident is known to be unemployed and at the same time seen to maintain a reasonable lifestyle, it was frequently inferred that he/she is working undeclared while receiving benefits. Lifestyle and access to consumer goods was the most common signifier used by residents to indicate the extent of benefit fraud on the estate, as illustrated by the following remark:

> "Look round here and most people do alright. They drive cars, they've got mobile phones, satellite telly, their kids are in Chelsea shirts and trainers and who pays for that? It's not the 'social'."

Although some non-employed residents do manage to maintain a lifestyle in excess of the subsistence level of state benefits, this does not necessarily indicate that they are working undeclared. The financial support of family is an important source in allowing their offspring to display the consumer items and status symbols that are a reflection of the household's standing in the community. Christmas and birthdays are vital in providing these goods, often purchased through catalogues and the repayments spread over the following year. Finally, it is the supply of cheap goods circulating through the estate's underground economy that for many, make such purchases a possibility. Another reason that MacDonald (1994) cites for treating common-sense perceptions with scepticism is that people tend to project their own experiences as being representative of the wider community. Openings to cash work are not evenly available, but require access to certain networks and sources of information. Among those who did possess these prerequisites the constancy and stability of cash work influenced their search for work, and their beliefs over the availability of such work. Debby has managed to avoid the poverty that characterises many lone parents through a succession of undeclared jobs (see also Chapter Six). Her work history has involved a progressive submersion into the underground economy and a disassociation from the formal labour market:

> "I don't know about changes in the formal jobs, because I haven't been involved in that area for such a long time. But the informal doesn't seem to change really. As soon as one business buckles under, another's starting up and it just seems to be always there."

Those who partake in undeclared work are also inclined to socialise in networks whose members also work under similar conditions, and they may assume that such activities are commonplace. Due to the broadly similar labour market prospects of most of the sample and the localised confines of the networks through which these attitudes were formulated, they were also expressed in spatial terms.

> "Round here I'd say most people were signing on and working people are fed up slogging their guts out and not being any better off than someone that was signing on. A lot of people now would just rather do their own thing because there's plenty of ways to get by."

The remainder of this chapter will examine factors based in the local economic structure, and the internal factors based in the estate's social composition that sustain demand for informal labour, goods and services. The point is not how many people or firms participate in informal working practices, but how those practices operate on the fringes of, yet inseparable from, the wider economy. This will act as a precursor to exploring why the informal economy works for some and not for others, and how the responses of people to a series of wider economic changes and employment insecurity draw upon resources based in localised forms of knowledge and relationships.

The local economy and the estate's cash economy

Performing undeclared work in order to supplement formal wages was more common than working while claiming benefits. There is a high demand for the provision of cheap services and those with certain skills are able to capitalise on this demand. The extent to which undeclared micro-businesses permeate social life on the estate and their important function in the lives of the residents, was remarked on by a member of the estate's tenants association:

> "I could get my hair cut, have my clothes cleaned and ironed, my building work done, my car fixed, or buy cheap fags or booze without ever going half a mile from my front door and without a penny going through any books. There's a fair amount of poor people, and they need to get their hair cut, repairs done and the rest just like everybody else. What with the prices and the VAT, people spring up offering to do it cheaper. It's just a matter of undercutting the big firms and you're in business."

Participating in these transactions links the household into a vast underground trading network, which transcends the boundaries of the estate to include the adjacent area and neighbouring estates and initiate reciprocal relationships between previously isolated groups of individuals. Although it is more commonly concerned with everyday services, the range of activities frequently encompasses various forms of criminality or involvement in networks that are involved in illegal activities and are avoided socially by many of the more 'respectable' households. This constitutes a major source of distinction – between the minority who provide cheap goods and services and the larger proportion of households who benefit from their activities. The trading networks that supply stolen/counterfeit goods to the area require the custom of such households and could not operate without their complicity. These exchanges are rationalised in economic terms and in terms of acquiring a lifestyle – measured by ownership of certain consumer items – comparable to others in the community (Parker et al, 1988, pp 105-8). Lifestyle participation has been largely absent from current social exclusion initiatives, which have been concerned primarily with inclusion into a highly polarised labour market. A relational and perceptual understanding of social exclusion recognises that a sense of exclusion is engendered through comparisons with groups of people sharing similar economic and social positions (Runciman, 1972). Informal trading practices therefore can play an important role in counteracting the restrictions imposed by poverty wages and/or welfare benefits, and allow participation in consumption practices that are a visible indicator of social inclusion. One lone parent working full time explained:

> "My little boy, now he's at the age where he wants Nike and Adidas and so do I and I can't afford to buy them for both of us so if anything comes up cheap I'll take it straight away."

The impulse for material improvement and the opportunity for a surreptitious purchase allows many residents to suspend their repugnance towards the small-time criminals and drug addicts who constitute the majority of these door-to-door salespeople, and enter into mutually advantageous exchanges with them. The same parent continued:

> "Credit card fraud must be one of the most common crimes around here as a matter of course for a lot of people. A card

or cheque-book comes up for £70 to £80 and most people will jump at the chance because it's like Christmas; the jeans they've been wanting to get for months, those CDs you've been meaning to buy, a trolley full of decent food. I mean it is illegal and someone's paying for it in the end and that's the issue. You do it, get caught and you pay the price but they never want to know why you had to do it, do they?"

Although the bulk of informal work is performed on an individual basis within the estate and local area, much also takes place for small businesses and contractors. While recruitment through personal networks is not new, Sassen views the increasing prominence of the informal sector in the 'global cities' as emerging in the wake of a post-industrial economy. The occupational structures of sectors displaying the fastest growth generate a large number of well-paid careers and a high volume of low-paid jobs. At the same time, a growing informal sector services the needs and consumption practices of the affluent service class: office cleaners, delivery staff, gardeners, domestic cleaners and childminders (Sassen, 1990). Gregson and Lowe's study indicates a vast expansion of waged domestic labour since the late 1980s, with Surrey accounting for 25% of this growth, and it is the affluent households in the area that sustain much of the demand for informal work (Gregson and Lowe, 1994, p 19). The advances of liberal feminism, which have allowed middle-class women to pursue their careers, are largely reliant on the low-paid labour of working-class women, as one interviewee noted:

> "You've got a lot of career women round here and while they're out chasing their careers who do you think's ironing their blouses and looking after their kids?"

The trend towards outsourcing and subcontracting results in different labour systems, which coexist in tiered layers of subcontractors. Many major contractors in contract cleaning, catering and security resemble this decentralised and fragmented profile. Running parallel to and competing with the decentralised contract-service industries hiring the formally employed 'working poor', are the small informal family-type firms often employing low-wage, undeclared labour. Research by The East London Community Organisation highlighted the impact that the contracting out of support services has had for those workers. Their study discovered wages of £3.75 an hour cleaning buses for

ISS Stagecoach, £4 an hour for cleaning offices at Canary Wharf and
£4.05 an hour cleaning hospitals with ISS Mediclean. As well as low
pay, the report found that most experienced poor working conditions,
long hours, minimal holidays, no pension rights and minimum sick
pay and maternity provision (www.unison.org.uk/pfi/doc).

During the course of the fieldwork, several interviews were
conducted with cleaners, caterers and gardeners servicing some of the
large office developments and public services in the area who are
employed and recruited under such conditions. One contract
performing routine gardening was awarded to a locally based gardening
contractor. The contract was in turn passed to a self-employed gardener
based on the estate, who had secured the deal through a friend who
was an employee of the contractor. Part of the condition of securing
the contract was that the gardener would employ his friend's nephew
who was finding it difficult to gain legitimate employment due to
criminal convictions. At the time of the fieldwork, he employed
between four and six (officially) unemployed gardeners who were
paid on a piecework basis, earning an average of £120 a week. Unskilled
and without qualifications, mainly long-term unemployed and with
biographies marked by alcohol and/or drug abuse and two with
criminal records, these gardeners view themselves as unemployable in
the formal labour market except for the most menial of work, which
they all reject. While he could be seen to be exploiting his workforce
through paying them less than he would be obliged to under NMW
legislation, the employer also insists that he is motivated by altruistic
concerns:

> "I've known most of these lads since they were this high,
> and all of them have been in trouble with the law, in and
> out of prison, drugs and what have you. They might not be
> earning a lot but at least they're getting up in the morning
> and doing something. They do give me a hard time yeah,
> but at the end of the day nobody else is going to give them
> a job. Would you if they turned up at your firm looking for
> a job?"

The expansion of the service sector combined with efforts to reregulate
certain sectors of the labour market has, to some degree, curtailed
opportunities for undeclared working. Sutton, like many other local
authorities, has encouraged the development of a town-centre 'night-
time' economy. The town centre, deserted after nightfall 10 years ago
is now replete with restaurants, wine bars, pubs, nightclubs, a bowling

alley and a multiplex cinema. Redevelopment of town centres around consumption and leisure and the increasing encroachment of large corporations in the retail, catering and leisure sectors have altered the nature of informal opportunities as jobs that may have once been performed on a casual basis, have been formalised. Bar work long provided a fruitful site for cash work, especially suitable for women with families as it could be fitted around domestic arrangements. Leanne, a 38-year-old married woman with two children, has spent much of the past 20 years working largely undeclared in local pubs and bars. As she explained, the decline of the 'local' pub, and proliferation of theme pubs has made this type of cash work increasingly rare. Traditionally a low-paid job, pub work was only economically worthwhile for Leanne when performed without tax deductions:

> "I've always done bar work and it used to be easy when we were first married and the kids were young. There were more free houses then, owned by a landlord and he'd generally be quite happy to pay you in the hand. Now they're all owned by breweries, like theme pubs and it's virtually impossible to work in there cash in hand. You have to fill out an application form, have an interview, National Insurance number and the rest. It's all very formal and by the time you've paid tax it's not worth it. Go in these pubs now, and you don't see many older women behind the bar anymore, it's just students."

The same processes that have formalised some types of casualised work have also created contexts in which such forms of work can prosper. Over recent years numerous late-night shops, fast-food outlets, mini-cab offices and wine bars have emerged in the wake of the 'night-time' economy offering new opportunities for cash work. As Leanne remarked, while the openings to work undeclared remain, in her chosen job the opportunities are limited as drinking establishments have become targeted at a young, affluent clientele:

> "Wine bars are still owned by individual people, and virtually everybody that works in wine bars is cash in hand (…) They're looking for young dolly birds in mini-skirts to pull in the punters. Cafés, independent businesses, even a corner shop. You could probably go in there and come to some agreement. He's quite happy not to have to pay any money for you if everything's alright."

Encouraging entrepreneurship and small business formation has formed a central element of local regeneration schemes (see Chapter Four). In Sutton, firms employing less than 10 employees grew by 32% between 1993 and 1996 and companies employing one to four employees grew by 7% over the same period. Seventy-two per cent of firms in the hotel and catering sectors employ less than 10 employees and in the personal services sector the figure is 81%. There also occurred a rise of 6% in the number of firms employing over 200 employees with employment growth forecasted in construction, business services, public services and in the distribution, catering and hotel sectors (LBS, 1998). The dominance in these sectors of large firms and retail outlets with high profit-making capacities on one hand, and an abundance of small enterprises on the other, bid up the price of commercial space and make the position of small businesses uncertain (Sassen, 1996, pp 65-6). Increasing business rates and rents intensify competitive tensions as small businesses, contractors and retailers come under pressure to reduce overheads. Evidence points to growing disparities in income among the self-employed and a growth of low-income self-employed people claiming in-work benefits (Eardley and Cordon, 1996). For the small employer, cash workers represent the ultimate flexible labour force allowing them to adjust their demand for labour as business conditions dictate. The small businesses in the area that I gained access to all used undeclared labour to a varying extent, and from interviews with their owners it can be seen that a 'flexible' pool of labour is a key resource in the early years of a business, as one small retailer explained[2]:

> "I wouldn't survive unless I cut corners – you've got cab offices competing with taxis, Indians competing with pizza shops, wine bars competing against pubs. You've got small shops competing against big shops and if we didn't use them [cash workers] we'd go under ... nobody can put their prices up because more and more supermarkets are getting nearer and nearer."

Within this extremely competitive environment, and generally operating with very low profit margins, most of the small employers and contractors that employ workers under informal conditions insisted that this was a necessary stage in the transition towards becoming a stable, legitimate business. Following her divorce, Angela invested £2,000 to form a domestic cleaning business. At the time of interview, she was still in her first year of business and employed between three and six cleaners. Employing them on a casual basis, she explained, allows her to adjust her workforce to weekly variations in demand. The lack of form-filling and bureaucratic obligations to which she would normally be subject is removed. This frees her time, letting her perform cleaning duties herself instead of employing another cleaner:

> "Every business starts off small and wants to dodge as many overheads as possible. It's just a way of insuring myself like if I pay cash in hand I can just rent an office, get a van, put some adverts around then pay people at the end of the week if the work's there and if it's not there's no one to find work for (...) I'll use these workers to get to the point where I can be a certified, legal business and that is what I want at the end of the day. I don't want to run my business like this permanently, it's just a way of tiding myself over until I can get to that point."

It is this unacknowledged labour force drawn from the ranks of the non-employed, the 'unemployable', the retired, students and those who move between short-term formal employment, welfare benefits and paid informal work that helps to sustain the micro-business sector. It is this sector that local authorities enthusiastically endorse in their economic regeneration strategies, while condemning the 'informal economy' and criminalising its workforce. Efforts to reregulate the labour market through programmes such as the New Deal, note Jordan and Travers, fail to recognise that those participating in the cash economy have little incentive to cooperate and that the strategies of employees and employers in the informal sector undermine attempts at regulation. The introduction of the NMW and employment legislation is likely to accelerate the trend towards self-employment, as firms attempt to gain a competitive advantage and absolve themselves from any obligation to the worker (Jordan and Travers, 1998). One of Angela's cleaners, employed on a cash-in-hand basis, told me:

> "Small businesses rely on people like us because they've got to get around paying taxes and that. They get around it like Angela: if anyone comes for a job she says to them 'you have to be self-employed and you can sort out your own tax and national-insurance'. Then it's not down to her."

Similarly, increasing regulation of the mini-cab industry and the recent trend of requiring drivers to register with local authorities in order to

receive a permit has diminished opportunities to work undeclared. Another factor has been a series of raids by DSS and Inland Revenue officials on local mini-cab offices and a joint DSS/police raid on a local cab office that was 'fencing' stolen goods. However, the advent of mobile phones has removed the need for potential mini-cab drivers wishing to work informally to obtain their work via cab offices. Start-up costs are negligible and the only requirement is a car that works and a mobile phone. These drivers are able to undercut the rates charged by firms since they do not have to obtain Hire and Reward insurance or pay either a flat rate or a percentage of their profits to the firm that supplies the work. Neither do they have to maintain the safety standards on their cars that most firms insist on these days. Several independent mini-cabs operate on the estate on this basis. Although their customer base is generally limited to friends and neighbours in their immediate locality, the level of demand for their services, particularly at weekends, makes this work financially worthwhile.

Employer and employee rationales

Informal recruitment operating through webs of locally based networks reduces costs to an employer and divides the labour market between a competitive impersonal formal one, and a set of informal labour markets rooted in personal ties and locality (Leonard, 1998). These increasingly refined divisions of labour further atomise and subdivide labour within a social class and within particular localities. The actions of both employees and employers in the undeclared sector can be understood as a reciprocal risk-reduction strategy and as a means of mitigating uncertainty in their respective economic environments. For the employer, expectations of the worker's productivity and reliability are lower, although this is offset by the advantages of employing labour under informal conditions. G.T. operates a small site clearance firm employing three undeclared workers, and a bank of casual labour that he employs occasionally. He explained the benefits of informal workers in terms of the absence of any obligation or responsibility towards his workforce outside of paying them. The fact that workers may not arrive at work is pardonable so long as an alternative source of labour is easily available, and it is acknowledged that the workers are liable to be laid off at a moment's notice.

> "They come and go and more often than not they'll get their money and that's the last I'll see of them. The good

ones I keep using. It's doing us both a favour so long as everyone knows the score. When a job's finishing and I say 'don't bother coming back tomorrow, I'll call you when something comes up' they're alright about it. See when the job's finished I don't owe them nothing and that's one less hassle that I've got to deal with."

The main source of undeclared work among males in the sample was in construction work. Because this sector is prone to labour market instability and work is often sporadic, it has traditionally lent itself well to the use of short-term labour. The irregular nature of the work means that it is often not viable to sign off the unemployment register, while the practice of keeping a week's wages in hand further encourages the worker to keep signing on until wages are received. For Patrick, a 32-year-old builder, continuing to receive Unemployment Benefit for the first couple of weeks of a new job is necessary due to uncertainty as to how long the job will last, and to prevent debts accumulating while he is waiting to receive his wages:

> "You'll phone a job and the governor will be like 'yeah mate, there's three month's work', then you'll get on site and find out there's a fortnight if you're lucky. I've been caught like that before then had to go through all the shit of signing back on again so now I wait and see – if the job's going to last less than a month I won't bother signing off."

Twenty-seven-year-old Mark (see also Chapters Five and Six) has worked in various building jobs – legal and informal – since leaving school. Despite professing to want to 'go straight', his efforts are thwarted by the actions of employers who prefer to employ their labourers undeclared:

> "I wanted to go legal but my governor was like 'hmm if I take you on the cards I've got to pay you more, give you holidays, bank holidays' and he doesn't want to do that does he? I remember that job in Balham. I was supposed to be like double, double legal. I started and I thought this was the one where I was going to get it sorted and he went 'no mate, I don't want to do it, I'll pay you cash'."

For cash workers, undeclared work and welfare benefits can serve as an insurance against insecurity in the formal labour market. Frequently, informal employees are working in similar jobs for similar rates of pay to the formally employed working poor. Low wages among the latter are subsidised through in-work benefits while among the former group, low wages are supplemented through Unemployment Benefit and Income Support (Smith and Macnicol, 2001). Little distinction is made between the two spheres as they represent different means to the same end. Cash work is often preferable, because of low wages, insecurity and the labour relationships at the bottom of the formal labour market and the way that these interact with the social security system. Howe notes that there is no reduction in the work ethic but what is being reassessed is the belief that households can only be sustained through legitimate employment (Howe, 1990, p 68). As argued in Chapter Five, a reassessment of available economic opportunities often occurred during a period of transition in the respondent's lifecycles. Julie, a 28-year-old lone parent of two children, moved onto the estate following her divorce (see Chapter Six). The change in status and lifestyle that this involved was accompanied by a period of adjustment between her previous aspirations and her objective location. She jettisoned conventional routes to economic security and followed more locally available routes offering a more feasible and readily accessible means of attaining a reasonable lifestyle. Remaining 'respectable' requires distance from the social relationships that provide avenues to material and informational support.

> "If I contrast living on the estate to before, we weren't on a council estate and I wanted my own home, the nice car, good job. You know that the people aren't any nicer than people round here but on the outside, what they've got and what you're aspiring to is a normal way of life. On an estate the homes aren't yours and nobody's got any regard for their surroundings. You get a few people that make the best of their situation and try to maintain their houses and gardens and live a straight life but they live in their own little world. People don't mix with them but if you're young and especially if you're young and on your own with kids you want to mix with people, and everybody's up to something and it's so common it changes your outlook. I know lots of people now and can usually find something if I need it. Saying that, I've done things I'd never have dreamt

of when I was married, so I'd say that areas can change your outlook."

Crucially, the tactics and knowledge that allow individuals to circumvent formal institutions and to construct lives either outside of or on the margins of formal employment, are based in a generational consciousness among those who have known little different. The belief that the world of work offers the route to a better life has been eroded through years of experience to the contrary. As one 28-year-old discussing the relative advantages of undeclared labouring and the realities that justify it, put it:

"The labouring I've been doing is 35 quid a day, nine till six. It's not big money and it's bloody hard work, but that's not much less than they're paying in the Job Centre these days and those blokes are working and still struggling (...) I wouldn't knock them for doing it because they're just trying to do something with their lives but I cannot see the point because for me, the idea of working is to give you a better life but if it's not going to do that then why bother?"

As important as economic aspects in influencing labour market behaviour among those who perform undeclared work, is the greater degree of security and autonomy offered by cash work compared to low-wage work in the formal economy. These considerations represent an important and often neglected aspect of social exclusion, since economic insecurity represents a major impediment to the sense of control over the quality and constancy of one's environment (Doyal and Gough, 1991, pp 210-11). As state surveillance for people to remain in formal work at the threat of forfeiting access to the benefit system gathers pace, the lack of control over working lives is heightened. Undeclared work underpinned by the benefit system is an increasingly reasonable option in securing a regular income and, vitally from the respondent's viewpoint, gives the freedom to leave jobs that are often too menial to perform for sustained periods of time. Several respondents working undeclared, often for long and/or unsociable hours in physically taxing work and for little remuneration, still considered themselves at an advantage to those employed in legitimate jobs. Colin (see also Chapter Eight), a 26-year-old working as a driver's mate explained:

"I have this feeling of freedom and that's why I keep doing this. Even though I hate the work you're free just to go 'I don't want to do it no more – I'm not going in' but people I talk to that have got proper jobs, it seems like they have to do them because they need the money and it's a real downer and seeing as you spend that much time at work I'm not prepared to feel that down really."

Many accounts of the informal sector emphasise the social relations in which such work is located. Informal work is based not on contractual agreements, but on obligatory relationships between employer and worker. The degree of mutual trust necessary for such relationships derives from shared backgrounds and localised understandings. As such, the relations surrounding informal employment are viewed as representing a return to pre-modern social relationships, and contrasted with the impersonal cash-nexus characteristic of employment relationships under modern capitalism (Roberts, 1994). Mutual trust produced through networks of personal relations is an important element, especially during recruitment to informal jobs. Long-standing associations grounded in locality, school, friendships and/or kinship mean that communication channels are based on what Suttles terms a 'personalistic social order'. This assumes a great deal of shared knowledge and individuals are judged, not according to public standards of morality but by personal loyalties and against an individual's known history (Suttles, 1968, pp 186-7). Such sources of information are ideally suited for testifying to the suitability of both worker and employer in the absence of any formal regulation, and the circumstances in which the work is performed.

However, the benefits of informal employment were often described as the lack of any obligations on behalf of both parties. For the worker, it is the lack of commitment towards the employer that increases independence, making the work relatively attractive, as Colin implies. The advantages of informal employment were frequently described in negative terms – as an absence of mutual obligations or responsibility with the only tacit agreement between worker and employer being that should any dispute or conflict arise, the authorities will not become involved. Indeed, it is within the networks that provide access to work that disputes are mediated and the likelihood of any deception between worker and employer reduced. A discernible pattern emerged, where the lowest grades of informal workers viewed a lack of any commitment either to the work or to the employer, and the control that this allows over how to spend one's day, as positively beneficial. One interviewee employed as a delivery driver/cleaner for a takeaway remarked:

> "You don't mind blowing them out and they can't say anything. It's like a mutual thing where they might treat you badly because you've got nowhere to turn to if they do, but you can be treating them as badly because they're employing you without any acknowledgement of it and they're not paying tax or your stamp and it's underhanded on both parts (…) In a proper job where you had colleagues and people relying on you and you end up getting involved with it and taking it home with you, it's quite a different scenario altogether."

In practical terms, the liberty to leave these jobs is rarely exercised. Outside of a minority that did have access to multiple sources of income, the majority retained their mostly short-term and sporadic jobs for as long as possible and took whatever opportunity arose. Still, the perception that they maintain the capacity to quit jobs when they see fit, is a significant element in shaping attitudes to work in the formal and informal economies despite the lack of congruence with their objective practices. Most have adapted to life on benefits or in employment that affords a lifestyle almost commensurate with that level. Subsequently, this provides for necessities and becomes the criterion anything above which is considered a bonus. As Sarah, one of Angela's cash-in-hand cleaners, remarked:

> "It's easier to have everything paid for and not to have to worry if you get sick or anything happens. It's all taken care of and at least you've still got a roof over your head and the money for the shopping … most people have learnt to survive in that way because they've been on Income Support for a long time. I can actually survive just on Income Support if I have to. I don't know how but I can."

Dean's research among those engaged in petty social security fraud indicated that while economic and materialist considerations featured prominently, the erosion of a sense of social citizenship and perceptions of injustice made many respondents more accepting of 'justified disobedience' (Dean and Melrose, 1996). Similarly, many vindicated their behaviour by pointing to the increasing inequality of society over previous decades, and the incomprehension to the daily realities of poor lives expressed by well-paid politicians:

> "Its easy to talk about benefit fraud when you're on 50 grand a year, because you're never going to face a situation where working for 30 quid a day cash plus your benefits is the best you can get (...) there's such a gap between doing alright and not doing alright, and unless the government do something about it, this fraud crackdown won't make an ounce of difference."

For cash workers, the constancy of such work increases in proportion to their immersion in the networks that supply such work. This means that it is constructed as more secure than formal opportunities in terms of minimising the risk of experiencing an unacceptable decline in living standards. Formal employment is often viewed as positively disadvantageous, since it involves a loss of personal autonomy and locks one into rigid structures that are subject to close surveillance by the state. Surviving on one's wits in the underground economy is viewed as preferable to the monotony of poorly paid formal work, and most viewed themselves as enterprising and resourceful risk-takers constantly on the lookout for further opportunities. However, beneath these sentiments, a marked ambivalence towards their situation was apparent as most were aware that they are exchanging what they consider as social inclusion – in terms of lifestyle – with labour market exclusion. This implies that various dimensions of exclusion exist among different networks of shared interests and beliefs and that social inclusion, on whatever basis it is defined, involves a trade-off between those dimensions. Andrew, a 33-year-old casual labourer remarked that his aspirations to gain legitimate work conflicted with his responsibility to provide for his partner and two children. The progressive detachment from the formal labour market that this has entailed has been accompanied by increasing anxiety that he will be permanently expelled from mainstream society through his exclusion from the formal labour market:

> "It's hard because I've been doing alright for a long time – bits of work here and there, labouring or whatever on top of the dole and Housing Benefit. That gives us not a bad income if you compare it to what they're paying people these days (...) this sort of life's alright when you're in your twenties and your kids are young, but by the time

you get to your thirties, you're starting to look at those nine to fivers and thinking I'd better get myself sorted out."

None are oblivious to dominant discourses surrounding unemployment and welfare dependency. The autonomy that they attribute to themselves co-exists with trepidation that dead-end jobs, either undeclared or legitimate, are their likely lot. This raises the important question over whether an individual who 'voluntarily' withdraws from the labour market is socially excluded. Certainly, the scope of 'voluntary' decisions is limited by structural factors and expressed through varied collective adaptions to those factors. Their ability to take up entry-level, formal employment is undermined by competing obligations to one's dependants, the fall in accustomed living standards that this would involve and the loss of relative material security and stability that their social networks yield. These tendencies are intensified through policies to expand the supply of subsidised, low-wage labour. As Debby remarked:

> "There's nowhere to go, it's just four pound an hour cash in your hand at the end of the week and they're usually crap jobs (...) and it gets frightening to let that go in the end. I mean if they phoned me up and said get a job, what would I be able to get a job as? I don't want a mundane job because I'd be walking out every few weeks and having to try and get money out of them again and the wages are so poor that we wouldn't be left with as much."

Social capital and the reproduction of informal working patterns

The main determinant of whether an individual had access to informal work was their social relations, which have a significant bearing in understanding how different groups of people become disassociated from formal work and the strategies that emerge in response. Although the concept of 'strategy' raises problems such as the degree of rational calculation that the term implies, it also avoids the agency–structure dichotomy through revealing how structural conditions provide the circumstances for particular strategies (Crow, 1989). Swidler (1986) has argued that the preoccupation with identifying distinctive cultural values among the poor fails to address class variations in culture and the extent to which culture organises patterns of action. The focus on cultural values has led to a neglect of other relevant phenomena such as culturally shaped skills, styles and practices. The causal significance of culture, she argues, is not in designating the ends of action, but in providing the elements that are used to construct lines of action. "Action is not determined by one's values. Rather action and values are organized to take advantage of cultural competencies" (Swidler, 1986, p 279).

Economic ties and the necessity of material survival provide a basis for reciprocity among network members through increasing the circulation of 'social capital', defined by Coleman (1990, p 314) as "the aggregation of knowledge and information stemming from sources other than formal education and training, in providing access to scarce resources". The benefits that accrue from those social relationships are the foundations of the group's solidarity, through encouraging mutual recognition and knowledge:

> Exchange transforms the things exchanged into signs of recognition and, through the mutual recognition and the recognition of group membership, which it implies, reproduces the group. (Bourdieu, 1986, p 250)

The relationships that surround undeclared working are important in understanding how collective responses to social exclusion are generated and reproduced. Morris' (1994) study in Hartlepool found that the major source of informal information was received from old friends, close relatives and acquaintances. This is against Granovetter's (1973) argument that it is the wider and more distant social ties that are vital in finding work, by increasing potential sources of information. The reason strong ties are vital, argues Morris, is that when competition for jobs is high, information is channelled on a preferential basis (Morris, 1995). Nevertheless, different degrees of interaction exist within different parts of a network, ranging from the dense ties of the 'effective network' to the weaker ties of the 'extended network'. It is the latter ties that are vital in finding and diversifying income opportunities, argues Granovetter (1973, pp 1370-1):

> not only in ego's manipulation of networks, but also in that they are the channels through which ideas, influences, or information socially distant may reach him. The fewer indirect contacts one has, the more encapsulated he will be in terms of knowledge beyond his friend-ship circle: thus, bridging weak ties (and the consequent indirect contacts) are important in both ways.

Those opportunities may then be distributed according to the preferential criteria suggested by Morris. Under conditions of insecurity, loose ties have an important adaptive value since they provide multiple sources of information, allowing for new strategies to emerge in response to the problems that unpredictable environments pose (Staber, 2001). The maintenance and preservation of previous relationships and contacts are vital in connecting members of different networks, initiating the potential for new channels of exchange and information to emerge. The individuals who provide those connections are pivotal and stand in high status within their own 'effective' network due to this fact. Their position as 'gatekeepers' ensure that those outside the network remain unaware of such opportunities, as Fukuyama (1997, p 70) notes: "Within the patronage network, information passes readily, but its outer boundaries constitute a membrane through which, information passes much less readily."

The temporal rhythms of cash work and other informal opportunities serve as a stimulus to preserve and utilise previous relationships. Contacts established in previous employment, often short-term jobs where immediate workmates are themselves part of the same casual and marginalised labour market, are a useful source of knowledge relating to future jobs. Central to Morris' study was whether there were distinct work histories comprising sporadic employment and recurrent spells of unemployment. Her data indicated that while there was an age and skills dimension to broken employment, it was closely related to the individuals' social relations. By their second job, informal recruitment was the main method of access to jobs for 32% of her sample. Because of the short-term jobs yielded through informal methods, it is the contacts that emerge around casual work that perpetuate fractured work histories (Morris, 1995, p 70). Through linking individuals to similarly placed networks in terms of labour market location and engaged in similar forms of economic activity, informal working patterns are reproduced. Sarah, the cleaner introduced earlier, observed:

> "It's easy to get really just by asking about. If you've got a lot of friends either working cash-in-hand jobs or know a wide circle of people then you'll always find something. It helps if you've got friends that are working, depending on what kind of jobs they're doing, like if you're a bloke and a lot of your friends are builders, say, then you're going to find it easier than if they are civil servants or teachers."

The ability to manipulate previous contacts established in formal and informal labour markets, and a willingness to move between these spheres as and when opportunities arise, is essential to securing a living in the absence of regular employment. Several respondents indicated the close interrelationship and fluidity between these areas of economic activity as the contacts and information established in one sphere enhance opportunities in another. For Steve (see also Chapters Five and Eight), previous employment in a timber yard provided an outlet for his cannabis dealing over the counter to incoming tradespeople as well as various 'fiddles' that the trade-counter staff engaged in with their customers. These exchanges established and affirmed relationships that would later become an important source for cash work once the timber yard job ended.

> "Through my time at the timber yard I got to know loads
> of builders and I used to sell a lot of draw on sites so I got
> to know loads of them and they've been regular customers
> for years now. If they need a hand they'll just call my mobile
> and say 'what are you doing next week?'."

Informal work relationships particularly of the unskilled, sub-contracting type are inherently exploitative. The potential for exploiting informal workers by paying them less and avoiding the overheads and employment rules that regulate formal work relations, is what makes them a useful resource for small employers. The sociability on which these relationships are based means that they are contrasted sharply to the coercive and instrumental attitudes that are perceived to predominate in the formal economy. These relationships provide a common basis upon which material cooperation operates, through concealing and stabilising otherwise impersonal commercial transactions (Bourdieu, 1985, p 186). The strength of the friendship ties that provide avenues into informal work is often exaggerated or romanticised to disguise the material dependence that is often an intrinsic element of those relationships. Gary is a 29-year-old unemployed crane operator, who had been labouring for an acquaintance from school while waiting for his next job to start:

> "My mate Tom who I've been working for, well we go
> back years (...) if he needs me for a few days it's doing us
> both a favour so we don't owe each other nothing but I'll
> graft for him because he's a mate. Come the end of the
> week, we'll go for a beer and he'll listen out for any other

work and I'll do the same (...) now the 40 quid a day's not
the point is it? It's the old you scratch my back and I'll
scratch yours thing. Work on site for a firm and it's like you
will scratch our back or you can piss off down the road
because there's plenty that will if you won't."

The personal relationships on which these opportunities are based
allow the employer to build a tried and tested bank of labour, and give
a cumulative advantage to those in certain networks while excluding
others. Anecdotes of benefit inspectors' raids on building sites and of
unscrupulous employers who fail to pay their workers wages, tie casual
workers to known and trusted employees who can offer relatively
'safe' employment. A more recent impetus in guaranteeing a loyal and
submissive labour force has been the influx of legal and illegal
immigrants willing to work harder, for longer hours and for less pay
than their native counterparts. This results in a closed and non-
competitive informal labour market where the employer, not the
market, sets rates of pay. Regularity of employment is determined
more by favouritism and nepotistic practices than by performance.
Employers' ranking is fluid and provides the employer with a potent
source of labour control, as workers vie to enter the employers' favoured
circle of regular employees. The reality of the employee's marginal
labour market location is submerged beneath the autonomy that they
attribute to themselves, yet confirmed through the sycophantic attitudes
that they display towards their employers. Colin explained how these
methods operate – resulting in a 'core' and 'periphery' workforce akin
to developments said to be transforming the formal labour market:

"G.T.'s got his regular crew that's three or four blokes he'll
give work to near enough full time. Then when he needs
extra, there's about five blokes like me that he'll call. He
knows we're alright because it's one of the regulars that
put us onto him, and that's how it works with G.T. If you're
in you're in, but if he don't like you, you're down the road."

This chapter has outlined some of the factors that sustain demand for
informal labour and services within the context of local economic
conditions and discussed employer and employee rationales for
participating in this sort of work. The important role of social
relationships in supplying access to informal resources and the shared
ideologies and lifestyles that underpin those relationships, have notable
consequences in shaping patterns of sociability and in influencing

perceptions of social exclusion. Informal practices provide an important supplement to welfare benefits or low wages for some but also constitute a further dimension of division in terms of sociability, lifestyle and consumption practices. The case studies in the next chapter allow these issues to be explored in greater depth, through delineating the 'cultural competencies' and lifestyles that emerge outside of formal institutions. Regardless of their employment status, few residents were isolated from support networks, but the structure and forms of support differ among different networks defined by their labour market location. The distinctions that they produce are underpinned by the perceptions of each other held by different groups and shape community-based patterns of exclusion and social divisions on the estate. These are the subjects of the next chapter.

Notes

[1] In 2000, £6.2 million was spent on a media campaign to combat benefit fraud. This included a television advertising campaign to persuade the public to inform on people committing benefit fraud. Criticism from opposition MPs and the government's own evaluation concluded that the campaign actually made many people realise that benefit fraud was easier to commit than they had previously believed (*The Independent*, 2001).

[2] This included a small grocery shop, a domestic cleaning firm, a removals/delivery operation, a building contractor and the self-employed gardener previously mentioned.

EIGHT

Labour markets, exclusion and social capital[1]

Chapter Seven revealed how the chances to augment income and consumption through informal activities are hierarchically structured through the employment relationships and the social relations that surround such work. The benefits that flow from these closed labour markets accrue over time to the same groups of people, and lead to the capture of sets of opportunity through the network's role as an agency of information and/or an agency of influence (Grieco, 1987). The salience of this aspect of stratification is that they provide avenues to resources, which allow access to forms of consumption and participation in lifestyles that represent distinct styles of life. Lifestyle was a major determinant in shaping residents' perceptions of their own and their households' status in relation to their neighbours and those around them. Such distinctions are important in understanding intra-class patterns of exclusion, since they function as a visible means of communicating social categories and of making and maintaining social relationships (Douglas and Isherwood, 1979, pp 60-1). They also fracture social relationships through their role in denoting a sense of difference between groups and in promoting division through the allocation of socially designated notions of failure. As discussed, the display of status symbols is just as important a signifier of group membership within low-income communities as among elite groups. Status symbols provide the visible markers that allow distance from the impoverished 'failures' that share the same social space, and evidence that one is able to prosper outside of, or on the margins of, formal employment. Darren remarked:

> "You've got a lot of people round here with nice cars, and that's because people like to give the impression that they've got money and they haven't really, they've got a motor on finance that's costing them £70 a week, and they're borrowing money off their mum till the giro or wages come."

Working-class access to spheres of consumption has always been tenuous and experienced alongside the chronic threat of poverty and dependency, encouraging sectionalism and social closure (Mann, 1991). This can occur through institutions such as trades unions erecting barriers to entry and restricting the benefits of membership to insiders, or through processes of informal group affiliation. As Parkin (1979, p 89) notes, modes of closure can occur both between and within social classes. Differences in lifestyle provide a useful tool for analysing how cleavages between groups of people sharing similar socioeconomic characteristics are generated and reproduced, and the processes through which social closure occurs and resources monopolised.[2] The emphasis in this chapter is not on how patterns of social exclusion and disadvantage emerge as an outcome of socioeconomic changes or of political priorities, but rather on the exclusionary strategies employed by one section of a community against another. Those excluded from informal opportunities are detached from the localised forms of knowledge through which particular strategies and paths of action can be followed. This is not to imply any clear segregation between groups of people and any distinction is an analytical one. In reality spatial proximity, similarities in demographic and socioeconomic characteristics and associations between people sharing common histories meant that networks did overlap, and there was no clear segregation in patterns of association, only tendencies. However, certain factors both internal to the network and in the collective perceptions that different groups of people pursuing distinct strategies in respect of work and welfare held towards each other, played an important role in the preferential distribution of opportunities.

In Stack's classic study among a poor black community, *All our kin*, reciprocal exchange relationships "pervade the whole social-economic life of participants" and constituted a "profoundly creative adaption to poverty" in the absence of surplus scarce resources, through providing a constant circulation of goods within a community (Stack, 1974, pp 38-44). Analysing patterns of exchange through a network approach may redress the classification of low-income communities as 'disorganised' through revealing the cohesive aspects of exchange networks. It is inherent to participant observation that the cohesive aspects of exchange relationships are emphasised, due to the focus on small-scale patterns of interaction. Nevertheless, an account of group cohesion is not inconsistent with overall community fragmentation although the extent of such divisions may not be apparent if not marked by ethnic, cultural or other visible features (Granovetter, 1973). Reciprocal relations constitute a major dimension of division, since it is within localised networks that information and resources are transmitted and exchanged and resources harnessed and distributed, according to exclusionary criteria. Patterns of exchange and information divide communities internally between groups loosely sharing similar lifestyles, and pursuing similar strategies in relation to work and welfare.

Outside of household-based relationships, social relations on the estate are based largely around peer group, gender and employment status. Homogeneity in patterns of association is reinforced through institutional arrangements such as education, recreation, leisure activities and a lack of geographical and social mobility (Suttles, 1968, pp 67-8). Approximately half of the respondents on the estate had grown up in the surrounding vicinity and attended local schools. Some of the friendships dated back to middle school, although more commonly they derived from adolescence. Many had moved onto the estate after being housed there by the local authority or as a result of cohabitation or marriage, and experienced their major lifecycle transitions at similar ages and in similar sets of conditions. This pattern of analogous experiences fosters similar world views and a body of shared 'collective knowledge'. This encourages the development of enduring 'strong ties' since it is length of association, argues Collins (1992, p 199), that "produce(s) the moral solidarity of the group which might also be called its ideological construction (or distortion) of reality". Through case studies of three individuals, the next section explores how these processes translate into distinctive economic strategies that draw on these cultural resources. Through the provision of services to the surrounding community, their activities play an important function in boosting the consumption levels of low-income areas. At the same time, such activities are also significant in generating material and ideological divisions between different groups.

The issues presented have notable policy consequences given the current welfare-to-work emphasis in reducing social exclusion. The case studies do not represent the experiences of the majority of residents on the estate. However, it is clear that a significant minority of people have developed, quite successfully, their own solutions to social exclusion. The assumptions on which current policy towards worklessness is based needs to recognise that both the economic and the more intangible incentives of formal work – job security, status, the capacity for self-control and creative enterprise – need to be significantly enhanced. Otherwise, the 'socially excluded' will have little incentive to enter and remain in jobs in the formal economy, when lengthy apprenticeships spent refining their skills in the cash economy have taught them alternative, and more dependable, routes to social inclusion.

Surviving in the cash economy: three case studies

At the time of fieldwork, Steve was 31 years old and unemployed. He lives on the estate with his girlfriend who was pregnant with his child and her six-year-old daughter from a previous relationship. After leaving school unqualified he worked in a variety of short-term jobs before starting a City and Guilds course in carpentry that he failed to complete. Since then he has worked in several legitimate jobs between spells of unemployment, which have become more protracted over time as he has developed an extensive network of contacts through which alternative sources of income can be earned. Many of these contacts date back to his childhood or from high school, these early associations later proving instrumental in providing income opportunities. By the age of 14, Steve was a habitual truant and along with a group of school friends engaged in petty crime besides doing the odd day's work labouring when the opportunity arose.

> "All my mates from middle school went up to the same high school and most of us lived near each other so we hung around together after school too, so school was no different from after school."

Steve was socialised into the junior end of the underground economy of small-scale crime. This invariably involves little financial return, as the impetus for a quick return means that stolen goods are usually sold or traded with local middlemen who have outlets for such goods, and who make the real profits from youthful crime. The long-term outcome of this short-term burst of criminal activity was to provide contacts into further forms of economic activity, which transcended the previously localised confines of his network. Occasionally, goods were exchanged for cannabis, which he sold locally, providing him with an income ever since. At the time of interview, he supplemented his erratic income from assorted driving and labouring jobs through weighing and delivering marijuana to local dealers. The risk of detection is minimised through a complex division of labour in the supply chain. Length and intensity of association generates the loyalty and conformity to established standards of behaviour on which such an operation is based although as he recognises, these relationships are always based on power and overshadowed by the implicit threat of repercussions:

> "Somebody picks it up, drops it off at my place and I weigh
> it up, and drop it round to a few people who knock it out
> for him. I don't have to collect any money, somebody else
> does that, I just deliver it. I've known the bloke since I was
> about 15 and he trusts me, well it's not just trust, he's a
> mate but you wouldn't want to get on the wrong side of
> him."

Status based on an individual's knowledge and competence of a
particular area constitutes a further factor in the allocation of economic
opportunities. Darren is 29 years old and lives on the estate with his
partner and their three-year-old daughter. He was introduced to me
through Steve, the two having known each other since high school.
His undeclared business repairing and selling second-hand cars
represents the successful, but small end of working informally since
his income is sufficiently stable that he receives no state benefits. This
marks an important distinction between Darren and the lower echelons
of the informal labour force whose members work and receive benefits,
thus exposing themselves to a higher risk of discovery from the
authorities.

> "I can make enough so I don't need the 'social'. I'm still
> taking a risk but not as big a risk as them. Most of them are
> not earning much so they need to stay on getting their
> rent paid and the rest because they can only make 20 quid
> a day on top of that. But for me the risk's less because
> where's the proof? Everything's cash, I don't keep records
> and I haven't got a bank account. My brother opened an
> account for me in his name, so no one's any of the wiser."

Like Steve, the ties and identities established in adolescent youth culture
would later prove vital in establishing a niche for Darren in the
unregulated sector of the economy. Hobbes (1988, pp 135-6) notes
that, for many, the transition to adulthood often involves reaffirming
identities established in teenage years, although this is no longer
'magical' but grounded in problems that emerge from their labour
market position. Darren's employment history is inseparable from his
long-standing passion for cars and his membership in the 'boy-racer/
casual' subcultures of the 1980s and early 1990s. Despite localised
variations and periodic shifts in outward style they have long been the
dominant youth style on the estates of South London, retaining the
'focal concerns' of expensive designer/sports clothes, the latest black

American soul/R&B music and the fetishisation of the car as the ultimate status symbol.[3] He has never attended a formal course in car mechanics, learning his trade as a boy by hanging about on the margins of older groups of car enthusiasts.

> "I've always been into cars since I was a kid and there was always blokes fixing up cars. There were blocks of these lock-ups and I used to hang about. The other kids'd be playing football, and I was their errand boy and run down the shops for them or clean the cars and I'd just hang about and ask questions. They used to like me, so they started showing me how to do things, what a carburettor did, and how an engine worked."

Later, the knowledge and contacts that he acquired in these networks of shared interests provided him with various income options ranging from the illegal, through to the less risky but more secure business that he currently runs. His business is almost entirely centred on the local area. He rents two lock-up garages and in addition rents a few front gardens from local residents where he stores and repairs cars. His customers are mainly local residents, their friends, families and mini-cab drivers. Most of his cars are sold through word of mouth, with the remainder parked on a local main road and the price and a mobile phone number pasted in the window

> "Working with cars was natural, I didn't really know much except cars (...) I've got a lot of mates in the car trade, a few doing what I'm doing, some who work in the parts industry, I know a lot of cabbies because I do a lot of work for them. A good mate of mine works at the car auctions and a lot of that goes back about 10 years when we were all getting our first cars and we worked together."

The spin-off benefits of his associations are distributed principally to kin and friends. Exchange relationships with older relatives and residents are encouraged through spatial proximity and link them into these overlapping networks of reciprocal obligation. Darren aims at the local market and sells his cars for between £500 and £1,000. He attributes the success of his business to his close knowledge of the local market, and the manner in which to conduct business given the financial constraints that surround those relationships:

"I'd say most of the families of our age are sort of on the edge and financially there's not a lot behind most of them, if they weren't I wouldn't be knocking out so many cheap cars. If they need a big repair I'll tell them how much it'll cost, then they might ask to pay over a month or two."

Darren derives a regular and relatively good income through providing his services cheaply, and in ways that make such expenditure feasible for many residents who would be unable to afford the services of a local garage. His workload has grown through the information channels that circulate information within the area, and it is within those channels that the relationship between Darren and his customer is regulated. These understandings result from the 'practical sense' that operates on the basis of shared normative assumptions, and understandings about common interests that can be advanced through social exchanges (Bourdieu, 1985, pp 80-1). Because they belong to this sphere, exchange relationships are a potent means of reproducing social ties and of excluding others from the benefits of such ties, especially should one renege on those understandings. Cornuel and Duriez (1985, p 190) note that:

> Within this framework black activities are perfectly understood but denunciation is reserved exclusively for those who do not play the game – 'the stranger', the person who attempts to achieve as much as he can from services rendered and whose isolation makes it impossible to make demands in return.

The maintenance of Darren's enterprise depends on the continuation of a good reputation, and on offering his services on terms attuned to the economic lives of his customers. Informal arrangements such as those between Darren and his customers, which allow payment to be spread or deferred, play an important function in the lives of the unemployed and working poor. With limited resources and little savings, they require frequent recourse to these neighbourhood-based enterprises through which cheap goods and services can be acquired. Benefiting from these services requires a guarantee that one can be relied upon to uphold one's side of an agreement, and can be quickly curtailed should anybody revoke the arrangement.

"I get dole-heads bringing their cars in, they're always right shit heaps, no MOT, nothing. And they'll pay half and say, 'can we pay you the rest when the giro comes?'. If I know them I'll usually say, 'go on then', and if they knock me that's the last time but it don't happen much (...) dole-heads always need to borrow something, usually money, and if they knocked me that'd be the last time they'd get credit from anyone else round here."

Colin is the partner of Tina and is 26 years old with a history of various unskilled manual jobs, unemployment and a series of employment training schemes. He was introduced through Steve, and the two have been good friends since he went out with Steve's sister some years ago. At the time of interview he was economically inactive after sustaining injuries in a car accident, although he has occasional cash work doing removals/house clearance and also works for G.T. builders when needed. Being recruited through locally based relationships has placed him within the core of G.T.'s most regular workers. As discussed in Chapter Seven, these practices result in highly segmented and tiered labour markets. These processes also act as a form of closure through restricting access to informal openings and restraining competition among members, thereby serving to replicate informal working patterns. For the worker, the benefits of such relationships accumulate over time and form an important element in shaping attitudes and orientations to work.

"I got it through Steve who I've known for years since I was going out with his sister, and we still go out for a beer and a game of snooker most weeks. His brother's going out with G.T.'s sister and he's given Steve a bit of work in the past so he put in a word for me and he gave Steve his number and told me to call him. I turned up over Docklands and did a few weeks labouring and this was about five years ago, and since then he'll always call me when he needs the hands."

He supplements his income from the removals job by selling any furniture of reasonable quality to second-hand furniture shops. Flexibility and opportunism are the key 'human capital' factors required in order to maximise a living from various and irregular flows of income. He also has an additional income through collecting household items and bric-a-brac, which he sells at car boot sales:

> "I do some work for a removals come delivery 'man with a van'-type set up (...) when we do a house clear he'll take the best stuff, and I'll take what's left. It's usually old tat but I'll take anything that I can sell and after about three house-clears we've got enough stuff to do a boot sale and that makes about £50 to £70 a go."

His plan is to set up as a self-employed trader through investing the profit he makes from the car-boot sales. The ability to utilise potential openings largely depends on what Swidler (1986) terms one's 'cultural competencies'. Success, she points out, cannot be pursued where the established skills, styles and informal knowledge are alien. Instead, one does better following lines of action for which one has the appropriate cultural equipment. These skills include not only styles of dress and speech, but "an image of the world in which one is trying to act, a sense that one can read reasonably accurately how one is doing" (Swidler, 1986, p 275). The small-scale entrepreneurs like Darren who manages to thrive outside of the system are respected, and the seemingly independent lifestyles that their work allows is aspired to:

> "I'm going to get into the boot sales on a regular basis like every Saturday and Sunday. I do the hospital on Sundays and it's packed, like some blokes are pulling in over a hundred pounds. When I get sorted out I'm going to the auctions and buy a load of stuff, get a few hundred pounds behind me first, which is where I'm aiming at the moment, then build it up. Before you know where you are you've got a regular business and that's a fact. I mean, that's reality, there's people making a living from boot sales I tell you."

Social divisions on the estate are maintained through lifestyle differences and form a parameter within which exchange relationships operate. These are reinforced through access to the shared patterns of consumption that provide routes into informal work, and which further segregate the poorest sections of the community. Komter's (1990) research suggests a strong relationship between the giving and the receiving of aid, with those giving most also the greatest recipients. Given the tendency for reciprocal relations to operate on the basis of balanced reciprocity, she argues that the sociological and psychological rules of reciprocity tend to disadvantage those who are always in the weakest social position (Komter, 1990). The ability to circulate in networks within which informal opportunities are found, requires a reasonable level of consumption and duplicate localised patterns of exclusion. This bears directly on Rowntree's notion of 'secondary poverty' since earning often requires wide-flung sources of information, which can only be reached through shared consumption (Douglas and Isherwood, 1979, p 91).

Those discussed in this and the previous chapter do not represent the majority of the (formally) workless, whose isolation from these networks restricts their chances of boosting their income or levels of consumption. A marked feature of the networks discussed here is a high proportion of employed friends, either formally or informally, and a near absence of the (genuinely) unemployed, except in contexts where they play an economic function. As Colin observed, it is the inability of the unemployed to participate in forms of sociability, which excludes them from alternative openings:

> "Most of my friends are working, a few are in and out of different things (...) I know some that are not working but they're mostly just people I know from the area. It'd be hard wouldn't it, like, when we go out you're looking at 20 quid a round, and if you're on the dole you're not going to blow half your giro on a round of beers are you?"

When seen from the insider's view, the ways in which individuals and households combine various sources of income with benefits do not provide evidence of an economically and socially excluded group, isolated from the mainstream institutions of society. Rather, the responses of this sample appear more as a response to avoid social exclusion as understood by those for whom such a status remains an ever-present possibility. Social exclusion among this group is understood as comprising not only exclusion from work, but from the networks that provide access to work and from the consumer symbols that denote inclusion in the activities of the wider society. It is the genuinely unemployed and economically inactive who are designated as excluded. They are often criticised through their rejection of the work ethic, as witnessed in their failure to generate their own opportunities in the cash economy. Lone parent Debby (see also Chapters Six and Seven) was especially critical, arguing that morality should be situationally shaped and that primary responsibility should be to one's dependants:

> "You can tell the real people on Income Support because they're really raggedy and scruffy, blankets for curtains and

all that. There's a few families like that on every street, and that's really living on the 'social'. I don't know why they don't work, well they're usually impaired in some way so maybe they're not in the market for work (...) maybe they don't believe in it, which is a bad attitude if you've got kids. If I still lived with my parents and did cash-in-hand work, it'd be unthinkable for me to sign on as well but now it's different, I've got a kid to bring up."

Castigated for their inability or reluctance to participate in the cash economy, the unemployed and economically inactive remain outside of the lifestyles and networks that could provide routes to alternative sources of income. In local classifications they are at the bottom of an increasingly fragmented localised social structure. As one resident observed:

"It's a mixed up area. Most people are working and buying their places or renting, but you've got a lot of other people that do alright in one way or another, signing on and working or whatever. Then you've got your scum, the junkies and then the ones living on the 'social'. I don't know why they don't work. I don't really know, I don't have much to do with them."

Employment histories and work orientations

A central theme in much of the literature on social exclusion and poverty has been the relationship between the social isolation of the poor and the potential for the social reproduction of these groups. W.J. Wilson relates the concept of 'social isolation' to the combined effects of discrimination in housing markets and industrial relocation, resulting in increasing concentrations of deprived households, often far from industrial and business districts. This restricts employment opportunities and curtails contacts with the world of work, while poverty limits the social activities of the unemployed, excluding them from wider social activities. Finally, isolation from mainstream values and activities results in changes in behavioural patterns and attitudes that, when prolonged, may corrode work commitment (Wilson, 1987, pp 57-61). Intuitively the social isolation concept should have less relevance in an area of relatively low unemployment and a more diverse social structure. As demonstrated in Chapter Four, deprivation occurs on the estate amid relative affluence, at a much finer level than the ward or even Enumeration District (ED) level, with both extremes of working-class experience and lifestyle represented within the same streets. Despite finding little evidence that unemployment leads to either extensive social isolation or less frequent contact with friends, research suggests that even in areas marked by low unemployment levels the unemployed largely associate with each other (Russell, 1999). Few of those detached from either formal or informal work on the estate, or among those attending Job Club, displayed a lack of ties to kin and locally based networks. What did differ were the types of support that they could draw upon. While their networks were high in social support they possessed few material and informational resources due to the similar circumstances of their friends (Gallie et al, 1994).

Over time, unemployment may result in a fracturing of the individual's contacts from the world of work. Current policy aims to re-socialise the unemployed into this world, through attendance on employment programmes such as Job Club. Mike was contacted through the programme and was 42 years old and married with two children at the time of interview. He had been unemployed for two years, since losing his job as a quality control supervisor for a local company that made surgical equipment. The skills that he acquired in his employment were in short demand, and he was retraining through learning computer skills. At the onset of unemployment, he had assumed that the work-based relationships he had established during his nine years at his last job would assist his search for employment. Although he initially attempted to maintain relationships with his former colleagues, his efforts were not reciprocated:

> "After they laid me off I kept in touch for a while but it got too awkward, like it was always me doing the contacting. As soon as I had gone it was like they'd forgotten me, so I haven't seen anyone from work for over a year. Of course I've still got mates that I see from time to time but most of my socialising is done here [Job Club] these days."

The one-sidedness of his efforts discouraged Mike and had a detrimental impact on his self-confidence. Having constructed his identity around being the sole provider for his family and belonging in the public sphere, he found his failure to fulfil these expectations difficult to adjust to. After a year of unemployment he entered a period of self-imposed withdrawal and began to internalise individualistic explanations for his failure to find another job.

> "I knew it weren't my fault I'd lost the job, it'd been on the cards for months, but I started to wonder 'what the fuck's wrong with me?'. You know, I had 20 years of work behind me, but the employers wouldn't even look at me (...) It got hard having to explain myself to people – at the Job Centre, the 'social' and especially to my wife and kids."

Of relevance is Beck's thesis concerning the 'individualization of social inequality'. He argues that the requirements of the labour market and geographical mobility disrupt traditional support networks. Increasing competition in the labour market, argues Beck, forces people for the sake of economic survival to make themselves the centre of their own life plans and conduct. Consequently, they need to become connected through "self-selected and self-created hierarchies and forms of stratification" that tend, as discussed, to form around the work situation and work contacts (Beck, 1992, pp 92-9). For Mike, voluntary attendance at Job Club had positive psychological and social effects through bringing him into contact with those similarly placed, and reducing his sense of isolation and self-criticism. Walsgrove (1987, p 53) argues that for the unemployed, "the overshadowing of the more individualistic moments by collective experience helps to negate any form of self-blame".

> "It [Job Club] is a help and I think it's not so much the practical side, it's getting me out the house and coming here. We're all in the same boat here and there's no pretence. We take the piss out of our situation and ourselves. It helps to see the funny side of things."

While aggregate unemployment figures in Sutton are among the lowest in Greater London, they differ vastly between different wards, ranging from 13% in St. Helier to 3% in the Woodcote ward in 1998 (LBS, 1998). Spatial concentrations of the unemployed combine with their institutional concentration on employment schemes. Far from re-establishing links to the sphere of employment, contact with those similarly unemployed through employment programmes solidifies relationships by employment status. This makes them increasingly dependent on the formal labour market and more reliant on formal methods of finding work. Informal recruitment is fundamentally a matter of 'being known' and requires an investment of time and effort to establish and maintain the relationships that supply those opportunities. Forty-seven-year-old Terry's partner lived in a small village in Surrey. He argued that his chances of finding work were better in his partner's area, where the size of the community meant that opportunities were more readily found through the local grapevine:

> "There's plenty of work where my partner lives because it's an affluent area and there's plenty of little jobs around. Her house is empty in the day, and it's a good base to go into town, make myself known and because it's a small place and word soon gets around but I need to be down there not here. This is blocking my job search."

Processes of segregation are intensified through boundaries erected by those in work to safeguard their own positions. As discussed, this became especially marked in relation to the supply of informal work because of the preferential channelling of information within and between those who circulated within certain networks. As one unemployed participant remarked when discussing openings to work informally:

> "I know there's supposed to be some [informal work] going if you look but I don't know anyone who does. How would I find it, it's hard enough finding a proper job that's advertised for everybody to see? I don't think I'm going to find jobs that are not even advertised."

The timing of labour market entry has long-term effects in influencing later experiences and labour market attachment (Yeandle, 2003). A central contention of this book has been that collective responses to social exclusion are not only mediated and shaped through social relationships, but also represent particular generational responses that are formed through shared experiences and circumstances of work. Comparing the experiences of those who entered the labour market between the mid-1980s and early 1990s and older cohorts revealed marked contrasts in the ways that they accommodated to their labour market location. Workers who entered employment under earlier conditions and were socialised into the working patterns and expectations of an older order, bear a heavier burden than those whose experiences were formed in an era of short-term work, part-time hours and a general impermanence in their working lives. Unversed in the practices and conventions of the 'flexible' labour market, government training schemes and in-work benefits, accommodation to their new role in the labour market and the loss of a status and lifestyle achieved through a lifetime of work is a painful process. The manager of Job Club explained the downward process of adjustment that many participants make, and how this is conditioned through their previous experiences of work:

> ★ "People's expectations get less because they're tailored to the demands of the labour market. After the reality sinks in they realise that the lifestyle that they once had has gone. Some people can't handle it and others adjust. We get men here that are in and out of work and more often than not, that's because of the nature of the labour market that they're in. They've generally adapted to it and they cope better. But with redundancies, these blokes are devastated. Their confidence is at rock bottom and it's going to have an impact on their lives and families too."

Displaced workers entering the labour market after years spent in steady employment, often possessing specialised skills developed through internal labour markets in large companies, face a dual disadvantage. First, the job market that they face often entails 'lifecycle deskilling', a reduction in income and transience in their future working lives that erode occupational identity. This was repeated during several interviews at Job Club, where many of the clients who had held relatively well-paid, stable jobs had not learnt to adapt to the vagaries of a 'flexible' post-industrial labour market. The dismay that their future prospects were likely to be marked by downward mobility and coercion into low-wage jobs, was felt more acutely than among those who had never experienced stable employment:

> "In my last job, I could take home £400 a week because I was driving all over the country and doing loads of overtime. When I got laid off, I went to the Employment Service and they asked me how much I'd be willing to work for and I said £250 minimum. Now they're trying to send me to jobs where I'd be taking home £150 a week (…) they said you can claim a working credit that'd make me about £50 a week better off, but even if it made me £50 a week better off than on the dole, where's the sense in working my guts out all week just to be £50 better off?"

Second, although contacts established in formal work are important in providing access to formal and informal work, outside of a limited number of trades, their skills are rarely amenable to informal work of the individualistic, self-employed type. After spending 11 years as a machine operator for a tool manufacturer, 37-year-old Andrew was laid off after his department was transferred to another branch of the company in a different part of the country. He was offered his job on condition that he relocated but declined the offer, as his family did not want to move from the area. There are few demands for his skills in the formal labour market, while the sector that he spent most of his working life in has no openings for undeclared or casual work:

> "I'd take the work under any conditions and if a company was willing to take me on when they needed me and pay me a bit less and forego tax and the rest, that'd be fine by me. The thing is it doesn't happen in those type of jobs (...) most of my old colleagues are too worried about their own jobs and too busy covering their own backs to look out for me. It's the uncertainty of it all these days, like when you don't know what's around the corner you have to look out for number one."

Thus, if they do want to supplement their income through undeclared work they are obliged to seek openings through subcontractors offering low-skilled, poorly paid work. Given that information on this type of work circulates through closed networks of workers, they often lack the relevant contacts and knowledge. While a few were fortunate in having contacts that facilitated entry into alternative sources of work, most were excluded from those networks:

> "Some of the blokes here were in jobs for years and you start at the bottom and work your way up the wage scale, so the time they were laid off they were on good money. Now they've got to take another job and start at the bottom and it's going to take years to build up to what they're used to. That's as bad as not even having a job because even if they get one it's not going to give them the lifestyle that they're used to ... most of them wouldn't have a clue where to work on the side. How would they or why would they need to know if they've been in a steady job for years?"

Research indicates that social class differences in aspirations are situationally determined, with the working class placing a higher value on a steady income and a secure job than the middle class, who place more emphasis on career advancement and status (Agnew, 1983). A lack of knowledge of, and isolation from, the workings of the cash economy means that informal opportunities are often constructed as inherently risky and unpredictable. Twenty-three-year-old lone parent Jenny (see also Chapter Six) had trained as a hairdresser before the birth of her son. Despite several women on the estate earning an undeclared income through this fertile source, Jenny was relatively new to the area and had few local contacts. Although she occasionally cut hair for friends and family, she gave the following rationale for not using her talents as a more regular source of income:

> "It's handy with the hairdressing because I can make a bit of pocket money if a friend or my mum asks me but I don't earn much from it because it's just once in a blue moon. I could go freelance, but I'd need to take up driving lessons again, get a car, and buy all the equipment. Then I might only get one customer one week and 20 the next. It's too unpredictable and because of the overheads I need something more consistent (...) you need a customer base and I'm not from round here so I wouldn't know where to start."

Her aspirations are closely focused on the formal labour market since these opportunities are regarded as offering more stability. During a follow-up interview in March 2000, Jenny's son had started school and she had found a part-time job as a chambermaid in a hotel. Despite performing a mundane job for low rates of pay, the financial aspects are not her reason for entering work. Her primary motivation is grounded in a desire to escape the constraints and limitations on personal autonomy that the welfare system places on its clients. After moving onto the estate, she had fallen out with a group of young mothers who she had met at a toddler's playgroup. Later somebody informed the DSS that her boyfriend, who sometimes stayed overnight with her, was living with her. It was her desire to escape those constraints that influenced her decisions over work:

> "Knowing that I'm doing it myself is why I work. When I had my boyfriend some bastard grassed me up to the 'social' and they came round and said, 'You've got a boyfriend

who's been staying with you, and he's not allowed to'. But now, I can have who I want in my house and I haven't got to answer to anybody. It's like I live my life, I rule my life, and nobody else has got a say in it."

For those unable or unwilling to engage with localised networks and/ or the cash economy, formal employment can provide a route out of social exclusion. However, this is rarely due to any intrinsic or financial benefits to be gained through the work itself but to overcome the social isolation that unemployment entails, and to provide a structure and purpose to one's day. A common theme at Job Club was the continuing adherence to the formal labour market, despite the universal grievance that most of the available jobs are economically non-viable:

> "It's pointless going to work for so little. The money is appalling and you couldn't afford to live a normal life because it's impossible round here on nine, ten grand a year (…) I'll take one though not for the money but to get me out the house and keep me busy. I don't want to sit around thinking all day, that's why half the people round here are on Prozac. Ideally, I'd like a decent job but until then I'll take anything just to be working."

Comparing the diversity of individual biographies demonstrates the complex and nuanced ways in which social exclusion is articulated. Those expressions are shaped, and given meaning, through previous labour market experiences and their collective expression in networks of social relationships. Jenny expressed formal employment as a route to social inclusion through allowing her to recreate her social identity as a worker, and extend her previously limited circle of friends. Despite the practical and financial hardships of working, it is undertaken for the social and psychological advantages that it brings:

> "My work's not great pay, it's minimum rate and I'd be financially better not working but mentally that's not me. I like to be out and about, mixing with people (…) people might say it's not much of a job, but I like the girls I work with and we have a good laugh at work."

Labour market orientations and ideological divisions

Lack of knowledge of informal opportunities and of the relationships that surround and conceal the work mean that the perceived risks associated with benefit fraud and tax evasion are often exaggerated. The high-profile campaign against benefit fraud did influence the perceptions of many of the unemployed and influenced their search for employment. Internalising official discourses on benefit fraud and the efficiency of fraud detection measures results in a reluctance to seek out cash work. There was a marked contrast in the perceived risks of undeclared work and the effectiveness of policies to eradicate benefit fraud, between those who had undertaken such work and those who had not. The latter were more prone to reject such work due to fears of being caught, and processes of social segregation are reinforced through official ideologies surrounding benefit fraud. Those that claimed not to partake in cash work perceived the extent of such work as common, while beneath the contempt shown by some of the genuinely unemployed towards those that defraud the social security system, was a concern that they will also be stigmatised as 'dole scroungers'.

> "There's a lot of people say they need benefit and they don't, you know the bogus people claiming benefit, there's a lot of it still going on. They're starting to crack down on it but there's still a lot of it going on. People do get through the net but they catch up with them in the end which I do like to see because it's making it worse for people who do genuinely claim it, it gives us all a bad name."

Working illegally involves more than knowing the right contacts, but requires a willingness to partake in practices and adopt a role that many found abhorrent when their taxes were subsidising those practices. Joe was contacted through Job Club and lived on the estate. He had a wide network of friends and associates that could, he claimed, facilitate entries into cash jobs. He rejected them because he did not wish to be associated with the perceived lifestyles and attitudes of those who work while claiming benefits. As discussed in Chapter Seven, it is the more visible and blatant forms of undeclared work that are cited as indicative of those who undertake such work. Rarely mentioned are the lone parents and housebound who join home-working schemes and fill envelopes or perform other equally tedious activities for a pittance, or the invisible kitchen porters and washers-up who are a mainstay of the expanding restaurant and catering sector.

> "I don't mind if I do a favour for a mate and they give me a drink out of it, that's fair enough but those jack the lads that leave their houses the same time every morning and come back at six o'clock filthy because they've been on site all day, I couldn't do that myself. It's that whole attitude like, 'Why should I work and pay tax?'(...) 'I'll work and pay no tax, and I'll take your tax'. Well, they're taking from everyone aren't they, but when they knock on your door and offer you a bargain, people jump and are like 'yes please!', they don't see that these people are laughing at us."

Processes of social closure operate within the overall condition of unemployment and labour market marginality through the attribution of such stereotypical classifications, and generate intra-class distinctions. Those distinctions are based upon observable differences in lifestyle and practice and correspond with older notions of 'rough' and 'respectable'. Somerville argues that the dual labour process can explain the ideological distance between the two groups with the latter who adhere to dominant orientations to work and welfare, and the former who do not (Somerville, 1998). Integral to the maintenance of self-respect is the desire to distinguish oneself from the idle, the dole-fiddler and other 'spongers'. Having placed himself in the 'respectable' category through his rejection of undeclared income and commitment to the formal labour market, Joe continued:

> "… I think you've got to change it from way down because a lot of it's part of a culture and just saying to people you've got to go to work won't work because there's a group of people who really don't see beyond benefits. I don't know what you'd offer them as an incentive but it starts way down with the children and I don't think you can change that overnight with quick fixes."

Both the antipathy shown, and sense of injustice felt among many of the unemployed and (formally) 'working poor' was that such distinctions are blatantly clear to themselves, since they are reinforced daily in their observations of those around them and given further legitimisation through media and political discourses. However, the middle-class observers, policy makers and bureaucrats who are the source of those discourses are unable, in practice, to differentiate between such lifestyle differences. This is despite them forming a central element of welfare since the 1834 New Poor Law. Subsequently, the derogatory and stigmatising discourse directed towards the 'dependency culture' and the punitive attempts to eradicate it is also directed at themselves, as the following remark made at Job Club illustrates:

> They just think 'I'm entitled to this money, give me the money' and you can't tell them, well you can tell them until you're blue in the face, but most of them don't give a shit because they'll say 'but I'm entitled to it' and most of those people do need it, but you can't say 'well, I think you're entitled to it, but I don't think you are'. How do you say well you're a scrounger and you're not because you look a bit nicer, or speak a bit posher?"

Howe notes that ideologies are not fixed systems of beliefs, but a frequently contradictory set of historically specific and fluid themes. It is the inconsistency of ideologies, which allow them to be applied in a wide range of contexts (Howe, 1994). Many of the 'working poor' aware of the uncertainty of their own labour market location, expressed the sentiments of 47-year-old Jim, an agency-employed hospital porter:

> "I dare say there are welfare scroungers, I mean I know there are, but I don't think they're in the lower classes. How can they be scroungers for Christ's sake? They've got no money. If they were middle class, now they're the real scroungers, not working-class people because there's not a great deal to be earned out there, and let's face it we all know that."

While explicitly critical of those who defraud the benefit system, many of the unemployed gave pragmatic reasons for not working 'on the side' themselves. Many avoided those involved in various forms of informal activity on the estate because of the rumoured links to more serious forms of criminal activity. These suspicions were not entirely unfounded, although this had more to do with the higher degree of interaction between different networks and a higher volume of activity in different spheres among those working outside of formal employment. Despite lamenting the lack of opportunities to earn additional income this way, an unemployed respondent gave the following rationale for continuing to aspire to a formal job:

> "I could always answer an advert for house cleaning and probably make 30-odd quid a week. That'd make a real difference and I have thought about it but I'll hold on for something a bit more permanent and above board ... How am I going to find a proper job if I'm cleaning or whatever? I'm a terrible worrier and I'd worry myself sick that I was going to get caught. They've got the whole thing pretty well sewn up these days and unless you're lucky you're going to get caught sooner or later."

The well-publicised anti-fraud measures, which provided the context to these interviews, assume that welfare abuse is prevalent in low-income localities and depend largely on residents of those areas policing each other. Anonymous phone lines have been launched where people are invited to inform on those who are working while claiming benefits. The divisions that these policies create strengthen the boundaries between networks of people, and trust becomes something that only exists within networks of shared interest, eroding an awareness of spatially bounded common location and collective interests. Stories of raids on building sites, of officials who wait outside the houses of lone parents to confirm whether they are cohabiting and of petty grievances that result in people being investigated by the authorities were common. The apprehension that these anecdotes generate serves to confine resources and information within closely bounded networks, and has implications for the type and quality of support available. Patrick, the builder introduced in Chapter Seven, observed:

> "People stop trusting their neighbours and that shouldn't go on. We're all in the same boat and everybody's just trying to make the best of their situation (...) if I work cash I'm very careful about who knows about it, and it comes through people that are doing the same so you know its safe (...) they cut their own throats because on site they're very reluctant to give work to strangers now. It's got nothing to do with people not agreeing with fraud because everyone round here knows the score, but it's got everything to do with petty squabbles and screwing people you don't like."

While regeneration schemes aim at rebuilding 'communities', the simultaneous drive to stamp out fraud fractures those same communities, instilling doubts and suspicion among neighbours.[4] As one resident remarked:

> "They're always cracking down on it, yet they're not doing the cracking down, what they rely on are grasses. They can't check on everybody so they just sit back and let the grasses do their work for them (...) if you live on a council estate and live quite well, people will report you out of jealousy, spite, hatred, whatever. It's terrible making people turn against each other."

Social capital, regeneration and welfare reform

As discussed in Chapter Four, community-based regeneration schemes have recommended enhancing 'social capital' as an essential complement to investment in physical and human capital, and an important component in reducing social exclusion (DETR, 1998b). The centrality attached to the development of 'soft infrastructures' is incompatible with recent policy changes that aim to increase the labour force participation of lone parents and previously economic inactive groups, such as disabled people and pensioners. Policies that provide financial incentives for lone parents to work longer hours, proposals to expand formalised childcare facilities and the increasing proportion of women in the labour market weaken the networks that have long-provided the bulk of informal welfare and services. Accordingly, there is an increasing reliance on kin for financial and material support and the substitution of reciprocal-based exchange with cash-based relationships and/or commodified childcare services managed by the state. This point was a recurring theme raised by several lone parents. Tracey, for example, highlighting the incoherence of current policies, complained that:

> "They're trying to push single mums into work because they think we're sponging. What the men who make these rules don't understand is who's going to look after the kids if we're all out at work? All they're doing is setting up lots of new nurseries and creating a load more crap jobs as childminders so that the kids' mothers can leave their kids with them and go off and do other crap jobs. I ask you, what is the point of that?"

The unemployed and economically inactive among the sample were not isolated from locally based support networks. Many lone parents resorted daily to alternative means of material and financial support supplied largely through kin. These provided an essential supplement to benefit payments that are insufficient in meeting their weekly outgoings. The assistance of relatives was the primary means that allowed many of their children to possess the latest gadgets and items of fashion, and avoid social exclusion as it is understood and expressed in its social context. In line with earlier research, the economically inactive women appeared to have higher levels of emotional and practical support than males, largely due to them having fewer but closer friendships, which were centred on the immediate locality (Bott, 1957, p 52). The unemployed males in this sample socialised in networks principally composed of other unemployed men, although it must be noted that many of the unemployed were contacted through Job Club and many had work histories comprising of stable employment patterns. At the same time as they were experiencing difficulties in maintaining relationships with the employed, their daily interactions were with those similarly placed. The social relations that emerge around unemployment and informal work meant that their aspirations were largely focused on securing future employment in the formal labour market. This, in part, reflected different expectations of work that varied by age and was formed when they entered the labour market assuming stable working patterns. Adherence to the formal labour market was reinforced through a lack of access to the lifestyles and practices of those who, having never experienced a stable job, have developed as a means of attaining a livelihood outside of the world of formal employment.

Distance between different groups on the estate were sustained through the ideological distinctions that were employed in order to locate themselves in relation to the other. Different elements of dominant ideological discourses around work and welfare are applied in a critical and often contradictory manner towards each other, encouraging division and isolation. For the unemployed, benefit fraudsters epitomised the 'welfare scrounger' through their rejection of legitimate avenues to attain a living and were criticised for giving the genuinely unemployed an undeserved reputation. The visibility of certain forms of cash work was indicative of a decline in the area and of an ascendant form of selfish individualism. Cash workers, meanwhile, positively contrasted their own adherence to the 'work ethic' with the passivity of the unemployed and workless, who are regarded as 'scroungers' for having eschewed a commitment to work. The presence of poverty and deprivation on the estate indicated the extent of demoralisation, and provided a constant stimulus to prevent downward mobility into this group. As Dean and Melrose (1996, p 14) note, it is ironic that this element of the dominant ideological discourse is used to defend an activity that is denounced within dominant ideology.

Regardless of whether they were unemployed, working undeclared or the formally 'working poor', all were striving to maintain a positive identity in the light of the negative discourses that are directed towards them by politicians, the media and by the social groups that inhabit the same spatial locations. While this encouraged fragmentation between groups sharing objectively similar circumstances, few saw themselves as 'socially excluded'. This was because the social relationships, within which these attitudes were formed, provided the reference groups with which they compared themselves. Rather than being demoralised by the structural pressures that impact on their lives, all stressed the capacity for control and independence under testing material circumstances. Indeed, as the testimonies presented here affirm, exclusion is understood primarily as a lack of agency and control rather than the statistical indices of poverty and disadvantage attributed by policy makers and academics. Within the tight constraints of local labour market options, through combining different sources of income and reciprocal support, residents are making informed choices – within a restricted range of options – about the division between each. As Stack (1974, p 129) noted:

> The strategies that the poor have evolved to cope with poverty do not compensate for poverty in themselves, nor do they perpetuate the poverty cycle. But when mainstream values fail the poor, as they have failed most Flats' residents, the harsh economic conditions of poverty force people to return to proven strategies for survival.

Notes

[1] Throughout this chapter, ★ indicates that a quotation has been transcribed from notes. In the quotations, (...) indicates that part of the text has been omitted.

[2] The term is used in accordance with Jenkins who argues for the use of 'lifestyle' as a 'strategic concept' to analyse divisions within a working-class community. The concept refers to "observable patterns of social practices distinguishing groups of people who may be said ... to belong to the same cultural group". It is used in preference to 'sub-culture'

for two reasons. First, it focuses attention onto practice and away from the 'cultural realm of meaning'. Second, Jenkins argues, the latter term neglects the continuity between subcultures and implies a determinate and deviant relationship towards the dominant culture (Jenkins, 1979, p 41).

[3] The style represents a continuity with South London's 'hard mods' found on the terraces of Chelsea Football Club in the late 1960s and whose style, write Dunning et al, was "distinctly smart *and* violent, managing to combine elements of 'the upward option' provided by the mod style with at least some of the skinheads' predilection for group loyalty and violence". Their descendants were the stylish and label-conscious 'casuals' drawn from the same estates and areas and found on the same terraces two decades later (Dunning et al, 1988, pp 169–71).

[4] Jahoda (1982, p 29) observed that the social disintegration that accompanied high long-term unemployment in Marienthal in the 1930s "was expressed in the tripling of the number of anonymous denunciations to the authorities that somebody had found casual employment in neighbouring villages, while drawing unemployment relief. On investigation it was found that three quarters of such denunciations were unfounded".

NINE

On the margins of inclusion

In Chapter One the aims of this book were laid out. First, to examine how different groups of economically marginal people negotiate the offerings of a 'post-industrial' labour market and a welfare system geared towards reintegrating them into formal employment. Second, to explore the role of localised social relations in both shaping and supporting the varied adaptions and processes of accommodation made in response to these structural and institutional coordinates. The starting point for any analysis of social exclusion must be the restructuring of labour markets and the reformulation of welfare as an instrument to facilitate that process. These provide a framework through which the life chances of individuals and households are experienced and provide the context in which responses to the structure of opportunities are formulated. Through close analysis of a single locality, the book has attempted to demonstrate the micro-social expression of large-scale economic and social processes and their impact on working patterns, family formation, class identities and the quality of life as experienced by residents of the estate. Exploring the motives that influence economic behaviour revealed how decision making is mediated through a complex and frequently contradictory set of considerations. These represent attempts to avoid social exclusion within the constraint of low-paid work and the operation of social policies, which together may be increasing the precariousness and exploitation of low-income households.

Strategies of economic maximisation featured prominently in the respondents' accounts of the imperatives influencing labour market behaviour. In the absence of employment that provides any intrinsic satisfaction or alternative means of self-respect, the material rewards of employment are central since they provide the only incentive to enter formal work. However, 'rational' economic considerations were largely eclipsed by a variety of competing concerns that are informed by a more comprehensive understanding of social exclusion than the rather limited version that is providing an organising principle for 'Third Way' social policies. This suggests the need for a situational notion of rationality that encompasses socially negotiated and culturally constructed perceptions of security, autonomy and lifestyle participation and is fundamentally shaped through the primary obligation to family and kin. Social exclusion is not expressed primarily as a lack of labour market participation. Instead, it is experienced as an inability to achieve constancy in one's material environment and working life; a lack of control and independence over one's own life; and the sense of incompetence at being unable to provide adequately for oneself and family. The lack of congruence between 'top-down' and 'bottom-up' understandings of, and solutions to, chronic economic and labour market disadvantage has notable policy implications given the welfare-to-work approach adopted by the present government. These are expanded on in the remainder of this chapter, which will first draw some general conclusions from the research concerning the potential of current policy to assist social inclusion through labour market integration.

Changing labour markets and social exclusion

While new terms have arrived to describe the casualties of contemporary economic restructuring, the assumptions guiding social policy remain rooted in increasingly redundant models of economic behaviour that locate the key cause of social exclusion in long-term labour market inactivity. This overlooks fundamental changes in the nature of work following the period of labour market restructuring since the mid-1970s, and the project of welfare curtailment and privatisation that accompanied those changes. This shift in priorities has been driven by the increasing penetration of previously protected national markets by global market forces and the development of a 'flexible' labour market assisted by deregulation, privatisation and organisational 'delayering'. De-industrialisation and the spatial relocation of industry had a profound impact on the urban centres of the West. Widespread structural unemployment, an upsurge in poverty, homelessness, deprivation and growing class and spatial divisions became common features of urban landscapes. The relation between macro-economic restructuring, intensifying spatial concentrations of poverty and changes in economic behaviour and family formation patterns was captured in W.J. Wilson's influential account *The truly disadvantaged* (1987). In the context of the decimation of employment opportunities and demise of the Fordist-Keynesian era of demand management, full employment and universal welfare, Wilson's account challenged the growing dominance of conservative perspectives that located the causes of poverty in the pathological and dependent attitudes of the poor (Chapter Three). This book shares Wilson's basic premise that collective variations in behaviour and attitude represent a response to social-structural constraints and opportunities. Wilson, however, was examining the emergence of a distinctive culture that grew in response to the relocation of manufacturing industry in urban US in the 1980s and the cultural adaptions made by inner-city black people in the face of *sustained* joblessness.

Through the 1980s and 1990s, increasing spatial differentiation at the level of local labour markets has resulted in the decline and renewal of areas at increasingly local levels, depending on the nature and composition of the local labour force. In many localities the social consequences of depressed labour markets, large-scale redundancies and mass unemployment have been superseded by a growth of new employment opportunities and working patterns associated with the transition to a 'post-industrial' economy. Under the current phase of capitalist development, of greater significance than the sections of the population rendered superfluous to current economic requirements, is the growing inequality of income and employment opportunities between a 'core' and 'periphery' workforce that has been an adjunct of global economic restructuring. The decline of mid-level occupations and the apprenticeships and internal labour markets that those jobs provided, means that key labour market transformations have made occupational mobility less effective in reducing inequality (McKnight, 2000). A generalisation and widespread perception of employment insecurity is a defining feature of contemporary societies. In addition, more fractured working lives consisting of intermittent spells of work punctuated by spells of unemployment and/or retraining schemes, have become a normal feature of many working lives (Lee and Hills, 1998).

Far from providing a remedy to poverty and inequality, work has become a major mechanism in perpetuating and reproducing social exclusion. Economic fragility and a polarisation of wealth and opportunity occur not as a result of recession and unemployment but alongside economic growth, a massive rise in prosperity among the upper echelons of the service class and a steady fall in unemployment. For those employed in the flexible labour market of expanding peripheral work, employment is experienced as a further source of insecurity and fragmentation rather than the means to security, an improved standard of living and entry into occupations that provide a source of collective identity. Given the direction of economic and labour market restructuring these issues have a wider significance, and are currently more applicable to studies of social exclusion than the classic studies of the social impact of mass redundancies and widespread unemployment. Present thinking is ambivalent over whether the precariously employed should be grouped together with the long-term jobless as 'socially excluded'. The empirical sections and testimonies presented indicate that the nature of contemporary work, and exclusion from secure paid employment, is central to understanding the contemporary experience of social exclusion.

Alongside labour market changes, welfare states and social policies also play an important role in shaping, as well as alleviating, inequality and disadvantage. The centrality of global markets and the impotence of nation states in the face of these changes have dominated current thinking about the potential of social policies to alleviate social exclusion. Conceding that global markets place strict limits on tax and expenditure policies, the government's emphasis has shifted towards reducing access to public funds and promoting supply-side measures as a panacea for social exclusion. The dominant market discourse has tended to subsume social and political perspectives into individualistic economic ones and finds its contemporary expression in the prominent use of the 'human' and 'social' capital concepts in framing social exclusion policies. Fevre (2000) notes that 'capital' has the right connotations for a culture where economic rationality is hegemonic and rises to ascendancy in all aspects of our lives (Fevre, 2000, pp 94-6). The increasing centrality of individual and social capital in formulating policy reflects both the abandonment of a commitment to greater equality towards the fostering of equality of opportunity, and the diminished capacities for state action that globalisation is assumed to entail. As discussed, the general thrust of welfare reform has been to extend the requirement to work to previously inactive groups such as lone parents and disabled people, and is based on the 'universal breadwinner' model in which women can be citizen workers alongside men (Lister, 2001a, p 99). From this perspective, the problem of social exclusion is that those disengaged from work lack the appropriate skills and training to allow them to adapt to the rapidly changing requirements of a global economy. Therefore, enhancing 'human capital' within the framework of labour market flexibility is seen to represent the best route to social inclusion.

Despite the shift in political terminology to describe and analyse the condition of contemporary economic marginality, many of the underlying conceptual frames and assumptions that have dominated debates surrounding work and welfare since the reform of the Poor Laws remain. These focus on the role of cultural values in transmitting dependent modes of behaviour that have a corrosive impact on the work motivations of the poor, and detract attention from the structured inequality that disadvantages particular segments of society. The 'rights and responsibilities' discourse emphasises that the 'client's' right to social inclusion through participation in paid work and supported by training and education, is balanced by the obligation to behave responsibly and take up these openings. Individuals who fail to avail themselves of these opportunities are seen as excluding themselves to their long-term disadvantage, and become legitimate recipients of a coercive strategy that aims to re-socialise them into the work ethic that they shun (Deacon, 2003). Similar anti-dependency strategies, as discussed in Chapter Three, display a long historical lineage in Anglo-American social thought where the predominance of free market individualism has shaped the nature of discourse surrounding work, welfare and family formation. Central to this approach is the idea that welfare policy has the potential to change behavioural patterns through the principle of 'less eligibility'. Under its current guise, 'less eligibility' has involved a shift towards a disciplinarian approach of 'tough love' that takes its inspiration from Lawrence Mead's pronouncements on the resigned and passive attitudes of the workless. The shift from a 'passive' towards an 'active' welfare system has been accompanied by increasing surveillance and control over the lives of the unemployed.

The emphasis on compulsion and the extension of penalties for non-compliance may weaken the contractual basis and emphasis on rights and responsibilities that underpin the welfare-to-work strategy. In discussions with the unemployed, it was apparent that a policy of coercion heavily weighted towards the responsibilities side of the 'contract' further erodes a sense of control over their lives, and may be counterproductive to the aims of 'empowerment' that current policies intend to promote. State coercion to enter low-paid work while withdrawing the fundamental right to leave such jobs without incurring the risk of destitution through the suspension of benefits, reduces confidence and heightens insecurity further. This was a constant complaint throughout the interviews and is regarded as a serious impediment to entering paid work through locking one into rigid and potentially exploitative structures, which are subject to close supervision by the state. This diminishes labour mobility and the chance to experiment with different types and combinations of paid employment, in strict conflict with the claims made for the self-reliant and mobile worker required by flexible labour markets. These fears are intensified through tying Housing Benefit to Income Support and the serious implications that this entails. As one Job Club participant recalled:

"A friend of mine worked in a nursing home. This old dear kept propping the fire doors open with a chair so he kept closing them. Words were exchanged and she complained about him and he was sacked. Not only did he lose his job but he lost his home because he 'lived in' and it can be as fast as that (...) you lose everything because the Housing Benefit's tied to the unemployment system so if I walked out of a job for whatever reason I could lose my rent and it makes you reluctant when you know that you could lose your home and you'll be homeless."

Commentators have noted that the growth of low-income employment in a strictly segmented labour market severely limits the potential of paid work to assist inclusion, a conclusion supported by the findings of this research. The problem is not that government and policy makers lack the political will to balance achieving full employment with a corresponding commitment to protect those in low-paid, structurally insecure unattractive work. Rather, the expansion of available labour to fill poorly paid work subsidised through in-work benefits is vital to capital accumulation through maintaining a downward pressure on wages and inflation, thus allowing the market to generate more low paid-work. The present government has set out to 'make work pay' and increase the financial motivations to take up poorly paid, low-skilled work through the introduction of a National Minimum Wage, extending the role and generosity of in-work benefits and an increasing integration of the tax and benefit systems. The rights of part-time workers have been aligned with those of full-time workers through the adoption of EU directives, although in Britain these directives are interpreted less liberally than in other EU states (Dean, 2002). While such initiatives mark a significant advance, the rational assumptions on which they are constructed fail to comprehend the way that people assess the opportunity costs of formal employment.

In an area of low unemployment and a buoyant labour market the complaint is not an absence of jobs. On the contrary, many acknowledged that they could obtain formal work relatively easily. However, the lack of legitimate opportunities to attain a reasonable standard of living from the jobs on offer, their failure to offer any prospect of career advancement or to pay a 'family wage' means that they are often viewed as disadvantageous for people struggling to maintain a family. Expectations of work were relatively modest although all respondents emphasised that work should provide a 'fair wage', not subsidised through in-work benefits. In recognition of London's high cost of living, Mayor Ken Livingstone agreed to the formation of a 'living wage unit' at City Hall and has quoted £7.70 per hour as a fair living wage for the capital (TELCO, 2004). From the perspective of many residents, social inclusion in the formal labour market means being able to raise a family independently and without state support. Pursuit of the 'universal breadwinner' model and the dissolution of the worker–non-worker dichotomy may redress gender inequalities in income (albeit by undermining the equation of a 'fair wage' with a 'family wage'). However, given the tendency for people to form partnerships with others sharing similar socioeconomic positions, such a strategy may increase income inequality between households (Taylor-Gooby, 2001, pp 81-2). In areas like St. Helier, this may result in greater intra-class polarisation as the economic behaviour of partners in low-income households tends to mirror each other due to a combination of low wages and means-tested benefits. Despite the increasing generosity of in-work benefits, their interaction with other means-tested benefits and the absence of jobs that play a 'breadwinner' wage still make it pointless for a single earner to work. For couples with limited earning capacity, the dual-earner or no-earner households may be the only reasonable options, as 33-year-old Tony, a married man with two children, argued:

> "It's all very well the government encouraging women to go out to work and I mean that's the only way people like us can manage on what they pay. But what if you've got young kids, or your wife's spending two hours a day dropping one off at one school and one off at another or for whatever reason can't work (...) It's not always practical for both partners to be out the house all day and families with one earner on low pay, it's not giving much incentive."

Likewise, flexible working hours and the growth of part-time work may facilitate the 'dual role' as carer/worker to lone parents but it is unlikely to lift them above reliance on the benefit system. The equation of social exclusion with the labour market inactivity of lone parents does not sound especially convincing when discussing their own experiences and priorities. For many, motherhood, not labour market activity, provided their primary source of identity. The emphasis on paid work as a duty conflicts with culturally constructed notions of 'good mothering' that stresses commitment to their children as the primary obligation, and means that many have chosen to defer work and/or training until their children are older.

Equally significant were the divisive methods of labour relations at the lower end of the labour market where 'flexibility' provides a potent source of labour control. As discussed in Chapter Five, 'attitude' is a more prominent facet than formal qualifications in determining access to many of the service sector jobs on offer. The forms of disposition and modes of conduct required in such jobs are antithetical to many men who have grown up expecting to perform masculine work in highly gender-stratified occupations. For those who adhere to a rapidly archaic definition of a 'man's' job, far from providing inclusion and a source of respect, work is experienced as a source of humiliation when required to undertake tasks that are commonly regarded as 'women's' or 'kids' work. Steve captured these concerns when recalling a period spent early morning cleaning in a local department store:

> "It weren't too bad, you were left to get on with the hoovering and cleaning and you'd just go into a trance (...) come half eight all the shop girls'd turn up and sit in the tea room and get their counters ready, well I'd be cleaning around them and I'd just keep my eyes on the work and never look up at them (...) I mean I was 26 and dusting counters."

The present policy regime through channelling people into state-subsidised, structurally precarious work may inadvertently be undermining the potential of social inclusion via labour market integration, through breaking the association of paid (formal) employment with lifestyle inclusion. The inability of many to acquire work that provides material security and independence, has entailed reassessing the notion that families can only be sustained through paid formal work and many have more faith in their own abilities to provide for themselves and their families than the uncertainty of formal routes. When underpinned by welfare benefits, informal support mechanisms and the opportunities they provide are often regarded as offering greater stability than formal openings. This is because such practices minimise the insecurity associated with the combination of low wages, insecure work and the new 'politics of enforcement' that is necessary to implement the aims of welfare-to-work. Although many undeclared workers contrasted their own innovative and entrepreneurial activities with the perceived passivity of the unemployed and working poor, they displayed a marked ambivalence to their activities. The progressive detachment from the formal labour market that was a feature of many of these work histories, coexists with the fear that 'adverse inclusion' in poorly paid, low-skill jobs in either the formal or informal sectors was likely to be a constant throughout their working lives.

The ability to enter entry-level jobs or training schemes is frequently compromised by uncertainty over the outcomes of such a move, and the loss of relative material security that their social networks yield. On a daily basis, the lack of a decent minimum living standard and finding ways of attaining one remained the major preoccupation, leaving little scope for the formulation of long-term plans. These daily concerns have important policy implications given the primacy attached to increasing employability, and suggests a failure to appreciate the practical and psychological restrictions that poverty and insecurity impose on people. A reasonable minimum living standard, whether through undeclared earnings or from more generous welfare benefits, enhances the potential and likelihood of the unemployed to take up paid work. First, it reduces the discernible sense of isolation from mainstream society, which as Chapter Eight explored, is heightened through the increasing institutional concentration of the unemployed on employment schemes. This has the potential for patterns of sociability to become segregated in 'strong ties' that are high in emotional and practical support but low in informational and economic opportunities. What distinguished the informal labour force from the unemployed was its greater degree of interaction between different networks and a higher volume of economic transactions between their spheres. A corollary of this is that a modicum of material security and a minimal level of disposable income increases self-confidence, keeps people more connected with the world of work, preserves work habits and orientations and ultimately enhances the possibilities of entering formal work.

> "A friend of mine did some typing and paperwork on the side and she did mornings and earned about 60 quid a week and when she'd saved enough to get a little car she packed it in. Now she's got a real job because she's got a car and she can travel down to Reigate every day but you wouldn't make them see that at the job centre."

Insecurity while in work combined with a lack of scope to negotiate one's own working life is an important aspect in shaping attitudes to work and the welfare system. The research found little evidence of the defeatist and resigned attitudes attributed to welfare recipients, but instead found an ongoing relationship of conflictual encounters with the bureaucratic welfare system. While many had engaged in intermittent and petty benefit fraud, few regarded this as a viable long-term strategy not least because the increased emphasis on fraud detection has made such a strategy more difficult to sustain for long periods. However, the sceptical and punitive approach towards their clients by welfare administrators made many more accepting of an instrumental use of the benefit system to achieve short-term ends. At the same time, the option of combining cash work with benefits is itself becoming uncertain and restricted as efforts to reintegrate the informal labour force into the formal labour market, combined with a renewed emphasis on reducing benefit fraud, intensify. Following on from this, there remains the possibility that making support increasingly conditional under the threat of withdrawal of benefits will push people into more serious criminal activities and intensified forms of social exclusion. One of the most common justifications for working while claiming benefits was that it is more morally acceptable than stealing or drug dealing. Discussing the government's moves to get lone parents back to work, 28-year-old Julie (see also Chapters Six and Seven) remarked:

> "If you start forcing girls to take jobs that they had a baby
> in the first place to get out of doing, then you're steering
> them more into that direction like going out on their own
> and being a prostitute or dealing drugs or credit cards."

Since the outset of the research the composition of informal and casualised labour markets has undergone rapid change. As the unemployed are reintegrated into formal work and training schemes, they are being replaced as the ultimate 'reserve army' by rising numbers of immigrants and refugees. Recent years have witnessed an increasing monopolisation of construction, domestic/childcare and low-grade service sector work by foreign workers, willing to work under worse conditions and for less pay than their native counterparts. This provides for an intensification of exploitation and a significant challenge to the livelihoods of those who combine various undeclared sources of income with welfare benefits. The manner in which these changes are transforming the clandestine workforce in different spheres of activity and their variation across local labour markets, represents a significant restructuring of informal and casualised opportunities that warrants further research. The extent that these changes realign opportunities for informal labour among the native unemployed and intermittent labour force and the implications for the 'survival strategies' of this workforce represents fruitful areas for further study. Suffice to say the growing visibility and significance of the immigrant workforce, further confirmed through perennial media fears over illegal immigration, were frequently presented as a source of potential threat:

> "I don't blame them for coming, I'd do the same if I was living there (...) I've noticed a lot more of them round here and you go in any café or bar round here now and most of them have got foreigners and it's the same on building sites now. So it does make it harder for us, I mean those little jobs you used to pick up they're giving them to asylum seekers."

Irrespective of whether they were working undeclared, unemployed, the (formally) working poor or more commonly moving between these spheres, almost all of the respondents were supportive in theory of the broad objectives of current policy. However, its objective of achieving social inclusion through work was constantly compromised by the economic and labour market context that it operates within. This suggests that in the absence of a deeper scrutiny of the structural causes of labour market disadvantage, current policies are unlikely to increase cohesion and inclusion as it is expressed and understood in its social context. Instead, it may merely lead to prolonged spells of (in-work) benefit dependency in structurally insecure, unrewarding work, or else exploitative and unrewarding work in the underground economy with access to those jobs determined by personalised and nepotistic social ties. The economic incentives of work, as well as the stability and quality of the jobs that the 'socially excluded' are being persuaded and cajoled into entering, remain the central issue that will determine the success of a 'welfare-to-work' strategy for those to whom current policies are directed. This common sentiment was voiced by Gary, who argued:

> "A job where the pay's so low that you have to apply for the wage benefit is no better than having no job at all because if the wages are that low then it's gotta be a crappy job anyway. Any decent job would pay you above that line (...) I'll only fill out all the forms if I'm skint and have to sign on. I'm not going through that crap every six months for the privilege of doing a job that I'd probably hate and with the school dinners and Housing Benefit, Council Tax and the rest of the stuff we'd lose. We worked out I'd be about 20 quid better off at the end of the week."

Community and social exclusion

The final section will elaborate on the relationship between changing labour market opportunities and the emergence of new social formations in response to those changes. These have significant implications for redefining social relations in areas such as St. Helier and for the increasing centrality attached to 'social capital' as a policy solution to the problems of deprived communities. Re-balancing the preoccupation with individual rights and the neglect of wider social obligations that was the obverse side of two decades of free market individualism is central to 'Third Way' solutions, and has been enthusiastically endorsed by the EU, The World Bank and the OECD. Fostering community-based social enterprises and restoring moral cohesion in those communities represents part of a holistic approach that will boost human and social capital, and create sustainable development through the promotion of social enterprises and entrepreneurial activity. Such policies are seen as effective in combating social exclusion by actively promoting a 'sense of community' and attach central importance to the development of public–private partnerships that 'learn from individuals and communities' rather than imposing bureaucratic solutions from above (Social Exclusion Unit, 2001).

Fears over the decline of communities and traditional support networks have been given credence through the work of influential social theorists such as Anthony Giddens (1990) and Ulrich Beck (1992), who consider 'individualisation' and increasing 'reflexivity' as defining features of 'late modernity'. For Beck, this represents a 'categorical shift', which has removed individuals from earlier social ties and commitments. This process is double-edged and contains an inherent contradiction: as individuals are removed from traditional support networks and obligations, they become increasingly dependent on institutions such as the labour market, educational institutions and other state agencies. These institutions become the decisive factors in determining an individual's life chances and "stamp the biography of the individual and make that person dependent upon fashions, social policy, economic cycles and markets, contrary to the image of individual control which establishes itself in individual consciousness" (Beck, 1992, p 131). Several empirical studies have demonstrated the continuing relevance and important role of localised social networks and reciprocal relations. Indeed, the importance of those social ties may have increased as a result of the same global processes that theorists such as Beck and Giddens argue is eroding them. The demands of the labour market, the increasing labour force participation of women and the geographical dispersion of what were previously close-knit kin-based networks, are transforming rather than corroding support networks. The prominence given to building social capital in low-income areas is incongruous with the emphasis on developing individual human capital. The central objective of the latter is to reintegrate those who provide the bulk of informal care and assistance into the formal labour market. As women enter the labour market in increasing numbers the mechanisms of intergenerational family aid and informal support that they have traditionally provided, and which supplemented inadequate formal welfare institutions, are weakened. Accordingly there is an increasing tendency within kin-based support networks towards material and economic-based aid. This has important connotations for a strategy that intends to incorporate lone parents into formal labour, given the important role played by family-based childcare in influencing lone parents' decisions over work (Wheelock and Jones, 2002). Since evidence suggests that those who avail themselves of employment-based training were more willing to enter formal work anyway, this approach may add to the further decline of those areas by allowing those most able to move away from the area.

In policy formulation, social capital has been employed in a largely circular manner. The concept is used as an explanatory variable to explain the strength or otherwise of social cohesion and civic participation, and to describe that same phenomenon (Schuller et al, 2000, p 29). Community presupposes the existence of a degree of homogeneity and an awareness of commonly defined problems upon which cooperative relations of reciprocity can operate.[1] A sociological understanding of social capital requires a relational perspective that looks from different vantage points to capture the changing nature of social relationships, located within a historically specific context and set of institutions that combine to create a distinctive 'structure of feeling'. Following Raymond Williams' original use of the concept, this is understood as the forms of communication and the selection and configuration of routine social practices that produce particular 'ways of life' (Williams, 1980, pp 64–88). Key economic and demographic transformations have combined with the public housing priorities of successive governments to shape the character of social life in working-class locales and rendered the term 'community' redundant among residents of those areas. Regeneration policies that focus on the revival of civil society and its associational networks often fail to consider the economic and political context, which will either intensify or alleviate divisions and conflicts that are endemic to capitalist society and which shape the nature of relationships in civil society (Fine, 2001, p 43).

As shown in Chapter Four, changes in the local labour market and in public housing policies impacted on, and fragmented, this previously 'one-class' estate of young families resulting in a more diverse social structure. Changes in tenure patterns and an increasing polarisation of the estate's demographic structure have been accompanied by increasing social divisions according to how access to housing was gained. The sale of over half of the estate's housing stock through the Right To Buy meant that the interests of different sections of the estate – essentially the 'core' and the 'peripheral' working class – were often incompatible. Increasing (property) wealth of the former coexists with the increasing indigence of the latter, meaning that issues of diversity and conflict have come to shape the nature of social relations on the estate. This is expressed in a pervasive public apathy as patterns of association restrict the notion of community within distinct groups determined by their common location in respect to consumption, or else defined by their niche in a progressively fragmented productive process. This diversification thwarts efforts to build genuinely community-based associations, as remarked by a community worker:

> "During the consultation process we went door knocking and got out and about to find what the residents wanted done. Crime and teenagers was the only thing you could get any agreement on. Otherwise you had homeowners complaining about council tenants, people paying rent moaned about the people on benefits, you got the elderly complaining about the kids and the kids complaining that there's nothing to do and everyone picked on them (...) and I mean, where do you go because they all had valid points?"

The intersection of economic transformation and lifecycle stage are central to understanding how new solidarities and collective responses are constructed in response to broader social and economic currents, and the way in which they are redefining perceptions of community. Edmunds and Turner point out that generations have been largely neglected as an analytical principle in sociology, despite their important function as a source of collective identity (Edmunds and Turner, 2002, p 2). The 'lifecycle principle' means that historically located social and economic changes are experienced differently across different cohorts, and those in the most vulnerable positions will suffer disproportionately from them. Spatially bound networks of broadly similar labour market locations and lifecycle experiences, foster a particular generational consciousness and a body of shared collective knowledge that will have a lasting influence on the way that individuals negotiate and evaluate future opportunities. As Williams (1980, p 65) reminds us:

> The new generation responds in its own ways to the unique world it is inheriting, taking up many continuities that can be traced, and reproducing many aspects of the organisation, which can be separately described, yet feeling its whole life in certain ways differently, and shaping its response into a new structure of feeling.

Due to the network of existing social relations underlying snowball sampling, this tends to generate a sample that is relatively homogeneous. Most of the sample on the estate entered the world of work between the early 1980s and early 1990s, during a period that offered significantly diminished opportunities for entry into similar occupations to those of their parents' generation. Under earlier conditions of Fordist mass production and full employment, adolescence involved the reproduction of class relations and the sexual division of labour, as young men prepared for labour market entry and young women for marriage and motherhood. Social networks held a pivotal position in transmitting embedded knowledge and expectations about these gendered trajectories and provided an intergenerational vehicle for the establishment of an adult identity. Although these transitions were rarely as smooth as sometimes portrayed, full-time jobs and apprenticeships that provided the promise of a degree of upward mobility were certainly abundant until the mid-1970s (Vickerstaff, 2003). The decline of the local industries that had provided the material base of Ferdinand Zweig's (1961) 'affluent worker' identified in the area in 1961, began in the early 1970s and accelerated through the 1980s culminating in the near total decimation of the area's industrial base (see Chapter Four).

The rapid collapse of these mechanisms of social reproduction provides a focal point for understanding how the gap between cultural aspirations to adulthood and the objective chances of achieving them, are expressed through shared collective experiences. These produce new social formations and responses that are grounded in the material reality of their existence, and which represent a "mediation of the local labour market, in the historical past and in contemporary experience, and which might generate a sense of resistance or adaption to global economic transformation" (Taylor et al, 1996, p 14). Central to this process is the collapse of the class-based association between masculinity, dignity and individuality, which was related to mastery of a trade, and acquired through internal labour markets and apprenticeships. The types of work that have replaced these occupations are largely low-skill 'feminised' service work, as manual work loses its connotations as the bearer of independent male status (Savage, 2000, pp 152-3). Increasingly, heterogeneous labour conditions either in the peripheral sector of the formal labour market, in informal labour markets or fluctuating between the two, means that different cultures of manual work exist and it is experienced as a further source of fragmentation rather than cohesion.

Entering an emerging post-industrial credential-based labour market of lowly paid, non-unionised and structurally insecure work, the class- and gender-specific routes to adulthood followed by earlier generations became progressively untenable. As areas undergo rapid economic decline and renewal, multigenerational experiences of industrial change exist simultaneously in the same localities and result in an increasing divergence of the labour market experiences and lifecourse patterns of successive cohorts. Charlesworth argues that traditional forms of working-class sociability and solidarity persist alongside the emergence of new cultural formations and share the same experience, but unwittingly because the public forms of affability and communication of an older order have been replaced by "the atomisation of 'life-long' education, unemployment and small-scale working environments" (Charlesworth, 2000, pp 49-50). Instead of speaking of a distinct 'structure of feeling' it may be more applicable to examine how the splintering and fragmentation of working-class areas are generating distinct 'structures of feeling', which coalesce around increasingly spatially based and age-segmented social structures.

A common theme in the interviews was an increasing awareness of their objective labour market location. This generally occurred with the onset of family responsibilities, at the point in their lives where cultural expectations and the status passages followed by previous generations had expected the transition to adult status to occur. The responses of many to the inability of a post-industrial labour market to create materially and psychologically rewarding entry-level jobs, was to draw on social ties and relationships forged outside the regimes of manual work in adolescent peer groups and peripheral labour markets. The utilisation of these networks as a source of economic opportunities provides a powerful incentive to nurture and maintain social ties based on shared assumptions and understandings that can be advanced through social exchanges. Reciprocal relations operate on the basis of exclusionary criteria that emphasise kin/family relations, peer group and lifestyle, and constitute an important dimension of social closure within the overall condition of economic marginality. These processes divide communities internally between groups sharing similar lifestyles and pursuing similar strategies in respect of work and welfare. Although the strategies may change in response to economic restructuring, the values and aspirations embedded in specific social formations may change slower than the structure of opportunities, as Byrne (2002, pp 279-89) argues:

> The social, being of the past, both in terms of own experiences and in terms of the components of tradition, matters although to a degree which changes as the centrality of that past experience recedes in contrast with contemporary experience.

Culturally constructed notions that place a high value on autonomy and security remain, although within a new occupational and economic context. Avoiding social exclusion as it was expressed in the interviews meant being able to realise these objectives, although the idea that families can only support themselves through formal employment has been renegotiated. Importantly, the shared understandings and knowledge that allow individuals to survive either outside of, or on the margins of, formal work are based in a shared consciousness among those who have known no different. For those who have never held a stable job, occupational identity has ceased to be a prominent facet of personal identity and is established through displays of consumption, which are expressed through distinct age-graded lifestyles and practices. Status distinctions play a crucial role in demarcating divisions between different groups. These distinctions retain and realign traditional notions of 'rough' and 'respectable' in a new context, with the former stigmatised as of old through their inability to provide for themselves and their families and participate in the culture of consumption. Through implying an absence of the pressures of necessity, the ability to participate in lifestyles based around particular forms of consumption provides a visible signifier of material security under testing material circumstances. Such distinctions play an important function in defining the limits of social solidarity on the estate. Consumption practices distance oneself and family from the impoverished failures that surround them, and provide an impetus to avoid the enduring possibility of further downward mobility into this group.

Social exclusion policies often fail to understand that the 'socially excluded' identified by policy makers are often the most socially included within their own environs, since the ability to participate in these lifestyles and access different sources of information are vital in harnessing informal opportunities. This has important implications for a strategy that aims to enhance social cohesion through labour market integration and to improve the quality of life in depressed localities through engendering a sense of community. The lifestyles represented in Chapters Seven and Eight indicate the emergence of social formations separated from older generations through the different economic conditions that shaped their formative labour market experiences, yet connected to it through the continuing adherence to certain cultural aspirations and orientations. The critical stance to formal institutions was expressed by seeking alternatives within the locality and in networks pursuing similar economic strategies, rather than in developing alternatives to those institutions. The emergence of these collective and generationally based adaptions to economic marginality plays a vital role in alleviating a subjective sense of exclusion through generating a sense of 'fantasy equality'. However, it also negates the potential for collective action based on a shared awareness of objective circumstances, and increases grievances and antagonism among different sections of poor neighbourhoods.

> Those with invisible earnings will … [see] themselves as income equals of those above them on the visible income scale. Those with no invisible earnings are more likely to be aware of the invisible earnings of those in the same class grouping as themselves, than of the visible earnings of others; their reaction will be one of intra-class antagonism rather than class solidarity and inter-class conflict. (Ditton and Brown, 1981, p 529)

The lack of synchronisation between the historical context in which aspirations and expectations are formulated and the potential of achieving them when their economic and institutional supports are eroded represent a largely neglected focus of social exclusion research. Grasping the relationship between the differing temporal frames in which restructuring of the labour market and the development of cultural aspirations occur, has notable implications in understanding how different generations adapt to economic marginality and how this is mediated through formative labour market experiences and networks of shared experiences and world views. First, this perspective suggests that behaviour has changed less than the context that it operates in and assigns little causal significance to the role of transmitted values in explaining labour market behaviour and family formation. On the contrary, most were aspiring to the typical gendered lifecycle trajectories of manual labour and early family formation followed by their parents' generation, before a combination of structural economic changes and the changes that are transforming family structures made this possibility increasingly remote.

Second, the decline of stable employment and the emergence of more transient and tenuous working patterns leave little scope for the formulation of long-term plans. These structural forces have prolonged the adolescent lifestyles of many respondents, based around displays of conspicuous consumption and recreational drug use, into their late twenties/thirties. While this also represents a wider pattern of cultural change, these trends are intensified in low-income areas through economic necessity and as an alternative source of self-esteem in the absence of an occupational identity. Further, the failure of flexible post-industrial labour markets to provide stable careers means that many respondents occupy a similar labour market location to their teenage offspring. The divergence of lifecycle experiences between those socialised into post-industrial working lives, and those socialised into an older order represents a major source of division, antagonism and incomprehension. These tensions represent a significant challenge to policies that aim to rebuild communities in polarised and fragmented areas such as St. Helier, and generate conflicts that are acted out both in the localities that they share and within their families. Twenty-nine-year-old Dean had not held a 'proper' job for five years and supplemented his benefits through a combination of working part time in a friend's video rental shop and unlicensed mini-cab driving:

> "When I see my mum and dad they're always on my back because they don't like me signing on and working. We always end up arguing about it and my dad goes 'you're an effing parasite' and threatens to shop me though he knows he won't (...) but he's only had four jobs since he left school and he's 54, I mean what does he know?"

Regeneration initiatives emphasise civic engagement in a social economy, and focus policy on the spaces where poverty is produced rather than the structural forces that create exclusion and disadvantage.

Changes in the labour market and in welfare and housing policies are not only contributing to this process but diminish the solidarity-building capacities on which the success of those policies ultimately depends. Furthermore, promoting social enterprises on the basis of 'proximity services' rarely achieves sustainability and, like the area's underground economy, may contribute to isolating disadvantaged communities further by drawing them into a localised circuit of capital isolated from the mainstream economy (Amin et al, 1998, p 9). The spatial bases of exclusion are generated and reproduced not from within those communities, but through spatial concentrations of people in a weak labour market position and through unequal access to public services, especially educational opportunities. Several of the respondents had children who were entering adolescence during the fieldwork stage. Those parents were acutely aware of the importance of educational credentials in determining lifecycle trajectories in post-industrial labour markets, an awareness grounded in their own experiences. They were also conscious of the competing concerns weighing on their children, and the potential for intergenerational disadvantage transmitted through an increasingly competitive process of educational stratification. This was a source of great anxiety to many parents, as expressed by 39-year-old Amanda, a married woman with two children:

> "My son, he's 14 now and he's a bright lad, always done well at school. We applied to all the selective schools. He sat the entrance tests but didn't get in so he ended up in Eastfields because it was the lesser of two evils (...) he won't get on with his work anymore because he's fallen in with the wrong crowd and walks round thinking he's Eminem or somebody, I mean it's only fashion but we despair of where he's going to end up sometimes."

Her son will be part of the second generation of youngsters to enter a highly segmented labour market offering few opportunities for the unqualified. Evidence suggests that these processes of educational failure are translating into continuing disadvantage in the labour market (see Chapter Four). The reaction of this generation to educational failure and whether their responses, like those of their parents, will involve continuing adherence to the 'work ethic' in a new context, or whether they will pursue more marginalised strategies in crime and drug dealing remains open to further study. As we have seen, the estate's youths were not slow to capitalise on the vacuum left in the market for drugs and stolen goods following the demise of the St. Helier Arms. This raises the potential for a further divergence in the lifecycle experiences and economic strategies between this generation and their parents, who largely use undeclared earnings as an alternative to crime. The way that these processes will shape the future trajectory of social life in areas like the St. Helier estate and whether they will further isolate those localities suggests the need for periodic follow-on studies of working-class localities. This would indicate a significant advance in research into social exclusion, through capturing the dynamic and historically situated nature of social relationships as they adapt and evolve in specific locales in response to the structural constraints that they face.

Note

[1] Robert Putnam, for example, points to an inverse relationship between social capital and inequality, noting that community and equality are mutually reinforcing. In the US, civic engagement was at its height during the 1950s and 1960s post-war boom of expanding employment opportunities, a levelling of inequality and a general improvement in the conditions of the manual working class. It was under such conditions that the solidarity of working-class and ethnic social movements was able to gain social and political advancement, notes Putnam (2000, pp 358-60).

References

Abel-Smith, B. and Townsend, P. (1966) *The poor and the poorest: A new analysis of the Ministry of Labour's Family Expenditure Survey of 1953-54 and 1960*, London: Bell.

Agnew, R.S. (1983) 'Social class and success goals: an examination of relative and absolute aspirations', *The Sociological Quarterly*, vol 24, no 3 (summer), pp 432-52.

Alcock, P. (2003) *Social policy in Britain* (2nd edn), Basingstoke: Palgrave.

Allen, A. and Macey, M. (1994) 'Some issues of race, ethnicity and nationalism in the 'New' Europe: rethinking sociological paradigms', in P. and R. Crompton (eds) *A new Europe? Economic restructuring and social exclusion*, London: UCL Press.

Allen, J. and Henry, N. (1996) 'Fragments of industry and employment: contract service work and the shift towards precarious employment', in R. Crompton, D. Gallie and K. Purcell (eds) *Changing forms of employment: organisations, skills and gender*, London: Routledge.

Allen, J. and Massey, D. (1988) *The economy in question*, London: Sage Publications.

Amin, A., Cameron, A. and Hudson, R. (1998) *Welfare to work or welfare as work?: Combating social exclusion in the UK*, Durham: Department of Geography, University of Durham.

Anderson, M., Bechhofer, F. and Kendrick, K. (1994) 'Individual and household strategies', in M. Anderson, F. Bechhofer and J. Gerschuny (eds) *The social and political economy of the household*, New York, NY: Oxford University Press.

Atkinson, J. (1984) 'Manpower strategies for flexible organisations', *Personnel Management*, vol 16, no 8, pp 28-31.

Bagguley, P. and Mann, K. (1992) 'Idle thieving bastards? Scholarly representations of the "underclass"', *Work, Employment and Society*, vol 6, no 1, pp 113-26.

Bane, M.J. and Ellwood, D.T. (1994) *Welfare realities: From rhetoric to reform*, Cambridge, MA: Harvard University Press.

Banfield, E. (1970) *The unheavenly city: The nature and future of our urban crisis*, Boston: Little, Brown and Co.

Bardgett, L. and Vidler, G. (2000) *Regional social exclusion indicators*, Research paper 00/71, London: House of Commons Library.

Baron, S., Field, J. and Schuller, T. (eds) (2000) *Social capital: Critical perspectives*, Oxford: Oxford University Press.

Bauman, Z. (1998) *Work, consumerism and the new poor*, Buckingham: Open University Press.

Beck, U. (1992) *Risk society: Towards a new modernity*, London: Sage Publications.

Becker, H. (1966) *Social problems: A modern approach*, New York, NY: Wiley.

Bell, D. (1973) *The coming of post-industrial society: A venture in social forecasting*, New York, NY: Basic Books.

Beresford, P. (1996) 'Challenging the "them" and "us" of social policy research', in H. Dean (ed) *Ethics and social policy research*, Luton: University of Luton Press.

Biernacki, P. and Waldorf, D. (1981) 'Snowball sampling: problems and techniques of chain referral sampling', *Sociological Methods and Research*, vol 10, no 2, pp 141-63.

Bird, S.E. (2002) 'It makes sense to us: cultural identity in local legends of place', *Journal of Contemporary Ethnography*, vol 31, no 5, pp 519-47.

Bivand, P., Gordon, B. and Simmonds, D. (2003) *Making work pay in London*, London: London Development Agency.

Blanden, J., Goodman, A., Gregg, P. and Machin, S. (2002) *Changes in intergenerational mobility in Britain*, Centre for Economic Performance no 517, London: London School of Economics and Political Science.

Bluestone, B., Murphy, W.M. and Stevenson, M. (1973) *Low wages and the working poor*, Michigan, MI: The University Press.

Borgois, P. (1996) *In search of respect: Selling crack in El Barrio*, Cambridge: Cambridge University Press.

Bott, E. (1957) *Family and social network: Roles, norms and external relationships in ordinary urban families*, London: Tavistock Publications.

Bourdieu, P. (1985) *Outline of a theory of practice*, Cambridge: Cambridge University Press.

Bourdieu, P. (1986) 'The forms of capital', in J.G. Richardson (ed) *Handbook of theory and research for the sociology of education*, New York, NY: Greenwood Press.

Bourdieu, P. (1996) 'Understanding', *Theory, Culture, and Society*, vol 17, no 2, pp 17-37.

Bowyer, I. (1997) 'Problems with interviewing: experiences with service providers and clients', in G. Miller and R. Dingwall (1997) *Context and method in qualitative research*, London: Sage Publications.

Box, S. (1981) *Deviance, reality and society* (2nd edn), London: Holt, Rinehart & Winston.

Bruley, S. and Edwards, N. (1997) *Factory life and labour in Merton and Beddington, 1920-1960*, Merton: London Borough of Merton.

Buck, N. (1992) 'Labour market inactivity and polarisation: a household perspective on the idea of an underclass', in D. Smith (ed) *Understanding the underclass*, London: Policy Studies Institute.

Buck, N., Gordon, I., Hall, P., Harloe, M. and Kleinman, M. (2002) *Working capital: Life and labour in contemporary London*, London: Routledge.

Buck, N., Gordon, I. and Young, K. (1986) *The London employment problem: Inner cities research programme series, 5*, Oxford: Clarendon Press.

Buder, S. (1990) *Visionaries and planners: the Garden City movement and the modern community*, New York, NY: Oxford University Press.

Burchardt, T., Le Grand, J. and Piachaud, D. (1999) 'Social exclusion in Britain, 1991-1995', *Social Policy and Administration*, vol 33, no 3, pp 227-44.

Burchardt, T., Le Grand, J. and Piachaud, D. (2002) 'Introduction', in J. Hills, J. Le Grand and D. Piachaud (2002) *Understanding social exclusion*, Oxford: Oxford University Press.

Burnett, J. (1986) *A social history of housing* (2nd edn), London: Routledge.

Burney, E. (1999) *Crime and banishment: Nuisance and exclusion in social housing*, Winchester: Waterside Press.

Burrows, R. (1999) 'Residential mobility and residualisation in social housing in England', *Journal of Social Policy*, vol 28, no 1, pp 27-52.

Byrne, D. (1997) 'Social exclusion and capitalism: the reserve army across time and space', *Critical Social Policy*, vol 17, no 1, pp 27-51.

Byrne, D. (1999) *Social exclusion*, Buckingham: Open University Press.

Byrne, D. (2002) 'Industrial culture in a post-industrial world', *City*, vol 6, no 3, pp 279-89.

Byrne, D. and Rogers, T. (1999) 'Divided spaces – divided school: an exploration of the spatial relations of social division', *Sociological Research Online*, vol 1, no 2.

Callaghan, G. (1997) *Flexibility, mobility and the labour market*, Aldershot: Ashgate.

Campbell, B. (1993) *Goliath: Britain's dangerous places*, St Ives: Methuen.

Castells, M. and Portes, A. (1989) 'The origins, dynamics and effects of the informal economy', in A. Portes, M. Castells and L.A. Benton (eds) *The informal economy: Studies in advanced and less developed countries*, Baltimore: John Hopkins University Press.

Chambaz, C. (2001) 'Lone-parent families in Europe: a variety of economic and social circumstances', *Social Policy and Administration*, vol 35, no 6, pp 658-71.

Chamberlayne, P. and Rustin, M. (1999) *From biography to social policy: Final report of the Sostris Project*, London: Centre for Biography in Social Policy, Department of Sociology, University of East London.

Charlesworth, L. (1983) *One hundred years of public health in Sutton: 1883-1983*, Sutton: Environmental Health Department, London Borough of Sutton.

Charlesworth, S. J. (2000) *A phenemonology of working class experience*, Cambridge: Cambridge University Press.

Christopherson, S. (1995) 'The fortress city: privatised spaces, consumer citizenship', in A. Amin (ed) *Post fordism: A reader*, Oxford: Blackwell.

Coffield, F., Robinson, P. and Sarsby, J. (1980) *A cycle of deprivation? A case study of four families*, London: Heinemann Educational.

Coleman, J. (1990) *Foundations of social theory*, Cambridge, MA: Harvard University Press.

Coleman, J. (1994) 'A rational choice perspective on economic sociology', in N.J. Smelser and R. Swedberg (eds) *The handbook of economic sociology*, Princeton, NJ: Princeton University Press.

Collins, R. (1992) *Sociological insight: An introduction to non-obvious sociology* (2nd edn), New York, NY: Oxford University Press.

Community Safety Unit (1998) *Crime and disorder audit, 1998*, Sutton: Sutton Community Safety Steering Group.

Cook, D. (1989) *Rich law, poor law: Different responses to tax and Supplementary Benefit fraud*, Milton Keynes: Open University Press.

Cook, D. (1998) 'Between a rock and a hard place: the realities of working "on the side"', *Benefits*, no 21, pp 11-15.

Cornuel, D. and Duriez, B. (1985) 'Local exchange and state intervention', in N. Redclift and E. Mingione (eds) *Beyond employment: Household, gender and subsistence*, Oxford: Blackwell.

CPAG (Child Poverty Action Group) (1998) *The Green Paper on welfare reform: CPAG's response*, London: CPAG.

CPAG (1999) *Working Families' Tax Credit: A CPAG guide*, London: CPAG.

Craine, S. (1997) 'The black magic roundabout: cyclical transitions, social exclusion and alternative careers', in R. MacDonald (ed) *Youth, 'the underclass' and social exclusion*, London: Routledge.

Crook, S., Pakulski, J. and Waters, M. (1992) *Postmodernization: Change in advanced society*, London: Sage Publications.

Crow, G. (1989) 'The use of the concept of "strategy" in recent sociological literature', *Sociology*, vol 23, no 1, pp 1-24.

Crow, G. (2002) 'Community studies: Fifty years of theorization', *Sociological Research Online*, vol 7, no 3.

Daguerre, A. (2004) 'Importing workfare: policy transfer of social and labour market policies from the USA to Britain under New Labour', *Social Policy and Administration*, vol 38, no 1, pp 41-56.

Dahrendorf, R. (1987) 'The erosion of citizenship and its consequences for us all', *New Statesman and Society*, 12 June, pp 12-15.

Dawson, T., Dickens, S. and Finer, S. (2000) *New Deal for Lone Parents: Report on qualitative studies with individuals*, Employment Service Research and Development Report, London: HMSO.

Deacon, A. (2003) 'Levelling the playing field, activating the players: New Labour and the 'cycle of disadvantage', *Policy & Politics*, vol 31, no 2, pp 123-37.

Deacon, A. and Mann, K. (1999) 'Moralism and modernity: the paradox of New Labour thinking on welfare', *Benefits*, Issue 20, September/October, pp 2-6.

Dean, H. (1994) 'In search of the underclass', in P. Brown and R. Scase (eds) *Poor work: Disadvantage and the division of labour*, Milton Keynes: Open University Press.

Dean, H. (2002) 'Insecure families and low-paying labour markets', *Journal of Social Policy*, vol 31, no 1, pp 61-80.

Dean, H. and Barret, D. (1996) 'Unrespectable research and researching the unrespectable', in H. Dean (ed) *Ethics and social policy research*, Luton: University of Luton Press.

Dean, H. and Melrose, M. (1996) 'Unravelling citizenship: the significance of social security fraud', *Critical Social Policy*, vol 16, no 3, pp 3-32.

Dean, H. with Melrose, M. (1999) *Poverty, riches and social citizenship*, Basingstoke: Macmillan.

Dennis, N. and Erdos, G. (1992) *Families without fatherhood*, London: Health & Welfare Unit, Institute of Economic Affairs.

DETR (Department of the Environment, Transport and the Regions) (1998a) *1998 index of local deprivation*, London: DETR.

DETR (1998b) *Community-based regeneration initiatives: A working paper*, London: DETR.

DETR (2000) *Indices of deprivation 2000: Measuring deprivation at the small area level*, London: DETR.

Dewilde, C. (2003) 'A life-course perspective on social exclusion and poverty', *British Journal of Sociology*, vol 51, no 1, pp 109-28.

DfEE (Department for Education and Employment) (1998a) *Secondary school performance tables: Merton*, London: DfEE.

DfEE (1998b) *Secondary school performance tables: Sutton*, London: DfEE.

Dickens, R., Gregg, P. and Wadsworth, J. (2000) 'New Labour and the labour market', *Oxford Review of Economic Policy*, vol 16, no 1, pp 95-113.

Dingwall, R. (1997) 'Accounts, interviews and observations', in G. Miller and R. Dingwall (eds) *Context and method in qualitative research*, London: Sage Publications.

Ditton, J. and Brown, R. (1981) 'Why don't they revolt?: "invisible income" as a neglected dimension of Runciman's relative deprivation thesis', *British Journal of Sociology*, vol 32, no 4, pp 521-30.

Doeringer, B. and Piore, M.J. (1971) *Internal labor markets and manpower analysis*, Lexington, MA: Heath Lexington Books.

Douglas, M. and Isherwood, B. (1979) *The world of goods: Towards an anthropology of consumption*, London: Routledge.

Doyal, L. and Gough, I. (1991) *A theory of human need*, London: Macmillan.

Driver, S. and Martell, L. (2002) 'New Labour, work and the family', *Social Policy and Administration*, vol 36, no 1, pp 46-61.

DSS (Department of Social Security) (1999) *Press release*, 16 November, www.dss.gov.uk

DSS (2000) *Safeguarding social security*, London: HMSO, www.dss.gov.uk/hq/fraud/html/main/chpone.htm

Duncan, S. and Edwards, R. (1999) *Lone mothers, paid work and gendered moral rationalities*, London: Macmillan Press.

Dunning, E., Murphy, P. and Williams, J. (1988) *The roots of football hooliganism: An historical and sociological study*, London: Routledge.

Eardley, T. and Cordon, A. (1996) *Low income self-employment, work, benefits and living standards*, Aldershot: Avebury.

Edin, K. and Lein, L. (1997) *Making ends meet: How single mothers survive welfare and low wage work*, New York, NY: Russel Sage Foundation.

Edmunds, J. and Turner, B. (2002) *Generations, culture and society*, Buckingham and Philadelphia, PA: Open University Press.

Elam, M. (1995) 'Puzzling out the post-fordist debate: technology, markets and institutions', in A. Amin (ed) *Post fordism: A reader*, Oxford: Blackwell.

Employment and Social Affairs Directorate (1999) *Employment in Europe 1999*, Employment and Social Affairs Directorate–General for Employment, Industrial Relations and Social Affairs, V/A1.

Employment Service, AZTEC and South London Training and Enterprise Council (1998) *New Deal delivery plan: Sutton, Epsom and Esher district*.

Fainstein, S., Gordon, I. and Harloe, M. (1992) *Divided cities: New York and London in the contemporary world*, Oxford: Blackwell.

Fantasia, R. (1988) *Cultures of solidarity*, Berkeley, CA: University of California Press.

Featherstone, M. (1991) *Consumer culture and postmodernism: Theory, culture and society*, London: Sage Publications.

Fernandez-Kelly, M. (1994) 'Towanda's triumph: social and cultural capital in the transition to adulthood in the urban ghetto', *International Journal of Urban and Regional Research*, vol 18, no 1, pp 88-111.

Fevre, R. (2000) 'Socialising social capital: identity, the transition to work and economic development', in S. Baron, J. Field and T. Schuller (eds) (2000) *Social capital: Critical perspectives*, Oxford: Oxford University Press.

Field, F. (1995) *Making welfare work: Reconstructing welfare for the millennium*, London: Institute of Community Studies.

Field, F. (1997) 'The underclass of '97', *New Statesman and Society*, 17 January, pp 30-31.

Fine, B. (2001) *Social capital versus social theory: Political economy and social science at the turn of the millennium*, London and New York, NY: Routledge.

Finer, M. (1974) *Report of the Committee on One-Parent Families Vol 1*, London: HMSO.

Finlayson, L. and Marsh, A. (1998) *Lone parents on the margins of work*, DSS research report no 80, London: HMSO.

Finn, D. (2003) 'The "employment-first" welfare state: lessons from the New Deal for Young People', *Social Policy and Administration*, vol 37, no 7, pp 709-24.

Ford, R. (1999) 'Welfare to work and financial incentives for families with children: strategies from three liberal regimes', *Benefits*, April/May, Issue 25, pp 6-10.

Ford, R., Marsh, A. and Finlayson, L. (1998) *What happens to lone parents*, DSS research report no 77, London: HMSO.

Ford, R. and Millar, J. (1998) 'Lone parenthood in the UK: policy dilemmas and solutions', in R. Ford and J. Millar (eds) *Private lives and public responses*, London: Policy Studies Institute.

Franklin, D.L. (1997) *Ensuring inequality: The structural transformation of the African-American family*, New York, NY: Oxford University Press.

Fraser, D. (1984) *The evolution of the British welfare state: A history of social policy since the industrial revolution* (2nd edn), Basingstoke: Macmillan.

Fukuyama, F. (1997) *The end of order*, London: The Social Market Foundation/Profile Books.

Furlong, A., Biggart, A. and Cartmel, F. (1996) 'Neighbourhoods, opportunity structures and occupational aspirations', Sociology, vol 30, no 3, pp 551-65.

Gallie, D., Marsch, C. and Vogler, C. (1994) 'Unemployment, the household and social networks', in D. Gallie, C. Marsch and M.Vogler (eds) *Social change and the experience of unemployment*, Oxford: Oxford University Press.

Gans, H.J. (1962) *The urban villagers: Group and class in the life of Italian-Americans*, New York, NY: Free Press.

Geremek, B. (1994) *Poverty: A history*, Oxford: Blackwell.

Gibbon, G. and Bell, R.W. (1939) *History of the London County Council 1889-1939*, London: Macmillan.

Giddens, A. (1973) *The class structure of the advanced societies*, London: Hutchinson.

Giddens, A. (1990) *The consequences of modernity*, Cambridge: Polity Press.

Glasgow, D. (1980) *The black underclass: Poverty, unemployment and entrapment of ghetto youth*, San Francisco, CA: Jossey-Bass Publishers.

Glass, R.L. (1939) *Watling: A survey of social life on a new housing estate*, London: P.S. King.

Goldthorpe, J.H. and Payne, C. (1986) 'Trends in intergenerational class mobility in England and Wales, 1972-1983', Sociology, vol 21, no 1, pp 1-24.

Gorz, A. (1989) *Critique of economic reason*, London: Verso.

Grabiner, Lord, QC (2000) *The informal economy: A report by Lord Grabiner QC*, March, HM Treasury, www.hm-treasury.gov.uk/docs/2000/grabiner.html.

Granovetter, M. (1973) 'The strength of weak ties', *American Journal of Sociology*, vol 78, no 6, pp 1360-79.

Granovetter, M. (1985) 'Economic action and social structure: the problem of embeddedness', *American Journal of Sociology*, vol 91, no 3, pp 481-510.

Gray, A. (2001) 'Making work pay: devising the best strategy for lone parents in Britain', *Journal of Social Policy*, vol 30, no 2, pp 189-207.

Green, A.E. and Owen, D.W. (1996) *A labour market definition of disadvantage: Towards an enhanced classification*, DfEE research studies RS11, London: HMSO.

Greenstone, J.D. (1990) 'Culture, rationality and the underclass', in C. Jencks and P.E. Peterson (eds) *The urban underclass*, Washington, DC: Brookings Institution.

Gregson, N. and Lowe, M. (1994) *Servicing the middle classes: Class, gender and waged domestic labour in contemporary Britain*, London: Routledge.

Grieco, M. (1987) 'Family networks and the closure of employment', in G. Lee and R. Loveridge (eds) *The manufacture of disadvantage*, Milton Keynes: Open University Press.

Grover, S. and Stewart, J. (1999) 'Market workfare: social security, social regulation and competitiveness in the 1990s', *Journal of Social Policy*, vol 28, no 1, pp 73-96.

Grover, S. and Stewart, J. (2000) 'Modernizing social security? Labour and its welfare-to-work strategy', *Social Policy and Administration*, vol 34, no 3, pp 235-52.

Guardian, The (1990) 'Carriage lamps light the social ladder', 24 January.

Hales, J., Roth, W., Barnes, M., Millar, J., Lessoff, C., Gloyer, M. and Shaw, A. (1999) *Evaluation of the NDLP: Early lessons from the phase one prototype – findings of surveys*, DSS research report no 109, London: HMSO.

Hamnett, C. (2003) *Unequal city: London in the global arena*, London: Routledge.

Handler, J. (2003) 'Social citizenship and workfare in the US and Western Europe: from status to contract', *Journal of European Social Policy*, vol 13, no 3, pp. 229-43.

Harding, P. and Jenkins, R. (1989) *The myth of the informal economy: Towards a new understanding of informal economic activity*, Milton Keynes: Open University Press.

Harrington, M. (1962) *The other America*, New York, NY: Macmillan.

Harvey, D. (1992) *The condition of postmodernity: An enquiry into the origins of cultural change*, Oxford: Blackwell.

Harvey, D. (1995) 'Flexible accumulation through urbanization: reflections on 'post modernism' in the American city', in A. Amin (ed) *Post-fordism: A reader*, Oxford: Blackwell.

Harvey, D. (2003) *The new imperialism*, New York, NY: Oxford University Press.

Haskey, J. (1998) 'One parent families and their dependant children in Great Britain', in R. Ford and J. Millar (eds) *Private lives and public responses*, London: Policy Studies Institute.

Henry, S. (1981) 'Introduction', in S. Henry (ed) *Can I have it in cash? A study of informal institutions and unorthodox ways of doing things*, London: Astragal Books.

Hernstein, R.J. and Murray, C. (1994) *The bell curve: Intelligence and class structure in American life*, New York, NY: Free Press.

Hills, J. (1998) *Income and wealth: The latest evidence*, York: Joseph Rowntree Foundation.

Hills, J. (2004) *Inequality and the state*, Oxford: Oxford University Press.

Hills, J., Le Grand, J. and Piachaud, D. (eds) (2002) *Understanding social exclusion*, Oxford: Oxford University Press.

Hirst, P. and Thompson, G. (1996) *Globalization in question: The international economy and the possibilities of governance*, Cambridge: Polity Press.

Hobbes, D. (1988) *Doing the business: Entrepreneurship, detectives and the working class in the East End of London*, Bristol: Clarendon Press.

Hobcraft, J. (1998) *Intergenerational and life course transmission of social exclusion: Influences of childhood poverty, family disruption, and contact with the police*, CASE paper no 15, London: Centre for Analysis of Social Exclusion.

Hobcraft, J. (2002) 'Social exclusion and the generations', in J. Hills, J. Le Grand and D. Piachaud (eds) *Understanding social exclusion*, Oxford: Oxford University Press.

Hope, R.S. (1941) *Nuffield College Reconstruction Survey. Reports on the London boroughs: Carshalton*, Oxford: Nuffield College/London: Greater London Regional Development Committee.

Hopkins, E. (1991) *The rise and decline of the English working classes, 1918-1990: a social history*, London: Weidenfeld and Nicolson.

Howe, L. (1990) *Being unemployed in Northern Ireland: An ethnographic study*, Cambridge: Cambridge University Press.

Howe, L. (1994) 'Ideology, domination and unemployment', *The Sociological Review*, vol 42, no 2, pp 315-40.

Hyder, G. (1977) 'St Helier Estate: the planning and establishment of an LCC estate', Unpublished thesis, Brighton: Brighton College of Education.

Independent, The (2001) 'Labour's £15m bill for wooing the grey vote', 26 July.

Independent on Sunday, The (1994) 'The most dangerous pub in Britain', 7 August.

Independent on Sunday, The (1995) 'How Hayley keeps the scrotes in their place', 3 September.

Jahoda, M. (1982) *Employment and unemployment: A social-psychological analysis*, Cambridge: Cambridge University Press.

Jenkins, R. (1979) *Lads, citizens and ordinary kids: Working class lifestyles in Belfast*, London: Routledge.

Jessop, B. (1995) 'Post fordism and the state', in A. Amin (ed) *Post fordism: A reader*, Oxford: Blackwell.

Jordan, B. (1996) *A theory of poverty and social exclusion*, Oxford: Polity Press.

Jordan, B. and Duvell, F. (2002) *Irregular migration: The dilemmas of transnational mobility*, Cheltenham: Edward Elgar Publishing, Inc.

Jordan, B., James, S., Kay, H. and Redley, M. (1992) *Trapped in poverty?: Labour market decisions in low-income households*, London: Routledge.

Jordan, B. and Travers, A. (1998) 'The informal economy: a case study in unrestrained competition', *Social Policy and Administration*, vol 32, no 3, pp 292–306.

JRF (Joseph Rowntree Foundation) (1995) *Joseph Rowntree inquiry into income and wealth, vol 1*, York: JRF.

JRF (2003) 'Monitoring poverty and social exclusion 2003', *Findings*, December, York: JRF.

Jupp, B. (1999) *Living together: Community life on mixed-tenure estates*, London: Demos.

Katz, M.B. (1989) *The undeserving poor: Fom the war on poverty to the war on welfare*, New York, NY: Pantheon.

'Key Facts' (2004) *End child poverty once and for all*, www.ecpc.org.uk/keyfacts.asp

King, D.S. (1987) *The new right: Politics, markets and citizenship*, Basingstoke: Macmillan Education.

Komter, A.E. (1990) 'Reciprocity as a principle of exclusion: gift giving in the Netherlands', *Sociology*, vol 30, no 2, pp 299–316.

Kornblum, W. (1984) 'Lumping the poor', *Dissent*, vol 31, no 6, pp 295–302.

Kumar, K. (1978) *Prophecy and progress: The sociology of industrial and post-industrial society*, Harmondsworth: Penguin.

Kumar, K. (1995) *From post-industrial to post-modern society: New theories of the contemporary world*, Oxford: Blackwell.

Lampard, R. (1994) 'An examination of the relationship between marital dissolution and unemployment', in D. Gallie, C. Marsch and M. Vogler (eds) *Social change and the experience of unemployment*, Oxford: Oxford University Press.

Lash, S. (1994) 'The making of an underclass: neo-liberalism versus corporatism', in P. Brown and R. Crompton (eds) *A new Europe?: Economic restructuring and social exclusion*, London: University College London Press.

Lash, S. and Urry, J. (1987) *The End of Organized Capitalism*, Cambridge: Polity Press.

Lash, S. and Urry, J. (1994) *Economies of signs and space*, London: Sage Publications.

LBM (London Borough of Merton) (1994) *The economic development strategy, 1992/3*, London: Economic Development Unit, LBM.

LBM (1999) *The economic development strategy for Merton, and action programme for 1999/2000*, London: Economic Development Unit, LBM.

LBS (London Borough of Sutton) (1981) *Census: Facts and figures, borough and ward profiles: Ward profiles: St. Helier North and St. Helier South*, Sutton: LBS.

LBS (1998) *The economic development strategy 1998/1999*, Sutton: LBS.

LBS (2001) *Census: Facts and figures, borough and ward profiles*, Sutton: LBS.

Lee, A. and Hills, J. (1998) *New cycles of disadvantage?: Report of a conference organised by CASE on behalf of the ESRC for HM Treasury*, CASE report no 1, London: Centre for Analysis of Social Exclusion/London School of Economics and Political Science.

Lee, P. and Murie, A. (1999) 'Spatial and social divisions within British cities: beyond residualisation', *Housing Studies*, vol 14, no 4, pp 625-40.

Lee, R.M. (1993) *Doing research on sensitive topics*, London: Sage Publications.

Lemann, N. (1992) *The promised land: The great black migration and how it changed America*, USA: Vintage.

Leonard, M. (1998) 'The long-term unemployed, informal economic activity and the 'underclass' in Belfast: rejecting or reinstating the work ethic', *International Journal of Urban and Regional Research*, vol 22, no 1, pp 42-59.

Levitas, R. (1996) 'The concept of social exclusion and the new Durkheimian hegemony', *Critical Social Policy*, vol 16, no 1 pp 5-21.

Levitas, R. (1998) *The inclusive society?: Social exclusion and New Labour*, London: Macmillan.

Lewis, O. (1966) *La Vida: A Puerto Rican family in the culture of poverty - San Juan and New York*, New York, NY: Random House.

Lewis, O. (1968) *A study of slum culture: Background for La Vida*, New York, NY: Random House.

Lian, G. (1999) 'All I want is a decent life: experiencing poverty in the East End's inner-city settings in Newcastle', Paper presented at Social Policy Association Annual Conference, University of Surrey, Roehampton, 26-27 July.

Liebow, E. (1967) *Tally's Corner, Washington, DC: A study of Negro street corner men*, Boston, MA: Little, Brown & Co.

Lister, R. (2001) 'Work for those who can, security for those who cannot: a third way in social security reform?', in R. Edwards and J. Glover (eds) *Risk and citizenship: Key issues in welfare*, London: Routledge.

LRC (London Research Centre) (1998) *1991 Census data for London, part 2*, London: London Research Centre.

LRC (1999a) *Annual employment survey and Census of employment: 1991-1996*, London: London Research Centre.

LRC (1999b) *Index of local deprivation, 1998*, London: London Research Centre.

Luard, C. (1998) *Expanding guidance services to young people in Wallington, Beddington, Roundshaw and the Northern Wards*, Prospects Careers Service/Sutton Regeneration Partnership.

Lummis, T. (1987) *Listening to history*, London: Hutchinson Education.

Lund, B. (1999) '"Ask not what your community can do for you": obligations, New Labour and welfare reform', *Critical Social Policy*, vol 9, no 4, pp 447-62.

MacDonald, C.L. and Sirriani, C. (eds) (1996) *Working in the service society*, Philadelphia, PA: Temple University Press.

MacDonald, R. (1994) 'Fiddly jobs, undeclared working and the something for nothing society', *Work, Employment and Society*, vol 8, no 4, pp 507-30.

Macmillan, R. (2003) 'Getting by', in P. Alcock, C. Beatty, S. Fothergill, R. Macmillan and S. Yeandle (2003) *Work to welfare: How men become detached from the labour market*, Cambridge: Cambridge University Press.

Macnicol, J. (1987) 'In pursuit of the underclass', *Journal of Social Policy*, vol 16, part 3, pp 293-318.

Maldonado, C. (1995) 'The informal sector: legalization or laissez-faire?', *International Labour Review*, vol 134, no 6, pp 705-28.

Mann, K. (1991) *The making of an English 'underclass'?: The social divisions of welfare and labour*, Milton Keynes: Open University Press.

Mann, K. (1994) 'Watching the defectives: observers of the underclass in the USA, Britain and Australia', *Critical Social Policy*, Issue 41, vol 14, no 2, Autumn, pp 79-99.

Mann, K. (1996) 'Who are you looking at?: voyeurs, narks and do-gooders', in H. Dean (ed) (1996) *Ethics and social policy research*, Luton: University of Luton Press.

Mann, K. (1999) 'Agency, modernity and social policy', *Journal of Social Policy*, vol 28, no 3, pp 413-35.

Manning, N. (1991) 'What is a social problem?', in M. Loney (ed) *The state or the market?* (2nd edn), Milton Keynes: Open University Press.

Marris, R. (1996) *How to save the underclass*, London: Macmillan.

Marshall, T.H. and Bottomore, T. (1996) *Citizenship and social class*, London: Pluto Press.

Martin, B. (1981) *A sociology of contemporary cultural change*, Oxford: Blackwell.

Martin, J.E. (1966) *Greater London: An industrial geography*, London: G. Bell & Sons.

Marx, K. (1976) *Capital: A critique of political economy, vol 1*, Harmondsworth: Penguin.

Matheson, J. and Babb, P. (eds) (2002) *Social trends no 32, 2002 edition*, London: HMSO.

Mawson, J. (1999) 'Continuity and change: a review of English regeneration policy in the 1990s', *Regional Studies*, vol 33, no 5, pp 477-91.

Mayhew, H. (1969) *London's underworld*, London: Spring Books.

McKnight, A. (2000) *Trends in earnings inequality and earnings mobility 1977-1997: The impact of mobility on long term inequality*, Employment Relations Research Series no 8, London: Department of Trade and Industry.

Mead, L. (1986) *Beyond entitlement: The social obligations of citizenship*, New York, NY: Free Press.

Mead, L. (1992) *The new politics of poverty: The nonworking poor in America*, New York, NY: Basic Books.

Mead, L. (1996) 'Raising work levels among the poor', in M.R. Darby (ed) *Reducing poverty in America: Views and approaches*, Thousand Oaks, CA: Sage Publications.

Merton & Morden News (1938) 'The cupboard was bare: so needy could not be helped', 4 March.

Merton & Morden News (1939a) 'Tales of hardship told by rate defaulters', 6 January.

Merton & Morden News (1939b) 'Life at St. Helier reduced to a mere existence', 19 January.

Merton & Morden News (1939c) 'Women discuss speech on estate poverty: effects of higher rents and travelling costs', 3 February.

Merton Guardian, The (1998) 'Watermeads to close after failure to raise standards', 24 September.

Merton and Sutton Health Authority (1994) *District health report*.

Michison, G.R. (1941a) *Journeys to work*, Greater London supplementary report no 2, Oxford: Nuffield College Reconstruction Survey, London: Greater London Regional Development Committee.

Michison, G.R. (1941b) *Reports on the London boroughs: Mitcham*, Oxford: Nuffield College Reconstruction Survey, London: Greater London Regional Development Committee.

Millar, J. (1997) 'State, family, and personal responsibility: the changing balance for lone mothers in the UK', in C. Ungerson and M. Kember (eds) *Women and social policy: A reader*, London: Macmillan.

Mingione, E. (1991) *Fragmented societies: A sociology of economic life beyond the market paradigm*, Oxford: Blackwell.

Mingione, E. (1994) 'Life strategies and social economies in the post fordist age', *International Journal of Urban and Regional Research*, vol 18, no 1, pp 24-45.

Morgan, D.H.J. (1985) *The family: Politics and social theory*, London: Routledge and Kegan Paul.

Morgan, P.M. (1995) *Farewell to the family?: Public policy and family breakdown in Britain and the US*, London: Health & Welfare Unit, Institute of Economic Affairs.

Morris, L. (1995) *Social divisions: Economic decline and social structural change*, London: UCL Press.

Moss, P., Holtermann, S., Owen, C. and Brannen, J. (1999) 'Lone parents and the labour market revisited', *Labour Market Trends*, November, pp 583-93.

Mount, F. (1982) *The subversive family*, London: Jonathon Cape.

Moynihan, D.P. (1967) 'The Negro family: the case for national action', in L. Rainwater and W.L. Yancey *The Moynihan Report and the politics of controversy*, Cambridge, MA: MIT Press.

Murard, N. (1996) 'The economy is destroying society: social exclusion in France', in *Social exclusion in comparative perspective: Sostris (social strategies in risk societies) working paper 1*, London: Centre for Biography in Social Policy, Department of Sociology, University of East London.

Murray, C. (1984) *Losing Ground: American social policy, 1950-1980*. New York: Basic Books.

Murray, C. (ed) (1990) *The emerging British underclass*, London: Health & Welfare Unit, Institute of Economic Affairs.

Murray, C. (2000) 'Baby beware', *The Sunday Times News Review*, 13 February.

Myrdal, G. (1962) *Challenge to affluence*, New York, NY: Pantheon.

Nelson, I. (1995) *Post-industrial capitalism: exploring economic inequality in America*, Thousand Oaks, CA: Sage Publications.

Nelson, M.K. (2000) 'Single mothers and social support: the commitment to, and retreat from, reciprocity', *Qualitative Sociology*, vol 23, no 3, pp 291-317.

Nielsen, K. (1991) 'Towards a flexible future: theories and politics', in B. Jessop (ed) *The politics of flexibility: restructuring state and industry in Britain, Germany and Scandinavia*, Aldershot: Edward Elgar.

Norman, M. (1993) 'Artful dodgers in suburbia', *The Times*, 25 June.

O'Byrne, D. (1997) 'Working-class culture: local community and global conditions', in J. Eade (ed) (1997) *Living the global city: Globalization as a local process*, London: Routledge.

ODPM (Office of the Deputy Prime Minister) (2004) *Tackling social exclusion: Taking stock and looking to the future: emerging findings*, London: Social Exclusion Unit.

OECD (Organisation for Economic Co-operation and Development) (2003) *Sectoral distribution of employed: ISIC classification (% of total employment)*, www1.oecd.org/scripts/cde/members/lfsindicators.

Ohmae, K. (1990) *The borderless world: Power and strategy in the interlinked economy*, London: Collins.

Okely, J. (1992) 'Anthropology and autobiography: participatory experience and embodied knowledge', in J. Okely and H. Callaway (eds) *Anthropology and autobiography*, London: Routledge.

ONS (Office for National Statistics) (2004) *First release: Households below average income statistics*, www.dwp.gov.uk

Oppenheim, C. (1999) 'Welfare reform and the labour market: a "third way"?', *Benefits*, Issue 25, April/May, pp 1-5.

Oppenheim, C. and Lister, R. (1996) 'The politics of child poverty, 1979-1995', in J. Pilcher and S. Wagg (eds) (1996) *Thatcher's children? Politics, childhood and society in the 1980s and 1990s*, London: Falmer Press.

Pahl, R. (1984) *Divisions of labour*, Oxford: Basil Blackwell.

Palmer, G., North, J., Carr, J. and Kenway, P. (2003) *Monitoring poverty and social exclusion 2003*, York: Joseph Rowntree Foundation/New Policy Institute.

Parker, H. (ed) (1998) *Low cost but acceptable: A minimum income standard for the UK: Families with young children*, Bristol: The Policy Press.

Parker, H., Bakx, K. and Newcombe, R. (1988) *Living with heroin: The impact of a drugs 'epidemic' on an English community*, Milton Keynes: Open University Press.

Parker, S. (1999) 'From the slums to the suburbs: Labour Party policy, the LCC, and the Woodberry Down Estate, Stoke Newington, 1934-61', *The London Journal*, vol 24, no 2, pp 51-69.

Parkin, F. (1979) *Marxism and class theory: A bourgeois critique*, London: Tavistock Publications.

Parsons, T. and Smelser, N.J. (1956) *Economy and society: A study in the integration of economic and social theory*, London: Routledge and Kegan Paul.

PAT (Policy Action Team) (1999) *Enterprise and social exclusion/national strategy for neighbourhood renewal*, London: HM Treasury.

Paugam, S. (1996) *Poverty and social exclusion: A sociological view*, Florence: European Universities Institute.

Peck, J. and Theodore, N. (1998) 'The business of contingent work: growth and restructuring in Chicago's temporary employment industry', *Work, Employment and Society*, vol 22, no 4, pp 655-74.

Phizacklea, A. (1990) *Unpacking the fashion industry: Gender, racism and class in production*, London: Routledge.

Piore, M.J. and Sabel, C.F. (1984) *The second industrial divide: Possibilities for prosperity*, New York, NY: Basic Books.

Plummer, J. (1983) *Documents of life*, London: George Allen and Unwin.

Pollack, M. (1993) 'Crime, public housing and social policy: a study of an inner city estate', Unpublished PhD thesis, London: London School of Economics and Political Science.

Power, A.E. (1987) *Property before people: The management of twentieth century council housing*, London: Allen & Unwin.

Power, A.E. (1999) 'Area problems and multiple deprivation', in J. Hills (ed) *Persistent poverty and lifetime inequality: The evidence: Proceedings from a workshop held at H.M. Treasury 17th and 18th November 1998*, CASE report no 5, Treasury occasional paper no 10, London: Centre for Analysis of Social Exclusion/HM Treasury.

Procacci, G. (1996) *A new social contract?: Against exclusion: The poor and the social sciences*, Working Paper RSC no 94/41, European Universities Institute.

Putnam, R.D. (2000) *Bowling alone: The collapse and revival of American democracy*, New York, NY: Simon and Schuster.

Rake, K. (2001) 'Gender and New Labour's social policies', *Journal of Social Policy*, vol 30, no 2, pp 209-31.

Reich, R.B. (1993) *The work of nations: A blueprint for the future*, London: Simon and Schuster.

Reynolds, F. (1986) *The problem housing estate: An account of Omega and its people*, Aldershot: Gower.

Richardson, L. and Le Grand, J. (2002) 'Outsider and insider expertise: the response of residents of deprived neighbourhoods to an academic definition of social exclusion', *Social Policy and Administration*, vol 36, no 5, pp 496-515.

Ritchie, S. (1990) *Thirty families: Their living standards in* unemployment, DSS research report no 1. London: HMSO.

Rodgers, J.J. (1996) *Family life and social control: A sociological analysis*, London: Macmillan .

Rodman, H. (1971) *Lower class families: The culture of poverty in Negro Trinidad*, New York, NY: Oxford University Press.

Rostow, W.J. (1960) *The stages of economic growth: A non-communist manifesto*, Cambridge: Cambridge University Press.

Runciman, W.G. (1972) *Relative deprivation and social justice*, London: Routledge.

Russell, H. (1999) 'Friends in low places: gender, unemployment and sociability', *Work, Employment and Society*, vol 13, no 2, pp 205-24.

Rustin, M. and Rix, V. (1996) 'Anglo-Saxon individualism and its vicissitudes: social exclusion in Britain', in *Social exclusion in comparative perspective: Sostris (social strategies in risk societies) working paper 1*, London: Centre for Biography in Social Policy, Department of Sociology, University of East London.

Rutter, M. and Madge, N. (1976) *Cycles of disadvantage: A review of research*, London: Heinemann.

Sainsbury, R. (1998) 'Putting fraud into perspective', *Benefits*, no 21, pp 2-3.

Sassen, S. (1990) *The global city: New York, London and Tokyo*, Princeton, NJ: Princeton University Press.

Sassen, S. (1996) 'Service employment regimes and the new inequality', in E. Mingione (ed) *Urban poverty and the underclass: A reader*, Cambridge, MA: Blackwell.

Saunders, P. (1989) 'Beyond housing classes: the sociological significance of private property rights in means of consumption', in L. McDowell, P. Sarre and C. Hamnett (eds) *Divided nation: Social and cultural change in Britain: A reader*, London: Hodder & Stoughton/Open University Press.

Savage, M. (2000) *Class analysis and social transformation*, Buckingham and Philadelphia, PA: Open University Press.

Scott, G., Campbell, J. and Brown, U. (2001) 'The contribution of childcare to local employment: poor work or work for the poor?, *Local Economy*, vol 16, no 3, pp 187-97.

Scott, J.C. (1985) *Weapons of the weak*, Westford, MA: Yale University Press.

Scott, P. (1999) *Women, other 'fresh' workers and the new manufacturing workforce of interwar Britain*, Discussion paper no 127, Portsmouth: Department of Economics, University of Portsmouth.

Segalman, R. and Marsland, D. (1988) *Cradle to grave: Comparative perspectives on the study of welfare*, London: Macmillan & Social Affairs Unit.

Sennet, R. and Cobb, J. (1972) *The hidden injuries of class*, Cambridge: Cambridge University Press.

SEU (Social Exclusion Unit) (1998) *Bringing Britain together: A national strategy for neighbourhood renewal*, London: HMSO.

SEU (1999) *Summary: First annual report on tackling poverty and social exclusion*, www.dss.gov.uk

SEU (2000) *National strategy for neighbourhood renewal: A framework for consultation*, London: HMSO.

SEU (2001) *Preventing social exclusion*, London: HMSO.

Shepherd, J., Westaway, J. and Lee, T. (1974) *A social atlas of London*, Oxford: Clarendon Press.

Silver, H. (1994) 'Social exclusion and social solidarity: three paradigms', *International Labour Review*, vol 133, no 5-6, pp 531-78.

Smith, D. (2000) 'Dealed out?: Welfare to work and social exclusion', *Local Economy*, vol 15, no 4, pp 312-35.

Smith, D. and Macnicol, J. (2001) 'Social insecurity and the informal economy: survival strategies on a South London estate', in R. Edwards and J. Glover (eds) *Risk and citizenship: Key issues in welfare*, London: Routledge.

Smith, G. (1994) 'Towards an ethnography of idiosyncratic forms of livelihood', *International Journal of Urban and Regional Research*, vol 18, no 1, pp 71-87.

Solotec (South London Training and Enterprise Council) (1999) *London Borough of Sutton Economic Assessment 1999/2000*, London: Solotec.

Somerville, P. (1998) 'Explanations of social exclusion: where does housing fit in?', *Housing Studies*, vol 13, no 6, pp 761-80.

Sparkes, J. (1999) *Schools, education and social exclusion*, CASE paper no 29, London: Centre for Analysis of Social Exclusion.

Spradley, J.P. (1979) *The ethnographic interview*, New York, NY: Holt, Rhinehart and Winston.

Staber, U. (2001) 'The structure of networks in industrial districts', *International Journal of Urban and Regional Research*, vol 25, no 3, pp 535-51.

Stack, C.B. (1974) *All our kin: Strategies for survival in a black community*, New York, NY: Harper and Row.

Standing, K. (1999) 'Lone mothers and "parental involvement": a contradiction in policy?', *Journal of Social Policy*, vol 28, no 3, pp 479-95.

Stedman Jones, G. (1971) *Outcast London: A study in the relationships between classes in Victorian Society*, Harmondsworth: Penguin.

Stewart, A. (2000) 'Never ending story: inclusion and exclusion in late modernity', in P. Askonas and A. Stewart (eds) *Social inclusion: Possibilities and tensions*, Basingstoke: Palgrave.

Strangleman, T. (2001) 'Networks, place and identity in post-industrial mining communities', *International Journal of Urban and Regional Research*, vol 25, no 2, pp 253-69.

Sullivan, M.L. (1993) 'Absent fathers in the inner city', in W.J. Wilson (ed) *The ghetto underclass*, London: Sage Publications.

Suttles, G.D. (1968) *The social order of the slum: Ethnicity and territory in the inner city*, Chicago, IL: University of Chicago Press.

Sutton & Cheam Herald, The (1992) 'Residents snub plans for a Conservation Area', 10 June.

Sutton Guardian, The (1982a) 'St Helier estate: built to be "perfect"', 6 February.

Sutton Guardian, The (1982b) 'Des. Res. Estate', 30 September.

Sutton Guardian, The (1994a) 'Murder pub in license fight', 24 February.

Sutton Guardian, The (1994b) 'Youth club plan "Immoral' claim"', 9 April.

Sutton Guardian, The (1994c) 'Police get tough on crime-ridden area', 5 August.

Sutton Guardian, The (1996) 'Police in action to ban club', 25 January.

Sutton Guardian, The (2001) 'Complaints onslaught to be launched from estate', 12 July.

Sutton Herald, The (1994) 'Pub license revoked', 9 March.

Sutton Regeneration Partnership (1999) *Annual report, 1998/99*, Sutton: Sutton Regeneration Partnership.

Swidler, A. (1986) 'Culture in action: symbols and strategies', *American Sociological Review*, vol 51, no 3, pp 273-86.

Taylor, I., Evans, K. and Fraser, P. (1996) *A tale of two cities: Global change, local feeling and everyday life in the North of England: A study in Manchester and Sheffield*, London: Routledge.

Taylor, M. (1998) 'Combating the social exclusion of housing estates', *Housing Studies*, vol 13, no 6, pp 819-32.

Taylor-Gooby, P. (2001) 'Complex equalities: redistribution, class and gender', in R. Edwards and J. Glover (eds) *Risk and citizenship: Key issues in welfare*, London: Routledge.

TELCO (2004) 'Breaking news – Ken wants Living Wage Unit!', *The Newsletter*, September-October.

Theodore, N. and Peck, J. (1999) 'Welfare-to-work: national problems, local solutions?, *Critical Social Policy*, vol 19, no 4, pp 485-510.

Tilly, L.A. and Scott, J.W. (1978) *Women, work and family*, London: Holt, Rinehart and Winston.

Tonge, J. (1999) 'New packaging, old deal?: New Labour and employment policy innovation', *Critical Social Policy*, vol 19, no 2, pp 217-232.

Townsend, P. (1993) *The international analysis of poverty*, Hemel Hempstead: Harvester.

Toynbee, P. (2003) *Hard work: Life in low-pay Britain*, London: Bloomsbury Publishing.

Travers, M. (1999) 'Qualitative research and social class', *Sociological Research Online*, vol 4, no 1.

Tripp, A.M. (1997) *Changing the rules: The politics of liberalization and the urban informal economy in Tanzania*, Berkeley, CA: University of California Press.

Turok, I. and Webster, D. (1998) 'The New Deal: jeopardised by the geography of unemployment?', *Local Economy*, vol 12, no 4, pp 309-27.

UNISON (2005) 'A fair wages clause: an end to the two tier workforce', www.unison.org.uk/pfi/doc

Valentine, C.A. (1968) *Culture and poverty: Critique and counter proposals*, Chicago, IL: University of Chicago Press.

Vickerstaff, S.A. (2003) 'Apprenticeships in the "golden age"', *Work, Employment and Society*, vol 17, no 2, pp 269-87.

Wacquant, L. (1991) 'Making class: the middle class(es) in social theory and social structure', in S. McNall, R. Levine and R. Fantasia (eds) *Bringing class back in*, Boulder, CO: Westview.

Wacquant, L. (1999) 'How penal common sense comes to Europeans', *European Societies*, vol 11, no 3, pp 319-53.

Walker, A. and Walker, C. (eds) (1997) *Britain divided: The growth of social exclusion in the 1980s and 1990s*, London: Child Poverty Action Group.

Wall, K. (2001) 'Families and informal support in Portugal the reproduction of inequality', *Journal of European Social Policy*, vol 11, no 3, pp 213-33.

Walsgrove, D. (1987) 'Policing yourself: social closure and the internalisation of stigma', in G. Lee and R. Loveridge (eds) *The manufacture of disadvantage*, Milton Keynes: Open University Press.

Walters, W. (1997) 'The active society: new designs for social policy', *Policy & Politics*, vol 25, no 3, pp 221-34.

Wheelock, J. and Jones, K. (2002) 'Grandparents are the next best thing: informal childcare for working parents in Britain', *Journal of Social Policy*, vol 31, no 3, pp 441-63.

White, M. and Forth, J. (1998) *Pathways through unemployment: Where do they lead?*, York: Joseph Rowntree Foundation.

Whyte, W.F. (1981) *Street corner society: The social structure of an Italian slum* (3rd edn), Chicago, IL: University of Chicago Press.

Wilkinson, D. (1998) 'Who are the low paid?', *Labour Market Trends*, December, pp 617-22.

Williams, C.C. (2000) 'Informal employment: implications for work and welfare', Paper presented at the Local Economy Policy Unit seminar, 'Precarious work: coping with the informal economy, South Bank University, 5 April.

Williams, C.C. and Windebanck, J. (1998) *Informal employment in the advanced economies: Implications for work and welfare*, London: Routledge.

Williams, C.C. and Windebanck, J. (1999) 'The formalisation of work thesis: a critical evaluation', *Futures*, vol 31, no 6, pp 549-51.

Williams, R. (1980) *The long revolution*, London: Penguin.

Willis, P. (1977) *Learning to labour: How working class kids get working class jobs*, Cambridge: Ashgate.

Wilson, W.J. (1987) *The truly disadvantaged: The inner city, the underclass and public policy*, Chicago, IL: University of Chicago Press.

Wootton, B.F. (1960) *Social science and social pathology*, London: Allen & Unwin.

Wright, J.D. and Devine, J.A. (1993) *The greatest of evils: Urban poverty and the American underclass*, New York, NY: Aldine de Gruyter.

Yeandle, S. (2003) 'Family, life course and labour market detachment', in P. Alcock, C. Beatty, S. Fothergill, R. Macmillan and S. Yeandle (eds) (2003) *Work to welfare: How men become detached from the labour market*, Cambridge: Cambridge University Press.

Yelling, J.A. (1992) *Slums and redevelopment: Policy and practice in England, 1918-45, with particular reference to London*, London: UCL Press.

Young, T. (1934) *Becontree and Dagenham: A report made for the Pilgrim Trust*, London: Becontree Social Survey Committee/S. Sidders & Son.

Yow, V. (1994) *Recording oral history*, London: Sage Publications.

Zweig, F. (1961) *The worker in an affluent society: Family life and industry*, London: Heinemann.

Index

A

Abel-Smith, Brian 45-6
absent males 2, 118, 132
active labour market policies viii, 104-14
active society 117
Adam Smith Institute 52
aesthetic of consumption 30
'affluent worker' 207
African Americans 48
age grading 209
agency vi, 39, 41, 45-51, 161, 191
Aid for Dependent Children 54
alcoholism 136
alienation 37
almshouses 42
anomie 91
anti-dependency strategies 197
anti-fraud measures 188-9, 202
antisocial behaviour viii, 2, 40, 52, 53
apprenticeships 108, 195, 207, 208
aspirations
  cultural 210
  occupational 89-93, 183
  of the unemployed 190
associative regulation 9
attitude 46, 55, 100-1, 159, 185, 194-5, 200
autonomy 141, 157, 161, 169, 183, 193, 209
axial principle 19-20

B

balanced reciprocity 139
Banfield, Edward 47, 48
bartering 9, 141
Barton, Dr Mary 65
basement dwellings 64
Basic Skills Agency 72
Beacontree Estate 64
Becker, Howard 40
Beck, Ulrich 204
Beddington 68
Bell, Daniel 19
benefit dependency
  adolescent pregnancies and 122
  as cause of worklessness 104
  current policy and 203
  detrimental effect on work ethic 58
  growth of in US and UK 53-5
  indicator of exclusion vii
  in African-Americans 48
  in 'underclass' debate 2, 118
  wage subsidies and 42
  Welfare-to-Work and 60
Benefit Fraud Inspectorate 144, 165
benefits

access to 35
augmentation of income with 5, 7, 42
conditional nature of 105
council tax 140
exclusive reliance on 7
integration with taxation 198
in UK and US 53-5
in-work 35, 130, 131, 152, 199
lack of incentive to end 83
lone parents and 115-136
means-tested 199
Benefits Agency 105, 114
biographical research method 11
Bishopsford Community School 76
black people 26-7, 48, 49, 50, 114, 168, 195
Booth, Charles 60
borrowing 141
Bowyer, Isabel 15
bread riots 43
breadwinner model 135, 196, 199
British Household Panel Survey 57
broken marriages 48
building boom 5, 92
bureaucracy 106-9, 111, 135, 153, 187, 204
business services 4,. 32, 152
Byrne, David ix

C

Cabinet Office Social Exclusion Unit vi
capital
  human vii, 84, 88, 104, 120, 174, 196, 205
  mobility of 18
  social vii, 1, 81, 161-92, 189-91, 196, 204-5, 213
career advancement 99, 183
Carshalton 64, 65, 67, 109-10
cash economy 9, 170-7; see also informal work
casualisation 31, 60, 151, 202
catalogues 141, 146
catering industry 30, 70, 129, 152, 186
CCTC, see Childcare Tax Credit
chain referral method 11, see also snowball sampling
child abuse 128
Child Benefit 118
childcare ix, 119-32, 137-8, 141, 189, 202; see also lone parents
Childcare Tax Credit (CCTC) 119
childminders 149
Child Poverty Action Group 106
children viii, 115, 121-32, 140, 199, 212
Child Support Act (1991) 118